13/7
7/3/18

Cont

KT-479-488

Matthew Fort's food writing career began in 1986 with a column in the *Financial Times Saturday Review*. Between 1989 and 2006 he was Food & Drink Editor of the *Guardian*.

He was Glenfiddich Food Writer of the Year and Restaurateurs' Writer of the Year in 1991, Glenfiddich Restaurant Writer of the Year in 1992 and Glenfiddich Cookery Writer of the Year in 2005. In 1998 he published *Rhubarb & Black Pudding*, a book about the Michelin-starred chef, Paul Heathcote. His second book, *Eating Up Italy*, was the Guild of Food Writers' Book of the Year in 2005. *Sweet Honey, Bitter Lemons*, a food portrait of Sicily, won the Premio Sicilia Madre Mediterranea in 2009.

On television he co-presented *Market Kitchen* with Tom Parker Bowles and he is currently a judge on *The Great British Menu*. He lives in Gloucestershire.

Rhubarb & Black Pudding

Eating Up Italy

Sweet Honey, Bitter Lemons

SUMMER IN THE ISLANDS

An Italian Odyssey

Matthew Fort

Unbound

This edition first published in 2017
Unbound
6th Floor Mutual House, 70 Conduit Street, London W1S 2GF
www.unbound.com

While every effort has been made to trace the owners of copyright material
reproduced herein, the publisher would like to apologise for any omissions and
will be pleased to incorporate missing acknowledgements in any further editions.

Text Design by PDQ
A CIP record for this book is available from the British Library

ISBN 978-1-78352-332-0 (trade hbk)
ISBN 978-1-78352-333-7 (ebook)
ISBN 978-1-78352-334-4 (limited edition)

Printed in Great Britain by Clays Ltd, St Ives Plc

For Lois
my beloved daughter

Dear Reader,

The book you are holding came about in a rather different way to most others. It was funded directly by readers through a new website: Unbound. Unbound is the creation of three writers. We started the company because we believed there had to be a better deal for both writers and readers. On the Unbound website, authors share the ideas for the books they want to write directly with readers. If enough of you support the book by pledging for it in advance, we produce a beautifully bound special subscribers' edition and distribute a regular edition and e-book wherever books are sold, in shops and online.

This new way of publishing is actually a very old idea (Samuel Johnson funded his dictionary this way). We're just using the internet to build each writer a network of patrons. Here, at the back of this book, you'll find the names of all the people who made it happen.

Publishing in this way means readers are no longer just passive consumers of the books they buy, and authors are free to write the books they really want. They get a much fairer return too – half the profits their books generate, rather than a tiny percentage of the cover price.

If you're not yet a subscriber, we hope that you'll want to join our publishing revolution and have your name listed in one of our books in the future. To get you started, here is a £5 discount on your first pledge. Just visit unbound.com, make your pledge and type **island5** in the promo code box when you check out.

Thank you for your support,

Dan, Justin and John
Founders, Unbound

CONTENTS

PREFACE

I fell in love with Italy through ice cream.

I first came to Italy in 1956 on a family holiday in Cervia, a resort town on the Adriatic coast. I was eleven. It was the only holiday we had on which my mother and father were both present, as well as my three brothers, James, Johnny and Tom. Our sister, Elizabeth, had not yet been born. My father, an MP, had to return early to take part in the parliamentary debate on the Suez Crisis. Not that such epic events impinged on my world view at the time. That was bounded by the here and now and the edible, and I was easily caught in the thrall of Italy.

Sunny, colourful, vibrant, different, it was far removed from the drab monochrome of post-war Britain. The warmth, the dappled shade, the resinous smell of pines, the spice-perfumed dust, the clear, amethyst waters and expanses of sand like caster sugar had a brilliance and shimmer that life at home never produced. There was a sense of excitement from simply staying in a grand hotel, the Mare e Pineta, with its pools, restaurants, terraces, gardens and a kind of ineffable allure. It was said that the owner had been part of the Italian underground during the war, and had been honoured for smuggling British pilots out of the country, which added dash to glamour for an imagination schooled on Biggles, Rider Haggard and Jack London.

Above all, there was the food. Each Thursday buffet lunches were laid out like gastronomic gardens. They were on a scale and of a dazzling variety of which we had never dreamed. Even sixty years on, I can still remember the undulating tablescape of lobsters, crabs, prawns, scampi, cold salmon, mussels, rare roast beef, cold chickens, salamis, hams, curious vegetable mixtures, salads, fruits of every variety laid out with casual abandon around a huge ice swan. It was a continent of temptation on which we feasted with a wild sense of pleasure.

Some evenings my father would take us to a particular café in town 'for a treat', ice creams. The centre of the town was marked by a small dusty area on which grew a stand of dusty umbrella pine trees to one of which was nailed a sign that read Divieto di Caccia (Hunting Forbidden). Even at the time, this struck me as extraordinarily optimistic.

Our ice cream palace of choice was a small café, the name of which has long vanished from my memory. Already the ice creams I had eaten in Italy had had the same effect on me as reading Chapman's Homer had had on John Keats – 'Then felt I like some watcher of the skies/When a new planet swims into his ken'. They opened my senses to a universe of pleasure at which Wall's bricks and Lyons soft ice cream had not even hinted, even if covered liberally with golden syrup or maple syrup.

One evening we arrived to find the proprietor in the act of making ice cream. No ice cream ready and waiting! I couldn't imagine such a disaster. I was outraged by the thought, ready to be inconsolable. Then disappointment was replaced by curiosity, and curiosity by fascination, as I watched the cream being poured into the freezing tub and the paddle churning it as it thickened. The gelataio added banana flavouring, and suddenly this mysterious, smooth, velvety substance smelt more of banana than any banana I had ever smelt and, as that first lick of cool, downy softness ran melting over my warm tongue, I fell in love. Any people who could lavish so much passion and care over ice cream must be a people worth treasuring.

Since that magical baptism, I returned to Italy as often as time, money, work and domestic responsibilities allowed, to Rome, Milan, Lake Bracciano, to Lucca, Pisa and Parma, to the Monte Lucretili and Naples. I spent summer holidays, principally on the mainland, but also visiting the islands – Elba, Sicily, Salina, Sardinia and Capri.

While filled with pleasure and discovery, these visits left me unsatisfied, my passion unquenched. Two weeks, three weeks, even a month, never quite seemed long enough. Just as Italy had soaked into my core, just as I'd adjusted to its rhythms and joys, it was time to go back home, to education, work, responsibility and humdrum reality.

But somewhere along the line the seed of passing an entire summer lotus-eating among Italy's islands was sown. There was the sheer romance of spending almost unlimited time playing in the clear, azure waters; eating and drinking in small, charming ports; chatting away to wizened, taciturn fishermen; turning golden brown in the sun. I dreamed of it in the quiet hours of the night, fantasised about it during meetings, pondered it when I should have been doing more productive things. But I never got round to actually doing it. Years drifted by. Summers came and went. The dream remained.

In 1999, I took three months off to ride a Vespa from Melito di Porto Salvo in Calabria, the southernmost town in Italy, to Turin in the north, to write *Eating Up Italy*. In 2008 I made a similar journey across and around Sicily and wrote *Sweet Honey, Bitter Lemons*. Exhilarating and full of delights as the journeys were, perhaps because of them, the notion of spending a whole summer in the islands still floated in my imagination.

There's something particular and fascinating about islands; about the very notion of islands. There they are scattered like crumbs across a vast blue tablecloth. It's easy to hold each in the mind's eye and in the imagination. Each is a discrete entity, identifiable and comprehensible and filled with possibility, each a world in itself, and yet connected by history, trade, inter-migration and by sea.

I've lived on an island all my life. Clearly where we come from shapes our sense of who we are and our relation with the rest of the world. But how? Is the mentality of islanders different from that of mainland dwellers, and if so, why? And in what way? Perhaps I could understand my own island better through exploring others, especially these islands swathed in myth and legend as well as historical witness. Could there be monsters lurking among them? Or sirens? Can any of the Aeolian Islands really be Aeolia of the Odyssey? Or Sicily the land of the Cyclopes? Would I find today's descendants of Homer's Lotus-eaters? Are there connections between past and present that a passing stranger could see?

And what of food? Someone had once said to me that Italians speak and eat in dialect, and that seems to me to be one of the keys to the country. Italy's food is rich in its diversity, and has always helped define Italians' sense of identity. Previous trips to Italy had been stuffed, you might say, with edible delights, each of the season and place, valley, village, even house. But would this be equally true of the islands? There was bound to be plenty of fish, I assumed, but did the dishes vary from island to island? Had the pressures of mass tourism and globalisation begun to erode the essential purity of individual cooking cultures?

The more I ruminated, the more enticing the idea seemed to be. Anyone in their right mind would want to spend six months or so loafing around the Mediterranean, I felt. Of course they would. On the other hand, I was about to be sixty-seven, in theory moving towards the quiet evening of my life, a time when a more responsible person might deem it foolish to set off on their own to travel through terrae incognitae mounted on a Vespa. But neither did I like the idea of sitting in a rocking chair in a home for toothless old food writers thinking, 'If only I'd had the bottle, if only I'd got organised... if only... if only.' Regret is a pointless emotion.

Everyone to whom I spoke about it said the same thing, expressed the same enthusiasm, the same wish. Six months moving in a leisurely fashion among some of the most beautiful and fascinating islands in the Mediterranean? Yes, please. Can

I come, too? Can I join you? Even for a little bit? The lure of escape was irresistible.

But I knew – and, in their heart of hearts, they knew – that they would never do anything so foolhardy, so indulgent. They were too sensible. They had jobs, businesses, children, mortgages, responsibilities. So, I reasoned, I would go on their behalf. It wasn't that I didn't have responsibilities, it's just that they didn't seem quite so important. Of course, it was foolhardy, irresponsible, indulgent, but it wasn't trivial.

'Take the Adventure, heed the call, now ere the irrevocable moment passes! 'Tis but a banging of the door behind you, a blithesome step forward, and you are out of the old life and into the new,' the Sea Rat says to Ratty in *The Wind in the Willows*.

Finally I heeded the call.

PROLOGUE

JUNE 2014

England

My brother, Tom, picked me up from Gatwick Airport to take me home to Gloucestershire.

'I've been thinking about what's happened,' he said. 'Do you know, Matty, I think this might be for the best.'

'How do you figure that out?' I asked.

'Well,' he said, 'the trouble with your other books is that they're too bloody cheerful. Nothing ever seems to go wrong. It has gone wrong this time, and treated properly, I think it could make for a much better book. You know, dark to temper the light, contrast, that kind of thing.'

'Hmmm,' I said.

The country was enjoying one of those perfect spells of still summer weather when everything seems to have been touched by a fine dust of gold, made all the more perfect because you know it's not going to last. But then, nothing seemed to last any more.

Swapping the bright clarity of the warm South for the lush green of the Gloucestershire countryside had not been exactly how I had thought I'd be spending the summer. I had anticipated all manner of stomach ailments, infections, strokes and domestic disasters that would force me to return home, but I had never foreseen something so improbable, painful or so final as a snapped Achilles tendon. I knew they didn't grow back overnight. I knew that it would be three months at least before I would be fit enough to travel again. With the best of fortune I wouldn't be able to be on the move properly until early September, too late

1

to be able to visit the remaining islands in a way consistent with how things had gone so far. That meant – well, what did it mean? Plan A was scuppered, but there never had been a Plan B.

It had all started so brilliantly.

1

THE WINE-DARK SEA

MAY 2014

Livorno – Gorgona – Elba – Pianosa – Giglio – Giannutri

Livorno

Livorno, or Leghorn as my grandparents and great-grandparents knew it, and how it's still known on Google maps, is on the Tuscan coast. It's mid-May, warm and sunny. The air's flush with salt, iodine and diesel. Sleek yachts, toothpick masts swaying, halyards tick-ticking; glossy cruisers heavy with money and gross taste; and scuffed, battered fishing boats in white and blue pack the interlocking harbours like sardines in a tin. Beyond, brood four gargantuan cruise ships, their presence as alien as space stations from another galaxy.

It's a long time since Livorno's days of glory as a porto franco, a free port, under the Medicis. It had become one of the most dynamic trade centres of the Mediterranean after Jewish traders settled here following their expulsion from Spain and Portugal around 1583. The British Levant Company established a trading house in the seventeenth century, trading cloth, bloaters from Yarmouth and wheat from Kings Lynn. Livorno's decline, which began during the Napoleonic wars, was completed after the Unification of Italy, when it lost its status as a free port. Its position still gave it a strategic importance in the Mediterranean, that cost it dearly in the Second World War. In 1944, a report by the US Army Corps of Engineers described Livorno as 'the most thoroughly demolished port in the Mediterranean'.

But the cruise ships are bringing back business, industry, money, prosperity. Once Livorno's wealth depended on youthful energy, entrepreneurial dynamism, and martial pragmatism. Now its survival depends on catering to the quieter needs of silver surfers.

As I ramble along the harbour fronts, canal-side quays and scuffed streets, I find it increasingly delightful. It doesn't have the obvious and trumpeted charms of Pisa, Florence, or Siena, no painstakingly preserved and achingly beautiful antique city centre, or World Heritage site. Instead it has a certain scruffy-cur charm, energy and character, a strong sense of its own identity and worth and place in the world.

According to my friend, John Irving, who's lived in Italy for over forty years, the character of the Livornesi is 'vulgar, rowdy, fiercely leftist, violently anti-Pisan... but soft inside. I have always seen them as a sort of race apart, with their very distinctive accent, cuisine etc. A bit like Neapolitans born in Tuscany by accident.' The city even has its own satirical magazine, *Il Vernacoliere*, printed in the Livornese dialect, a Livornese *Private Eye*, as funny and cheerfully irreverent, but more vulgar and political.

And so Livorno reveals its modest, but real, treasures little by little – fishermen selling their early morning catch from marble slabs on the promenade; a children's guitar orchestra performing in one corner of the imposing Fortezza Nuova, a monument to the trading power of the city and of the Medici family who built it in the sixteenth century; the Quartiere Venezia, which is Venetian in the same way that Bourton-on-the-Water is the Venice of the Cotswolds. Canals curve at random through the middle of the city, with quays and waterways cluttered with fishing boats, rowing boats, yachts, yawls, dinghies, cruise ships and gin palaces, rusty old freighters and natty new speed boats, boats of every size, shape and colour, engines phut-phutting, flags twitching.

Above all there's the neo-classical Mercato Centrale, where pushing, shoving, peering, poking, sniffing, waving, chatting market shoppers haggle over green candle zucchini with their flame flowers; fat, waxy, canoe-shaped pea pods; salted anchovies arranged in herringbone patterns in their tins; red and purple cherries, cherries the shade of ivory blushing faintly here and there, all shiny and perfect; rabbits looking queerly naked without their skins; clusters of purple-skinned onions, their withered stalks plaited together; and tomatoes, tomatoes, tomatoes – perfectly spherical, lumpy, bumpy, shaped like plums; tomatoes the size of crab apples; tomatoes the size of oranges; green striped tomatoes, blush pink tomatoes, tomatoes as scarlet as the Pope's socks – tomatoes for every dish, for every occasion, for every day.

All these delights are treated with a matter-of-fact briskness by the Livornesi, as if they have something better to be getting on with than blowing their own trumpet. Their existence doesn't depend on past glories, but on present opportunities.

———

I'm staying in the Hotel Gran Duca, overlooking the port. I'd assumed that the Gran Duca referred to a Gran Duca of Tuscany or Pisa or another of Livorno's former aristocratic overlords, but I'm wrong. A plaque on the wall of the hotel is dedicated to 'Roberto Dudley, Duca di Nortumbria, insigne nella scienza del mare e riordinatore del Porto di Livorno' (Robert Dudley, Duke of Northumberland, eminent in the science of the sea and co-ordinator of the Port of Livorno).

Unlikely as this seems, it's no more unlikely than the rest of Dudley's life. He was the bastard son of Queen Elizabeth I's favourite, the Earl of Leicester and his lover, Douglas, Baroness Sheffield, the daughter of William Howard, First Baron of Effingham. (Douglas may seem an odd name for a woman these days, nevertheless it was hers.) Born in 1574, Dudley lived a rumbustious life, leading expeditions to capture Spanish merchantmen in the West Indies and taking part in the defeat of the Spanish Armada in 1588.

Although a bastard, he laid claim to the peerages of Leicester and Warwick. His claim was dismissed, and England became a bit hot for him as a result. He headed off to Italy with his consort and cousin, Elizabeth Southwell, disguised as his page. Converting to Catholicism, he married Elizabeth. He had to gain a special dispensation from the Pope to do so, as they were blood relatives, and marriage between blood relatives was generally discouraged in those days, as it is in ours. He went to work for Ferdinand, Grand Duke of Tuscany, designing an arsenal for him, harbour fortifications, a palace, galleys and the breakwater at Livorno. He died in 1649 at the age of seventy-five, his life having reflected a time when buccaneering daring and dash characterised the English.

Livorno seems to have had a strong attraction for the English. Nelson and Emma Hamilton entertained here. Sir Joshua Reynolds and Inigo Jones both stopped off at Livorno. Byron and Percy Shelley rented houses briefly, and Shelley drowned while sailing his boat, the *Don Juan*, from Livorno to Lerici on the other side of the Gulf of La Spezia in 1822. Some twenty years later Robert Stephenson built the railway line from Pisa to Livorno that opened in 1844.

The most celebrated Englishman to have ended his days in Livorno was Tobias Smollett. He died of an 'intestinal disorder' here in 1771. Like Dudley, he had lived a rich and varied life. He trained as a doctor, but had the good fortune and good sense to marry a rich heiress, and so became a literary gentleman rather than a medical man. Few people read *The Adventures of Roderick Random*, *The Adventures of Peregrine Pickle* or *The Expedition of Humphrey Clinker* these days, but these early novels were best sellers in their day.

I look on Smollett the man rather more kindly than Smollett the novelist. Too many dreary hours ploughing through the picaresque adventures of the likes of Humphrey Clinker and Fielding's *Adventures of Tom Jones* during my years of education rather blunted my pleasure in his prose.

But there's a delightful portrait of him by an unknown artist in the National Portrait Gallery in London, that shows a wistful humour in his eyes, a certain melancholy sweetness of expression and a nose of unusual length. He was a man with a kindly and liberal disposition, by all accounts. With the help of his friend and great champion of all manner of liberties, John Wilkes, Smollett rescued Francis Barber, Samuel Johnson's black servant, from the press gang. Curiously, Abraham Lincoln's assassin, John Wilkes Booth, was a distant relative of Wilkes, one of those random associations that make history so entertaining. John Wilkes (not John Wilkes Booth) outlived his friend by many years, and was buried with full honours in the Grosvenor Chapel in South Audley Street, London.

Smollett's grave lies in the Old Protestant Cemetery in Livorno, tucked away off the via Ingegner Guido Donegani, itself tucked away off the via Giuseppe Verdi. Guido Donegani was a prominent local businessman, an enthusiastic fascist and supporter of Mussolini. However, he obviously lacked political judgement. He managed to get himself arrested by the Germans for siding with the British, and by the British for siding with the Germans.

Sadly, the gates to the cemetery are locked and chained to prevent any would-be visitor from wandering in. It's an unloved, neglected spot, but neither melancholy nor desolate. Through the wrought-iron gates I make out the forms of stone chalices, columns, urns, angels, pillars and pinnacles marking the graves, the splendid monuments of former times, shimmering as if underwater. Untended, it's become an unofficial nature reserve, shaded by that most English of shrubs, elderflower, as well as lanky oleander, cypress, and elms planted by American sailors in memory of loved ones buried here.

It's full of flickering and dancing shadows and bird song. For a moment I think of scaling the gate, but come to the conclusion that I'm no longer of an age or a fitness for such activity. And I'm not certain that, having got in, I could get out again.

As I turn away, I hear the deep cadences of bass voices coming from an impressive, neo-classical church on the other side of the road. It sounds very much like a Russian Orthodox choir. Is it possible that there's a service of some kind at this hour of the afternoon? I wander in. Sets of icons glitter in the gloomy interior; a few elderly women, with their heads bound up in scarfs like babushkas, gossip quietly. But there's no choir. Those splendid deep bass male voices are recorded. How churches benefit from the improvements in recording technology, I think, but I feel cheated, and irritated with myself for being such a simpleton.

As I come out, a Muslim woman in a burqa passes by pushing a baby buggy with one hand and holding the hand of another child with the other. Within a few minutes and a few paces there's been a conjunction of Protestantism, Russian Orthodoxy and Islam, a reminder of Livorno's long tradition of religious tolerance. The Protestant rebels Martin Luther and John Calvin, the rabbinical scholar Samuel Uziel and the financier and philanthropist Moses Haim Montefiore all found refuge in this Catholic city. It comes as no surprise to discover that the Italian Communist Party was founded in Livorno in 1921.

My favourite place to eat is a stand on the corner of the promenade and a bridge over a canal between two quays almost opposite the Hotel Gran Duca. The dishes of the day – ribollita, trippa alla fiorentina, fritto misto Modi (an unexpected reference to the painter, Amedeo Modigliani, a native of Livorno), stracotto di guanciale – are roughly scribbled on a board beside it. Copious helpings are ladled into baps and handed out for immediate eating. The stracotto di guanciale is a rollicking, refulgent stew of cured pig's cheek in booming tomato sauce, that I eat leaning over the parapet of the bridge. Any bits or bobs that don't quite make it into my mouth fall into the water below and are scooped up by waiting gulls.

If only all the food was as unpretentious and full-hearted as this. Too many Livornese chefs have discovered oversized plates, the kind that were fashionable in Britain a few years ago, and have adopted them with ill-considered enthusiasm. The problem with big plates is that they take a lot of filling up. Having plonked the main elements of the dish on a plate with the circumference of a hot air balloon, the chefs feel compelled to occupy the rest of the space with irrelevancies. One night in an all-white wood-and-shiny-surfaces newfangled trattoria down by the harbour I order mozzarella con gamberi crudi, out of curiosity. It turns out to be a tump of layers of mozzarella and raw prawns, with a lot of pointless chopped parsley deckling the rim of the vast plate. I haven't seen anything like it in a restaurant in the UK since about 1990. It's as pointless as it's horrible.

When restaurants stick to the classic, homelier dishes – gnocchetti con scampi, fritto misto, cacciucco, the great, blockbuster Livornese fish stew, baccalà con crema di ceci, cozze ripiene – I eat as I always want to eat in Italy, marvelling at the quality of the ingredients and the absolute assurance with which they're treated. This isn't food for messing about with. It's food for pleasure, pure and simple. Pasta and pulses are employed as heavy artillery, with sharply focused flavours enfilading on the back of them, and the occasional use of chilli for low-key explosive effect. It isn't subtle or clever, but it's mightily satisfying. And I become addicted to ponce alla livornese (also known as torpedine or bomba), that sharp combination of coffee and digestif, combining one part espresso, one part rum and a strip of lemon peel that, according to local legend, came about as a result of a Saracen felucca arriving at the port in 1614 stacked with coffee and barrels of rum. All of which seems unlikely to me, and some authorities suggest that it's actually a Mediterranean variant of the British punch or grog. Hmm.

Gorgona

It's 8.30 a.m. On the dock outside the barracks of the Polizia Penitenziaria, four grey, high-speed boats, as sleek as greyhounds, bob along the quay in sociable unison. Ten or so other people are hanging around, like me, chatting and smoking, waiting to be told which of the boats will be taking us to Gorgona.

Once Gorgona had been a refuge for monks and anchorites. Now it houses a prison. Is there a natural empathy between the asceticism of a religious calling and the enforced austerity of prison life? Italian authorities have used the islands as convenient dumping grounds for the country's criminals and political undesirables for millennia. The Roman emperors moved any unwanted figures, including members of their own families, to various islands. Mussolini deported his political enemies to them. And more recent Italian governments have turned some of the islands into fortresses – super-maxi prisons – to house the most dangerous Mafia bosses and terrorists. Gorgona doesn't have that kind of elite these days. Now it's more run-of-the-mill murderers, minor league drug barons and dealers, con men and armed robbers. One boat a week brings the curious tourists to the island, but I've managed to wangle a ride on the Polizia Penitenziaria ferry.

Promptly at 9 a.m. we ease away from the quay, wake bubbling, out under the towering cliff of a cruise liner, past the protective arm of the outer breakwater, into clear water, the engines opening up, planing the crests, rocking from side to side. Almost immediately one of the ladies is sick and spends most of the journey with her eyes shut and her mouth pressed to a bag, with laughing sympathy from her friends. It turns out that they're all relatives of the warders.

Suddenly there's Gorgona, a smudge, a shape, a 3-D isosceles triangle rising abruptly from the sea. The precision of its shape is blurred by trees around the slopes. Little by little it takes on greater definition: the seventeenth-century Medici castle keep jutting out from a cliff; the silhouette of the old abbey on the apex of the triangle; the village of Gorgona shovelled up a V-shaped incline from the small harbour; the sides of the hills around crowding in, groups of drab, utilitarian prison buildings sprawling over them. We swing within the arc of the port, slow, subside to a halt. Shouting, ropes thrown and caught and whipped smartly around bollards to hold us steady while we disembark.

'Would you like a coffee?' asks Commissario Mario Salzano as we walk up the steep, winding lane running from the tiny harbour to the Terrazza Belvedere. The commissario is wearing a natty blue uniform, baggy with pouches and pockets, a pale blue beret and impenetrable dark glasses. He leads me into a cavernous room that serves as a bar, shop and recreation area for the warders.

I explain that I'm curious how this multi-functional island – prison, farm, nature and marine reserve – works.

'There're about eighty prisoners here, serious criminals,' explains the commissario. 'Murderers, gangsters, drug barons. They come here towards the end of their sentences, and if they've behaved well. The great problem in prison is boredom. Prisons are boring places to be. And if prisoners are bored, they make trouble. The more active the prisoners, the better. Here on Gorgona we're unique in Italy. Here they're active. They look after the animals, grow the vegetables, prepare the food, bake the bread. It gives them some experience of normality. They even learn a skill they can use when they go back into society.'

He takes me to the bakery first, where two well-floured prisoners are sorting out the day's batch ready for the oven. That comforting, homely smell of fresh-baked bread is the same on Gorgona as it is anywhere. It's difficult to remember that this is a prison.

Accompanied by a small posse of colleagues we make our way up the hill to a building that houses a kitchen with good quality domestic equipment. A prisoner is preparing lunch for twenty people – slices of mortadella and cheese; pasta with freshly made pesto; and then hamburgers from freshly minced veal. It looks pretty appetising; plain perhaps, but good and fresh, and largely made from ingredients produced by the farm.

The cook's a chatty fellow from Naples, small-framed, sinuous, charming, bright-eyed as a ferret. It seems rude to ask what he's inside for. Instead, I ask him if he'd been interested in cooking before?

No, he says, he'd never cooked before coming to Gorgona. Other people always cooked for him. His granny, his mother, his aunts. His mother was a very good cook. But now he's happy cooking for others. He laughs.

It's difficult to resist his energy and charm. Manipulating people is part of his armoury. He crinkles his eyes, but their quick, wary expression never changes.

Some years ago I spent several illuminating days in the kitchens of Pentonville Prison. It was clear that preparing and serving food was more than simply an activity. It was a form of communication and an instrument of power. Whether a prisoner had a choice of dishes and whether his food was warm depended on which floor and which wing was served first.

Of course food is important, says the cook, in the outside world, and here. In Naples food's a religion. Ah, taralli! And sfogliatelle! And coffee's a cult.

He shows me the menu for the season – sgombro alla fiorentina, spaghetti alla campagnola, scaloppine di bovino, trenette al pesto, frittata alle erbette. The dishes on Gorgona are a far cry from the carb-heavy meals at Pentonville, although I suspect the part they play in prison politics isn't much different.

As we make our way further up the incline of the natural amphitheatre over which the prison sprawls, the commissario points out various sections of the farm. The place has an air of normality, and yet, beneath the placid outward appearance lie all the disciplines, restrictions and tensions of a penal institution.

'What about the wine you produce here?' I ask. I'd read that the prison had recently extended its rehabilitation activities to include vine growing and wine production in conjunction with the well-respected brand, Marchesi di Frescobaldi. This intrigued me because the Pentonville warders used to dread the disappearance of sugar more than anything else. If sugar disappeared in any quantity, it meant that someone was brewing hooch, and hooch meant trouble. 'Are the prisoners allowed to taste their own produce?'

He laughs. It's the same as in England. Alcohol spells trouble. Anyway, he adds, you don't need grapes or even sugar to make wine. All you need is pasta. Keep cooked pasta in warm water for a few days, and it ferments. This comes as something of a revelation to me. It adds a whole new range of gastronomic possibilities to that staple of the modern kitchen.

We come to a cluster of pens where pigs lie stretched out on the dusty earth in the sun. Chickens scratch in the dirt nearby. It looks bare and spartan, but these are lucky animals compared to the vast majority in Italy. They're not exactly free-range, but at least they have fresh air and space to move and lie in. I was once told there were a million pigs in the countryside around Mantua, but I never saw one. They were all indoors. Smelt them, though.

Beyond the pig and chicken pens is the kitchen garden where two prisoners are tying up tomato plants. One's Chinese, the other Nigerian, says the commissario.

I ask him how many nationalities they have at the prison.

'Seven or eight,' he says. 'Italians, the Spaniard, Nigerians, Moroccans, Jamaicans, Chinese, a Dutchman.'

'Any English?' I ask.

There had been one once, he thinks, but there're none now.

Around them are rows of zucchini, artichokes, onions, garlic and lettuce, all in neat ranks. The vegetables are grown from seed, all organic, says the commissario. They work closely with Slow Food, an organisation dedicated to preserving biodiversity, the traditional ways of agriculture and old varieties of fruit, vegetables and farm animals. The prisoners responsible for growing food are allowed to sell their produce to each other or to the groups of visitors who come to the island each Sunday in summer.

Around the corner we come across a man in beekeeping gear. The commissario explains that he's a repeat offender, a con man. The man takes off his protective veil. He has a serious, intense face beneath a cap of white curls. He breaks off his work to let us taste the products of his charges in his tidy, spotless shed. The rosemary honey – there are seven varieties of rosemary on Gorgona, he says – is pale as a primrose, light and elegant, with the penetrating flavour of the herb. The other honey from cistus, broom and clover is darker, richer and rounder, with a touch of caramel.

The beekeeper asks the commissario and the other warders if he could have permission to grow extra vegetables on the earth he's in the process of reclaiming. They're dubious.

'That's tricky,' says the commissario in a reasonable voice. 'It would upset the other gardeners.'

The bee-keeper pleads his case. The commissario becomes more intransigent. The beekeeper's face takes on a mask of stoic resignation. He knows the situation. He's seen it all before, been through it all before. He understands the power structures better than anyone. He shrugs his shoulders.

'In that case...'

'We'll ask, of course,' says one of the warders. They're decent men. They appreciate his needs, but they know they can't help him. In the end they're bound by the tacit collaboration between prisoners and warders that governs life in all prisons, and without which they would be hard to control. Beneath the worthy ambitions of the prison farm, there's a delicate balance of power and interests, in which the warders are trapped as much as the prisoners.

I thank the man for the honey tasting. Isn't it rather lonely, working on his own? I ask.

He chooses it, he says, not being with the other prisoners. He prefers the bees, admires their industry.

'They don't need us,' he says with forlorn passion. He seems wrapped in solitude.

Finally, just below the point where pines and scrub begin, are the other animals, cows wandering in to some ramshackle barns and pens from the slopes where they've been grazing freely; sheep and goats in for milking; sows for farrowing; calves for suckling.

'It's as natural as we can make it,' says the commissario. 'No artificial fertilisers or pesticides. The animals aren't stressed. They live in their natural groupings. They're born, reared, and, occasionally, killed on the island.'

He asks me what I make of what I've seen. I reply, truthfully, that I'm impressed. Even the animal shit has a different quality, smells cleaner and sweeter, than that on other farms I've visited.

'It feels like a family-run smallholding of a hundred years ago,' I say.

True, it isn't a model in the sense of modernity, order and productivity. It has that ramshackle quality of a working farm, with bits of abandoned machinery here and there, makeshift repairs, buckled fencing, battered corrugated iron roofing. But it's properly functional. It's for work, not for show.

I lunch with the commissario and other warders in their

canteen, and rather wish that I'd been able to eat what I had seen being cooked by the prisoners earlier.

I've no idea whether it works in terms of rehabilitation. I can't interrogate the prisoners on their views, and I wasn't investigating re-offending rates. I'm sure that for some, work on the farm, taking responsibility for the wellbeing of animals, tending plants, watching bees make honey, really does provide a portal to a more law-abiding life, but my experiences at Pentonville taught me that many prisoners view a return inside sooner or later as an inevitable consequence of their chosen lifestyle.

But in terms of animal husbandry, food production and human activity, Gorgona seems wholly admirable, even if it is ironic that the sheep, goats, cattle, pigs and chickens on the island live with a freedom that few farm animals enjoy on more conventional farms these days, precisely because their human managers do not.

Back in Livorno
I fall in love with Nicoletta the moment I see her in the Piaggio agency in Livorno. Not all scooters are ladies. On an earlier adventure I had ridden bloke-ish Bud, who'd been solid, sensible, dull and male. There's nothing remotely bloke-ish about Nicoletta. She's feminine in form and fibre, elegant of frame, bold of colour, steady of balance. Her voice has a seductive, half-a-bottle-of-scotch-and-twenty-Capstan-Full-Strength-a-day purr. She holds tight into the corners, and is steady on the straight run, given to the occasional shimmy as if saying 'Just pay attention'. She has fierce acceleration if needed, although I prefer to potter at lesser speeds.

We head south to Piombino to catch the ferry to Elba. Six months stretch out before me like a scroll without a mark on it. I have an intoxicating sense of freedom, exhilaration, and apprehension.

So we saunter along at an amiable pace, sliding past vineyards, fields of wheat, groves of olives, dinky hilltop villages, alien industrial plant and machinery, grubby holiday developments. The sun's bright. The tongue of tarmac unravels ahead. Into shadow, out of shadow, cool one moment, warm the next. Suddenly I smell the honeyed sweetness of broom – 'E tu, lenta ginestra,/Che di selve odorate/Queste campagne adorni' (And you, soft broom, gracing this vandalised countryside with fragrant bushes), as the poet, essayist and philosopher, Giacomo Leopardi describes it. Then the acid whiff of sheep. A little further down the road the taint of some industrial process. Now the tang of eucalyptus; now the rank reek of stagnant salt water.

Car drivers flash by in air-conditioned confinement. Motorcycle riders glide past wrapped in gleaming black and the fat noise of their machines. But I do not envy them their cocooned isolation. What do they know of the real pleasures of travel? The sun's high in the heavens. Wind tempers the heat of the day. I'm at one with Nicoletta, the elements, the world. The call of the wild, the romance of the open road, the joy of travel. Poop Poop.

I finally park Nicoletta in the bowels of the ferry, and make my way up on deck, exhilarated and relieved. The first major hike of the trip has finished without mishap, and that is to be relished.

Elba

'In ancient lays they sang the praise of purple Provencal and Samiotic wine/But I reserve my song to dwell upon the virtues of the Elban vine.'

I wrote those lines some forty or so years ago, after a visit to Elba with two friends, Paul and Charlotte. It'd been an epic summer, full of wine, food, exploration and laughter. We'd been staying near Lucca, and decided, on the spur of the moment, that we needed an adventure. We'd had enough of the formal beauties of the more celebrated Tuscan towns. Elba, an island looming tantalisingly off the coast, was the obvious candidate. And, aside from having been a temporary residence for Napoleon Bonaparte, we knew nothing of the place.

I'm not sure we knew much more by the time we returned to the mainland after two days. Elba struck us as being short on romance and visual splendour. The only detail that stuck in my mind was of a last lunch in a restaurant in Portoferraio before taking the ferry back to the mainland. We drank two bottles of red wine, not unusual then or now, but no one had warned us that Elban wines were routinely 14 or 15 per cent ABV. These days that level of alcoholic content has become pretty standard, but, at the time, when the only wines of a similar strength were port or sherry, the Elban bottles were liquid booby traps. Lunch became merrier and merrier. Suddenly it was time to get the car onto the ferry. This turned out to be easier said than done. I have a vivid memory of being at the wheel, Paul shouting at me and a sailor leaping nimbly to one side as we careered up the ramp and into the hold of the ship. Hence my rueful reflections on the potent charms of Elban wine. Attitudes to drinking and driving have changed since those carefree days. I hadn't returned to Elba since.

I turn up the narrow, winding road that leads along the Valle di Lazzaro. The hills curve round to form a natural amphitheatre. The crest of the hill is thickly wooded. The hillside below is neat with platoons of vines, sappy green with fresh foliage, and clumps of silvery-green olive trees. At the end of the road, nestled among the olive trees and vines, is the Azienda Agrituristica Farkas, the home of Stefano and Francesca Farkas.

Stefano bears an uncanny resemblance to the great French fisherman Charles Ritz, a boyhood hero of mine. He has the same lean features, sharp nose, elegant moustache, and clipped hair. He fizzes with energy and purpose. Francesca's more retiring, less forceful than her husband, but kindly and thoughtful.

Years before, Stefano tells me, the Valle di Lazzaro had been a farm producing wine, but it fell into disuse and disrepair. He and Francesca bought it and set about returning the land to its former productivity. As we stand in the evening light looking out over the serried ranks of vines turning gold in the sun, Stefano explains how they cleared away the undergrowth that had covered the terraces, and reconstructed them where they had collapsed, assessed the soil, measured the sunlight, put in the metal stakes that mark each line of vines, planted vermentino, chardonnay and aleatico vines and nurtured them. That was nine years ago; nine years of unremitting labour that had transformed the overgrown, raggle-taggle bowl in the hills into a series of orderly, productive terraces. It's been a prodigious undertaking. Stefano says that he has a helper, but he still works full-time, pruning, spraying and picking the grapes himself.

'I tell you one thing,' he says a little wistfully. 'This is work for a younger man.'

Elba has a rather confused history, in common with many Mediterranean islands. First the Etruscans arrived, and then the Romans, attracted like subsequent occupiers by substantial deposits of iron and related minerals essential for cutting-edge military technology of whatever age. The island's principal town/port, Portoferraio, means The Port of the Iron Works.

Later, Elba changed hands between Pisans and Florentines, as those city states vied for supremacy both on mainland Italy and in the Mediterranean. There was a short period under the somewhat unreliable wing of the Visconti of Milan. Barbary pirates made frequent and unwelcome visits. The Florentines eventually ended up in control, and Cosimo de Medici built a series of interlinking forts in Portoferraio – Stelle, Falcone and Inglesi – to protect his territory. These forts still stand as an impressive testament to sixteenth-century defensive strategy, with their systematic and linked communications, by which troops from one part could be moved swiftly and easily to another.

In 1596 Phillip II of Spain captured Elba, and like Sicily and much of Southern Italy, absorbed it into the Spanish Empire. In 1802 the island was sold to France, under whom it prospered for a while. But its more recent history has been one of decline. The mining that made Elba prosperous for so long dwindled and then died out, the last mine finally closing in 1981. Since then, agriculture, winemaking and tourism have occupied the energies of the Elbani, although they seem to take the business of growing things and making wine rather more seriously than they do tourism.

———

The sky is grey and lowering as I set off for Marciana Marina. The road loops inland and then loops back to the coast again. The main part of the island is low and lumpy. The highest part, Monte Capanne at 1,018 metres, is only a little higher than Scafell Pike in Cumbria. Much of the knobbly interior and coastline is covered in Aleppo and Corsican pines, and thick fragrant bush of macchia, that distinctive, dark green, prickly, fragrant mix of lentisk, myrtle, strawberry tree, juniper and heather. Here and there this dark green shag pile is broken by terraces of olive trees or vines lined up in methodical squares. The coast is as crimped and sculpted as a pie topping into a succession of bays. Here and there views open up along the craggy shore as I pass through dozy seaside villages.

If the sun were shining, Marciana Marina would be one of those idealised small Mediterranean villages. Low, cream and umber houses crowd along the curve of the seashore, sheltered by the shaggy hills behind. A long breakwater provides sanctuary for a mix of fishing boats and recreational yachts and cruisers. The centre of the town is very quiet in the cool grey of the day. The odd person goes about their daily business. Men line the benches of the well-kept municipal gardens on the front, like swallows on a telegraph wire. As I park, a small boy darts out of a baker's shop clutching the loaf of the day.

Carlo Eugeni is sitting outside the Café Roma, a large, unremarkable place on the promenade. Carlo is the local Slow Food supremo. He's a stocky man, dressed in denim for comfort, not for show. A shrewd, well-fed face watches the world with amused detachment from beneath a baseball cap. When he lifts the peak, there's a fine stipple of white hairs underneath.

He speaks excellent English, the result, he says, of the years he'd worked for Delta Airlines and Pan Am, organising gastronomic tours for their customers.

'Mostly widows and divorcees,' he says. 'I don't think they were really interested in food and wine.'

He retired and returned to the town of his birth, turning his energies and contacts to supporting local foods and wines.

I ask him what distinguishes the food on Elba.

'Well,' he says. 'There's food of the land and food of the sea, but both have the qualities of simplicity and frugality. It's not very sophisticated. It concentrates on flavour. Big flavours. La tonnina is a typical Elban dish.'

'La tonnina?'

'A salad made with salted tuna. Belly is best. Salt was used to preserve the tuna because oil was too expensive. And it meant that fish could be eaten inland as well as on the coast. You soak it overnight in milk. Then cut the tuna into pieces and mix it with chopped onion, tomatoes, black and green olives and capers. Add some olive oil and let it rest for a few hours before eating. Big flavours.'

I tell him of my experiences with Elban wine on my first visit to the island forty years ago.

Carlo smiles. 'Things have changed since then,' he says. 'Not all of them for the better. But some, yes.'

He summons Franco, a man with a comically lugubrious face, greying wavy hair, Marcello Mastroianni moustache and glasses, who's talking earnestly to two others at a table on the other side of the bar. 'Can you bring me a bottle of your wine. For my guest. A very important English journalist.'

Franco does his best to look impressed. 'As it's for him and not you…' He goes off to fetch the wine.

Carlo explains that Franco and his partner, Alberto, have a vineyard in the hills above the town where they grow trebbiano grapes and make wine in small quantities.

'It's about as natural as wine can be because Franco and Alberto are too lazy to do anything to it. Absolutely nothing. They don't spray because it's too much trouble and too expensive. They do a bit of pruning. Not much. They keep the weeds down. They pick the grapes, press them, ferment the juice and bottle it. That's it.'

Franco returns with the bottle. The label is a simple, elegant ox-blood rectangle with the letters TO in white on it. No flowery prose describing the terroir, family history or grape varieties. Not even a note on the alcohol level.

TO are simply the first letters of the surnames of the winemaking partners, Tonnino and Onetta.

Franco pours the wine. It's the colour of dandelions and has an unusual, peppery, astringent nose. Franco says we need to wait a little before drinking it, to give it time to open. Natural and unpretentious it might be, but that's no excuse for not treating it with respect.

Franco's wine-making partner, Alberto Tonnino, comes over to join us. He has one of those perpetually youthful faces and a mop of light brown hair. 'The vines are very old,' he says.'A hundred years or so. That helps give the wine its concentration.'

They only make about 300 bottles a year, he says.

'One hundred for him,' says Franco. 'One hundred for me, and one hundred to give away to friends like Carlo.'

Suddenly it's time for lunch.

'You must go to La Taverna,' says Franco. 'They've got fresh anchovies. In today.'

Carlo's reluctant. He isn't convinced that the anchovies can be as fresh as Franco tells him. Only very fresh anchovies are worth eating, he says.

Crossing the street outside, we bump into the chef of La Taverna. He confirms that the anchovies have just come in that morning. We'd be welcome. We're the only customers for lunch. I'm anxious to try the soppressata di polpo before the anchovies. As far as I'm aware, soppressata normally applies to a cured, pressed salami in Calabria and Basilicata. It turns out to be an ingenious variation on that favourite Mediterranean theme of potato and octopus.

I'm not quite sure why this particular team of ingredients should have such universal appeal. It comes with all kinds of variations – cold or warm; with capers; without capers; with parsley; without parsley; dressed; undressed – but a straight left to the tastebuds it isn't. Perhaps the attraction lies in the gentle nuttiness of potato, one of the few ingredients that don't mask the delicate, delectable sweetness of freshly caught octopus. In this case, rocket and tomatoes, parsley and olive oil all add their ha'p'orth to thin, firm slices of octopus, and very nice it is, too.

The anchovies come with similarly fried zucchini. Franco's right. The anchovies are very fresh, clean, lambent with a certain airiness within a crisp shell of batter as light as a butterfly's wing.

'Isn't it wonderful?' Carlo observes as we say goodbye. 'You come to meet me. I introduce you to two men who make very singular wine. And they tell us where to have lunch. Connections, it's a kind of magic.' He waves to me as I set off.

Francesca and Stefano invite me to dinner. Their house is comfortable, rooms lined with books and pictures, richly carpeted, wood gleaming in amber light. The table in the dining room next to the ample kitchen is loaded with bowls and plates are lined up – a gloriously fruity, gloopy pappa al pomodoro; zucchini in carpione, sweet and sharp; and la tonnina, the powerhouse salad of salted tuna Carlo Eugeni had told me about. Beside them stand sleek bottle after sleek bottle of Farkas wines with their Lazarus labels.

As I pile my plate, I ask Stefano and Francesca how they had come to live on Elba.

'It's a long story,' says Stefano. 'My grandfather was the painter, Istvan Farkas, one of the most famous in Hungary at the beginning of the twentieth century, a friend of Picasso, Modigliani and other artists of the time. He was also a publisher, which was the family business. Towards the end of the war, Hungary became very anti-Semitic and in 1944 the Germans occupied the country. My grandfather, who was Jewish, was sent to Auschwitz-Birkenau. He died there. My father, Paolo, went into hiding, and was then forced to leave Budapest in 1948 when the communists took over. He came to live in Italy and became one of the world's best-known textile designers. He bought Villa Cafaggio on the Tuscan mainland, and started making wine there, vino sfuso, which we sold to Pietro Antinori. Vino sfuso is bulk, unbottled wine.

'In 1972 there was a crisis and wine buyers stopped buying. So we had to do something. I took over the vineyard from my father, and began to make quality wines to build up its reputation.

'In 2006 someone offered to buy Villa Cafaggio, and we took the decision to sell my share and we came here, to the Valle di Lazzaro.'

'With our two daughters,' says Francesca. 'But then they fell in love and got married and went back to the mainland because that's where their husbands work.' She sounds wistful. She misses the easy contact with her children and grandchildren.

'How've you found it?' I ask.

'When we came here,' says Francesca, 'we invited our neighbours to lunch and dinner. They came and were very pleasant, but they didn't ask us back.' She speaks with a certain puzzled acerbity.

'I tell you one thing,' says Stefano. 'Gli Elbani sono isolani. They're insular, true islanders. They look inward, not outward.'

This sounds very like some places I know in East Anglia and west Gloucestershire. Perhaps they're isolani, too, looking inward, not outward. I wonder if Stefano and Francesca regret their decision to move to Elba, whether they feel trapped.

As we eat and talk, we drink, first the Lazarus Vermentino d'Elba, and then the Aleatico and then the Sangiovese. They're suave and elegant wines, and have the same vitality as their maker, a far cry from the natural wine of Franco and Alberto and even further still from the rough-hewn monsters of memory.

We talk about winemaking and families and food and fishing. It turns out that, as well as looking like Charles Ritz, Stefano's a fanatical angler himself, fishing the same waters in Slovenia, the Baca, Idriza, and Tolminka that I've fished in years past, for brown and rainbow trout, grayling, and the great marmorata, the marble trout of the Julian Alps. We compare notes on flies and rods, talk technicalities of line weights and cast lengths with the delight of strangers finding shared passions.

Eventually I drag myself away, filled with fine food, wine and wonder at the way the life of the Farkas family has meandered from Budapest to Florence to Elba by way of the rivers of Slovenia and elsewhere, and how this life has so delightfully intersected with my own.

Pianosa

'There was nothing funny about living in a bum tent in Pianosa between fat mountains behind him and a placid blue sea in front,' Joseph Heller had written in *Catch-22*, his great novel based on his war-time experiences as a bomber pilot.

It seems odd that Heller decided to set *Catch-22* on Pianosa because in reality, Pianosa has no mountains, fat or otherwise. Its name means flat, and so it is, a smudged green pancake suspended between sky and sea and far too small to make a suitable landing for giant American bombers. The creative novelist has the freedom to interpret or recreate landscape to suit their purposes. Sadly the travel writer has to be anchored more prosaically in reality.

I've taken the happily old-fashioned ferry, with sparkling white woodwork and manganese blue trim, from Marina di Campo to Pianosa. The sea's rumpled satin, the sky the colour of a blackbird's egg.

As we draw up to the quay the port looks substantial and normal, the civic buildings imposing, the private houses elegant and consequential. But there's something odd about it. There's no one on the quay to greet us, none of the buzz or bustle of a community. It's silent but for the chuckle of the sea and bird calls. The small, enclosed harbour is deserted. Trails of diminutive silver fish twist like tinsel in its clear water. And close to, I can see that the buildings are crumbling, windows boarded up, roofs caving in, scabs of plaster flaking from walls, doors sagging on their hinges, gardens gone to seed. Some of the houses appear to be held together by webs of electrical wires woven by drunken spiders.

The human absence is so palpable and unnerving that it's a surprise to see a woman come out of one of the houses, and a shock when a car emerges from a side street and moves slowly down the road to the jetty.

I feel as if I'm invading some private domain, like Augustin Meaulnes in Le Grand Meaulnes. Pianosa is an alien, urban Marie Celeste. It's as if the town has suddenly been engulfed by some apocalyptic disaster, eliminating all civic life at a stroke. And that, in a sense, was what had happened.

In the 1970s, Anni di piombo – the Years of Lead – when terrorism and criminal violence were at their peak in Italy, the government decided that Pianosa would become the site for a maxi-prison, the place where the most-feared Mafia bosses and terrorists were to be held. Suddenly the entire population who'd lived on the island at least since the Romans – Pianosa was mentioned in the Annals of Tacitus, the great historian of imperial Rome – and that had numbered 2,500 at one point, were told to leave. To judge by the buildings they left, these were not subsistence fishermen and farmers. The abandoned homes are mute testimony to a vigorous society. Over 1,000 years of communal life vanished almost overnight, and Pianosa's only inhabitants became prisoners and their keepers. The skies buzzed with helicopters night and day. Searchlights lit the walls. Heavily armed guards patrolled the walls. Now the total population is listed as ten.

But Pianosa and its lost people have not been forgotten. One building has been reclaimed by the Amici di Pianosa, the Friends of Pianosa. In it there's an illuminating exhibition of sepia and black-and-white photographs celebrating life on the island before the mass eviction. They show a vivid and active community, into which the prisoners and warders of an earlier prison appear to have been integrated. There are particularly poignant pictures of football teams down the years, in which it's impossible to distinguish prisoners from non-prisoners, almost every player sporting a formidable moustache.

In theory the maxi-prison closed in 1998, but it had recently been pressed into service again, even though the walls in some places are in no better state than the town buildings. Its presence determines life on the island, most of which is off-limits to the casual visitor, unless in the company of a guide.

Needless to say, I haven't booked a guide, so I wander off to the outskirts of the village, the limit of where I'm officially permitted to go, to explore what there is to explore on my own. Various tempting paths curve away into the scrubby bush of the island's hinterland, a nature reserve, with abundant birds and animals rarely disturbed by human traffic. As these paths are clearly visible from the offices of the Corpo Forestale dello Stato, the only occupied official building on the island except for the prison, I think it wiser to stick to the letter of the law.

Such prudence makes me realise that I'm not an explorer in the spirit of Burton, Speke or Percy Fawcett, or even a traveller in the mould of Norman Lewis, Paddy Leigh-Fermor, Eric Newby or Colin Thubron, forging on in the face of overwhelming odds, an enquirer after difficult truths. Mine's a meeker spirit. I may follow by-ways in preference to highways, but I always stick to a way of some kind. If a sign says 'Entry Forbidden', I tend to take it at its word.

Sticking to the permitted paths, I stumble on the island's cemetery, tucked away at the end of a track that runs through undergrowth fragrant with thyme, sage, wild fennel and curry plants. A protective thicket of shrubs grows on one side, and a tiny golden cove lies on the other. It's a sweet, shady place, crumbling from neglect, filled with resinous trees, aloe cacti, wild onions, daisies, wild iris and graves. It reminds me a bit of Swinburne's poem, 'A Forsaken Garden':

> In a coign of the cliff between lowland and highland,
> At the sea-down's edge between windward and lee,
> Walled round with rocks as an inland island,
> The ghost of a garden fronts the sea.

Here's another history of Pianosa, told in the inscriptions on the graves – 'Monzi Silvestro agente di custodia nato 10 Marzo 1890 Morto 24 Novembre 1918 i compagni posero' (Monzi Silvestro prison guard born 10 March 1890 Died 24 November 1918 erected by his companions); 'Qui dorme l'eterno sonno Frosini Elia d'anni 19 Caporale nel 10 Reggio Fanteria Vittima di giovanile imprudenza il 6 Gennaio 1808. I Cittadini di Pianosa e gli agenti di custodia O.M.P.' (Here sleeps eternally Frosini Elia19 years a corporal in the 10th Reggio Infantry Victim if a youthful indiscretion 6 January 1808. Citizens of Pianosa and prison warders O.M.P.). Quiet, plain homages to the people who lived and worked on the island. I can think of worse places to lie.

However, I'm not quite ready for that yet. I retrace my steps to the village, passing the Via Giovanni Falcone e Paolo Borsellino, the names of the two investigating magistrates assassinated by the Mafia, to the prison which has a – well, I wouldn't call it a trattoria, more of a canteen, a characterless, cavernous room with a bar, a vestigial shop and tables at which to eat food cooked by the prisoners and served by the prisoners. One prisoner, to be exact.

There's spaghetti con salsa di pomodoro followed by pesce spada alla griglia or chicken; and ice cream bought at the bar for pudding. Nothing fancy, but the cooking's sensible and sound, and at twenty-four euros including half a litre of white wine, there's not much to complain about. It's certainly better than the lunch with the warders of Gorgona.

There's not a lot to do before the ferry back to Marina di Campo at 5 p.m., other than visit the remains of the villa of Augustus Caesar, and loaf and swim or swim and loaf. The only beach open to the casual tourist lies beneath the long frown of the prison wall that curves the full length of the bay beside the ghost town.

At the end of the beach, Augustus's villa lies under a white structure shading it from the elements. It seems a modest structure for the man who founded the Roman Empire through a mixture of brutality, ruthlessness, mendacity, military nous and political sophistication. He understood that soldiers were happier to be paid for not fighting than they were to fight. Perhaps it had been the house for Postumus, the adopted son whom Augustus had exiled to Pianosa. Postumus, described as 'a vulgar young man, brutal and brutish, and of depraved character', lived there until he became involuntarily posthumous on the orders of his adoptive father.

Augustus ruled for forty-one years before retiring from politics, a rare thing to do in Rome of that time, and died of natural causes aged seventy-five, which was even rarer. Reputedly his last words were 'Have I played the part well? Then applaud as I exit.'

After inspecting the ruins and reviving my memories of Imperial Rome, I go for a swim, my first on this trip. Although the temperature's crispish, the sea feels like silk against my skin and the sun warms my head.

Elba (again)

If anyone knows anything about Elba, it's that Napoleon Bonaparte spent a few months in exile on it. He came reluctantly in April 1814 and left hurriedly in February 1815. Although he had a country residence island, he spent most of his time in the Villa dei Mulini, at the top end of the Portoferraio, that has been recently restored as part of the celebrations marking 200 years since his brief sojourn.

It has the air of the home of a well-to-do merchant, solid and handsome, with the central section slightly higher and grander than the two-storey wings on either side. It's freshly painted a curious, bilious rapeseed yellow, with bare grey stone surrounds framing the windows. It must have seemed constrictingly modest to someone used to the vaulting spaces, glitter and glamour of Versailles or Schönbrunn.

A covey of schoolchildren squats in the sun in the piazza outside. A teacher stands facing them. Her voice rises in a singsong monotone without, it seems, any oral punctuation. On and on she goes, her voice rising like that of a skylark, only less melodic. She knows her stuff, and by golly, she's going to give it to them whether they like it or not. Judging by the whispering and fidgeting, some of the children clearly don't.

My sympathies are with the kids. Their situation sharply brings back the ghastly tedium of visits to the mosaic-bedecked churches around Ancona and Cervia to which my parents dragged me all those years ago. Eventually the teacher's peroration comes to an end and the children are released. They pelt into the Villa dei Mulini as if released from bondage, clutching notepads and pens. I follow them in.

Inside the villa the rooms are sensible and comfortable and unmistakably bourgeois while the furniture is the grandiose, florid stuff of Empire. Little of it is actually Napoleon's own, but it is of the period, not modern counterfeit. The only exception is one of the Emperor's campaign camp beds, which is astonishingly elegant, minimalist and sensible, even with its baldacchino.

Is it the bed on which Napoleon lay while conducting the Battle of Waterloo, I wonder? At the time he had such a bad attack of piles that he wasn't able to sit on the back of his horse, thus depriving him both of mobility and the height he needed to survey the battlefield properly. It could be argued that haemorrhoids have played a pivotal role in European history. I don't suppose this interesting aperçu found its way into the teacher's discourse to her bored pupils. It might've livened up their afternoon.

For someone who never seemed inclined to stay anywhere very long, Napoleon had an impressive library. He was a ferocious and omnivorous reader all his life, committing chunks of Voltaire, Corneille, Molière and Racine to memory, as well as following philosophical, political and scientific debates. The bookshelves are spread over two rooms and made up of volumes he had chosen from his bigger library at Fontainebleau.

The way the light falls on the spines of the books and the rope preventing entry makes it nigh on impossible to see what volumes made up the Emperor's reading matter. I manage to decode the titles of volumes of Voltaire, *Année Française*, and *Le Moniteur Française*, but that's all. It's a pity, as the contents of other people's bookshelves are always illuminating about the collector.

Napoleon had a keen sense of family, and looked after them with typical Mediterranean patriarchal authority. Even so, he apparently found the presence of his sister, Pauline, in the villa rather trying. Pauline had sold her house in Paris to be able to join him on the island. With one of those delicious historical ironies, the buyer had been the British government, and the Duke of Wellington had acted as the intermediary. Indeed, he befriended Pauline, and had a picture of her in his residence. The building is still the British Embassy, and full of Pauline's own furniture and ornaments, including a pair of exquisite silver sauce boats said to be modelled on her breasts.

She might not have been dull, but she was unquestionably demanding, rackety and given to sex with just about everyone. She died in 1825 aged forty-four. I remember reading somewhere that she suffered from bad blood circulation in later years and was wont to tuck her toes up under the breasts of her ladies-in-waiting in order to keep them warm. Such learning is the product of indiscriminate reading and a memory in which the curious asides of history's trifles are retained more faithfully than its landmarks.

On 26 February 1815, alarmed by rumours that he was about to be transferred to a far less salubrious island in the Atlantic or even assassinated, Bonaparte left Elba, returned to France and began the last hurrah that led to Waterloo. Although his reign on the island was short-lived, he still managed to make a perfect nuisance of himself, issuing decrees, bossing everyone about to improve mining and modernise agriculture. The departure of this restless, Protean figure was probably greeted with a sigh of relief by the Elbani.

All in all, I think, the Villa dei Mulini's a fine, civilised and agreeable residence, and only an ass would want to leave it in favour of the uncertain cockfight of European politics.

From it, I wander down through the town. The streets are vertiginous. Pretty sun-washed pink, cream and yellow houses with green shutters cascade down the slope to the port.

In some ways, Elba presents the kind of Mediterranean scene nostalgia has fixed in my imagination, with some of the character, I fancy, that the South of France once possessed; an unspoiled, untrampled Eden of golden, sun-drenched coves and dramatic rocky outcrops lined with umbrella pines shading cottages with terracotta fish-scale tiled roofs, when Brigitte Bardot and Roger Vadim made it fashionable and it was colonised (cinematically, anyway) by the laughing girls, as brown as nuts and as scantily clad as shop window mannequins, frolicking in the sea with lads with the profiles of boxers and the minds of philosophers, before they picnicked on grilled fish, scarlet tomatoes, oozy cheeses and crusty baguettes, casually feeding each other grapes – or better still, figs – and drinking glasses of cloudy pastis or pink kirs, and smoking Gitanes or Boyards Caporal and talking all the time as they do so.

But I don't feel that the tough, self-sufficient, taciturn *Elbani* have the sophisticated worldliness or the cheery venality of the Provencals. Cecilia Pacini, a local journalist, had told me that the *Elbani* referred to mainland Italy as 'Il Continente' in much the same circumspect way that the British refer to Continental

Europe. Certainly, the *Elbani* don't have much truck with the demands of contemporary tourism.

Down on the quayside, deeply tanned, elderly men with silvery, wavy hair, black shades, trainers and jeans and shirts with the collars turned up to disguise jowls and scrawny necks, pose in front of a frieze of masts and cantilevered superstructures on boats. But Portoferraio is no Cannes or Beaulieu-sur-Mer, thank heavens. There's none of the grandiosity of sea-going palazzi. If there's just a bit of vulgar display, at least it's modest vulgar display.

Rather, Portoferraio has an air of distressed gentility, the elegant shabbiness, of a gentleman down on his luck. Collar and cuffs are frayed, suit and tie shiny with use, shoes in need of fresh soles and a lick of polish. But with a turn of fortune, an unexpected inheritance, Black Dog coming in at 100–1 in the 2.30 at Uttoxeter, the town will be as elegant and prosperous as it was in former times. Somehow, though, I feel that Black Dog isn't going to come in at 100–1 for Portoferraio any time soon.

Giglio

'Take the road to Giglio Castello. You can't miss the turning. It's just past the cemetery,' Francesco Carfagna tells me on the phone. 'It'll be a short journey for me when my time comes,' he adds, and laughs.

John Irving first introduced me to Francesco a couple of years earlier at Slow Food's great biennial food jamboree in Turin, the Salone del Gusto. It had been love at first sight on my part as I was drawn to Francesco's ebullience, generosity and idiosyncratic intelligence. He'd said that if I should ever visit Giglio, I must look him up. I'd taken him at his word.

I find the turning easily enough, bounce along the track past the cemetery, and come to a halt beside a circular stump of a building. Francesco is waiting for me outside.

'Matthew, you are welcome.'

Francesco's about my height, but thicker through the chest, and rounder in the tummy. He has a shock of fine white hair, and sideburns, the like of which I haven't seen since the 1970s, on either side of his cherubic face. His eyebrows are like two dark, spiky hedges above expressive brown eyes. His face, arms and hands are so deeply tanned that they might be mahogany all the way through. He's wearing a pink shirt with a frayed collar and a pale blue jersey that would be shapeless were it not stretched over a considerable girth. He has socks on and heavy work boots over them.

He explains that the house is round because it had once been a mill. Shorn of the superstructure that carried the sails, only the round base remains, looking out across the sea to Elba, the mysterious cone of Montecristo, and to Corsica beyond. The interior is as round as the exterior, with one room to each floor. Each room and the stairs between are cluttered with books, books and yet more books. The ground floor serves as kitchen and dining room. It's quite the tiniest kitchen I've ever seen.

Francesco leads me down some steps to the more conventionally configured base below the truncated tower. 'You will sleep with the bottles,' he says grandly, as if the bottles are sentient and responsive. The room with my bed is largely filled with boxes of wine stacked in partitioning walls, as is each of the other rooms, all part of a large order, he informs me, for a Japanese client and due for dispatch in a few days. It's snugly comfortable, with my own bathroom, shower and a small kitchen where I can make coffee and breakfast.

Presently his wife, Gabriella, joins us. She's beautiful, with broad, almost Slavic, lines to her face, high cheekbones, a full mouth, short light brown hair without a trace of white, and eyes the colour of toasted hazelnuts. She apologises for not being there to greet me, as she's been visiting a sick friend. Sadly she wouldn't be joining us for dinner either as she had to return to the friend. Her expression changes with almost every word she speaks, like wind passing over a field of wheat. She departs in a flurry of further apologies.

Before he starts cooking in the smallest kitchen in the world, Francesco brings up a couple of two-litre bottles of his wine, Ansonaco. It's the colour of winter sunshine. We drink it at cellar temperature, as he prefers. Chilling it, he says, reduces its distinctive flavours.

'It's from the bottom of the container,' says Francesco. 'It's – how do you say? – better than the clear wine. It has more character.'

The wine has a curious, astringent nose of crab apple and mirabelle plums, but tastes ethereal, gentle, sunny and fresh, with a slight resinous edge. It has an exquisite balance and dawdles expansively around my mouth.

'What's your philosophy of wine making?' I ask him, mindful of Stefano Farkas's eloquent expositions of his approach to making wine.

'I don't have a philosophy,' Francesco says. 'Philosophy is blah, blah, blah. The wine is the wine. That is the philosophy.'

'There are standard wines,' he goes on. 'And there're wines like mine, that aren't standard.'

He pours me a glass of sangiovese produced by a colleague in mainland Tuscany. It's smooth, handsome and immaculately tailored with suave, well-behaved fruit, something of a Savile Row wine. It's a style that I recognise immediately and enjoy.

'That's a standard wine,' explains Francesco. 'It's a good wine, well-made. The standard is high. But it's a standard. It has no individuality. It'll never be much better or much worse.'

Modern winemaking techniques and knowledge have improved the general quality of wines immeasurably since the days when I first started drinking the stuff. It's very rare to get an absolute stinker these days, while memories of Don Cortes Spanish Burgundy, Bull's Blood, Blue Nun and Black Tower of my student days still cause involuntary acid reflux. However, along the way, it seems to me that many wines have lost some of their distinctive character. Overall the palate of contemporary wines has narrowed, become smoother, sweeter and more predictable. The depths to which some wines were once prone to sink might have vanished, but so, too, have the individualistic heights.

As we drink, Francesco prepares dinner. He cooks as he speaks, with great deliberation, attending to each detail with meticulous care. It isn't a speedy process.

We start with salted anchovies that he's made himself.

'You can eat them after a couple of months, but they are better after a year,' he says.

He's already washed off the salt and taken out the backbones before submerging the fillets in olive oil for a day. He takes them out of the oil, and, while they drain, slowly chops a green shoot of a Tropea onion against his thumb with the scarred blade of an old Opinel knife. He slices some flakes of peel from a lemon and griddles a few slices of bread and rubs them with garlic. He heaps three or four of the anchovy fillets, onion shoots and lemon peel onto the bread and hands it to me. The anchovies have the texture of chilled butter and a mellow meatiness, carrying sweet onion and citrus oil and garlic and the slight bitterness from where the ridges of the griddle pan have burnt the bread.

Then Francesco cleans and descales the red mullet, bream and scorfano (scorpion fish) he bought from the fishmonger a few hours earlier. He chops a couple of onions and adds them to the olive oil in a sauté pan, mauled and dull from long use. He puts in a little chilli for good measure, scatters a handful of fresh broad beans on top and carefully places the fish in the pan so that they form a single layer, pours a glass of fresh water over them and sets the dish to a gentle simmer.

While he was cleaning the fish, he found a sac of roe. He washes the roe in salt water that he keeps in a bottle on the floor, and squeezes the raw eggs out of the containing membrane into a bowl. He splashes a little olive oil over them and beats them and oil vigorously with a fork. When there's a smooth emulsion, he hands the bowl to me.

'Fish mayonnaise,' he says. 'If you wash it in sea water, it doesn't need any salt. Put it on the toast.' It has a delicate but distinct fishiness. He pours a little more fresh water over the cooking fish. There's no sense of hurry about Francesco's cooking, just a steady deliberation about each stage.

He shakes a fine, brindled Mediterranean crayfish (aragosta) out from under a damp cloth in a plastic bag. The creature waves its long antennae in a kind of world-weary protest at its cavalier treatment. Francesco takes a large knife and forcefully cuts off the chunky tail. He sticks the head upright in a bowl to catch the juices. The antennae give one last, despairing twitch, and are still. Painstakingly and precisely he cuts the tail into sections and the head in half.

Before he puts the tail sections into the pan, he carefully extracts the bright orange sacks of raw roe. He pops one into his mouth, opening his eyes wide.

'Perche no? Why not?' he says, and adds more water and the crayfish juices to the simmering fish.

I try a sac of roe. It's gentle, sweet and creamy with a very slight graininess.

Francesco treats each ingredient as if it has a particular point, flavour or virtue. Each action is a stage in a closely observed ritual expanded over many minutes as he stops to tell a story, make an observation, reflect on this or that.

And so while he cooks, he tells me about his life as an engineer in Florence; how he once designed a building that was built without cement; about his daughters from his first marriage; how he met Gabriella, and why they came to Giglio; how they'd run a restaurant together, he cooking, she taking care of the front of house; the politics of wine production on Giglio. At one point he stops, searches for some missing piece of equipment and blames his inability to find it on Cincuit, which or who, says Francesco, is un diavoletto, a Triestino domestic goblin, who hides car keys, slips bills for payment into the wastepaper basket, trips you up with a shoe on the floor, who's responsible for those tiny, irritating hiccups that interrupt the smooth flow of a well-run life.

We finally begin eating the fish around midnight. With infinite patience Francesco scrapes away the skin and the bones of a mullet, before putting the pearly white flesh on my plate, along with a section of aragosta tail.

'Take some of the juices,' he commands, 'and the broad beans.'

'Perché no?' I say. Fish, crayfish, broad beans, juices, simple, complex, all the world in each mouthful, food to eat for the rest of my life. I wipe my plate clean with bread so thoroughly it gleams as if it's been washed.

The next day the weather bears a closer resemblance to the Lake District in November than the sun-drenched Mediterranean of my dreams. A heavy, wet mist shrouds the world. The shrubs around the house limply drip tears of moisture. Those beyond are just looming presences. Nothing moves.

I read and write up my notes and chat intermittently with Francesco and Gabriella as they come and go about their respective businesses. I log onto the BBC News website and try to relate to a world of mayhem, seedy court cases, political posturing and nastiness in a hundred forms, and can't. How unreal and meaningless it all seems, like a news broadcast from some far-distant galaxy.

And then my daughter, Lois, comes to join me for a short break, and the sun breaks through as she arrives.

Lois is a boon and a delight, the best of companions: curious, humorous, calm in the face of adversity (which I'm not), cheerful and determined to enjoy each adventure to the full. Above all, she's a warm, loving and generous soul, with a great appetite for life.

She was born in Columbus, Ohio, and my wife, Lindsay, and I adopted her at birth, flying to Columbus to collect her when she was three weeks old. When you adopt a child, it's like being a potter who's given a lump of clay by a stranger. We had no control over the qualities of the clay. All we could do was try to shape it through love and experience.

With Lois, Lindsay and I were fortunate beyond measure. It was soon apparent that the clay from which Lois was made was particularly fine, with a wide seam of purest gold running through her heart and spirit. I fell in love with her the moment I held her in my arms in the suite of the Ramada Hotel in Columbus in which we lived for a week after being given her. I've watched her grow with utter astonishment. There has been joy and wonder in every day of her existence.

I can't think of many people of any age who would have greeted the idiosyncratic arrangements of the Carfagna household with her delight, or adapted to the circumstances with such enthusiasm. Like me, she finds the beauty of the situation, the particularity of the house and the warmth of Gabriella and Francesco extraordinary and beguiling. She takes the dinners that begin at 8 p.m. and finish at 1 a.m. in her stride, observes the banter between Gabriella and Francesco with affection, sleeps easily among the wine bottles and embraces every day.

––––––

'Today, Matthew, we go to the vineyard, Altura, and you and Lois can pick lemons,' says Francesco one morning.

Altura feels as if it's at the end of the world because it slopes steeply to where the land falls abruptly 200 metres or so to the rocks and the sea. It's magnificently terraced, the old retaining walls, carefully restored, descending in a series of long steps beneath an aquamarine sky to an aquamarine sea. But instead of the metal stanchions with taut wires running between them of Stefano Farkas's vineyard at Valle di Lazzaro, wooden stakes form a pleasing, higgledy-piggledy, abstract pattern. The wires between them for supporting the vines don't exactly have the tension of violin strings. And the gaps between the vines are a riot of wild flowers, so that the fresh green vine leaves rear up out of a sea of yellow, white, red, purple herbage, beautiful and beguiling.

'Look at the generosity of those plants,' Francesco says, waving at the vines like the father of particularly precocious and talented children. He intervenes as little as possible in the way the vines grow, he says.

But doesn't thinning bunches of grapes help to improve the quality? I ask.

'The rabbits, birds, the weather, the gods, they reduce the grapes for me.'

What about herbicides or fertilisers?

He frowns.

The wild flowers are regularly cut with a strimmer, and, instead of being tidied away, are allowed to lie where they fall to shade the ground from the fiercest heat of the summer, help keep moisture in the earth, and improve the structure and fertility of the land as they rot.

Francesco's method of vineyard management resembles that of his cooking: gradual and deliberate, a series of carefully integrated but natural processes. He has help in the form of the tattooed, ponytailed and endlessly smiling Marco. At harvest, members of the family and their friends are drafted in. The nature of the topography makes the use of machinery impossible, so all picking has to be done by hand. Because the vines grow in more or less their own way, there aren't the neat and regular bunches of grapes that make for easy picking. 'Sometimes you really have to look for the grapes,' says Francesco.

He sends Lois and me off to pick lemons from trees in another part of the vineyard. We scramble over a low, lichen-blotched wall in the hot sun, and pick our way gingerly between lines of vines, leaping from one terrace to the next, scraped and scratched by thorns and brambles. It's a breathless, sweaty business.

The trees grow on the very edge of a sharp vertical drop. We balance precariously over the abyss, trusting to the branches not to break under our weight, reaching into tangles of sharp twigs for the fat, yellow, tear-drop fruit just at the very limit of our reach. We pick clusters rapidly, tossing them as if they are live hand grenades from one to the other, depending on who's holding the bag, floating in a lemon haze, of citrus oil and leaf. Presently the bag's full and the tree's empty, except for the fruit too remote to reach. We make our way, laughing and cursing, back through the spiny undergrowth, to the cool of the old shepherd's shelter in the main vineyard where Francesco's preparing lunch of pasta sauced with the remains of the previous night's fish stew for us.

Giannutri

Giannutri is an island the shape of a gnawed dog's bone, about forty-five minutes from Giglio Porto. Francesco has arranged for Antonio and his large inflatable to take Lois and me there and bring us back. The sun's bright. The sea's smooth and blue. The light sparkles on wavelets. A sense of adventure bubbles between us.

We disembark at the Cala dello Spalmatoio, a narrow bay where houses, holiday homes, and buildings are scattered through the trees above the landing stage, all apparently deserted. Suddenly a shrivelled raisin of a man materialises on the path. He appears to be the Ancient Mariner's elder brother, rather nattily done up in a striped shirt of many colours and shorts that are indecent on a man of that age, indeed, of any age.

'Tedeschi?' he asks.

'No!' I say firmly. He looks disappointed.

'Olandesi?'

'Inglesi,' I say more firmly.

'Ah,'he says, as if that information provides unexpected illumination. Without further ado, he launches into an account of the last few years of his life, which consist, it seems, of spending winters skiing at Cortona and summers in Giannutri. We listen politely for a minute or two, bid him good day, and, baffled, make our way through the deserted village.

Giannutri isn't as strange or striking as Pianosa, but it still has that slightly eerie quality of a place where human beings should be, but aren't. We strike out along the dirt path taking us to Cala Maestri, the other landing spot on the island, where, I fancy, we'll swim, lunch, snooze and swim some more. Ah, the idyll of summer in the islands.

Or, at least, the dirt path I think is taking us to Cala Maestri. Slowly I come to the conclusion that it isn't.

You may think it difficult to get lost on a small island with few paths, but it's really quite easy. The wayward signposting doesn't help. The solid wall of bush on either side cuts off any long view, making it difficult to identify landmarks. The paths, themselves, seem designed to disorient, more a series of interconnected mazes than logical connections between one place and the next. Some lead to the dead end of a holiday establishment festooned with 'Proprieta Privatà' signs. Others just twist and turn until they come to a fork. We study the forks. No signs. It's a lottery which one to take, a lottery in which invariably I make the wrong decision.

My spirits droop. I become cross. I moan. I feel that I've let Lois down. Where's the swimming I had promised? Where the clear, azure waters? The curious sights? The bold adventure? Even more disturbing, where and when are we going to have lunch?

'Stop complaining, Dad,' Lois says sharply. 'This *is* an adventure.'

'Not the one I had in mind,' I say.

'Well, I'm enjoying it,' she says, and stomps on.

Were there anyone to see us, we'd make an incongruous sight – a middle-aged man with a red, perspiring face, a straw hat, a rucksack on his back and a plastic bag in each hand, one bulging with lunch, the other with towels, being led at a fast clip by an elegant young woman in a coral T-shirt and black leggings, carrying a Mary-Poppins-sized handbag in one hand and another plastic bag containing God knows what in the other.

Presently, a truck carrying two men, one of whom appears to be North African and the other from Central America, passes us. They stop and give us clear instructions how to find Cala Maestri and, sure enough, with a right here and then a left, there it is: curious and beautiful, with Roman pillars, mysterious brick archway, landing stage and, best of all, empty.

We hurry down. Joy, rapture. A swim before lunch. A snooze in the sun. This is what it's all about. Then we notice jellyfish, flotillas of them, pretty pink umbrellas with dangly bits waving below, pulsating gently in the water at our feet. Suddenly swimming doesn't seem quite so attractive. Oh well, at least we can have lunch and relax in the sunshine. Swimming can come later.

And then a middle-sized cruise boat steams up, heaves to and begins edging its way towards a jetty on the far side of our little cove.

'It isn't going to— !' I exclaim.

'It is,' says Lois.

And it does – edges in, ties up and disgorges dozens of families on a day out, who make their way along various paths to our side of the cove. I feel as peaceful villagers on the northeast coast of

England must have felt about the arrival of the Vikings. We pack up again and march off.

After further fruitless exploration of Giannutri's path system, in desperation we make our way back to the bay where we landed, clamber along the rocks to a place of relative solitude and swim and eat our picnic and chat in a most amiable way. Balm at last.

I ask Lois what she makes of Giannutri.

'It's very pretty, Dad,' she says.

'Hmm.'

'And the sea is fabulous.'

'Hmm.'

'And we've had adventures.'

'Hah!' I say.

'Honestly, you expect too much.'

'But don't you think Giannutri is missing something?' I say.

'Well,' says Lois. 'I suppose it's a bit vacuous, sort of void. I kept feeling that someone had left a place just before we arrived there, that we'd just missed something, and the fun had vanished round the corner.'

Giglio (again)

Over the next few days Lois and I explore Giglio together, swimming at the Cala delle Cannelle, speculating about the relationships and histories of our fellow swimmers; eat fried anchovies, paccheri with squid, prawns, scampi, zucchini and tomatoes, and a fabulously indulgent apple tart at La Paloma down on the harbour; search out the best ice creams on the island at Da Rosa at Giglio Porto; peer at the *Costa Concordia*, the cruise liner that alerted the wider world to Giglio when it crashed into rocks just off the island and sank killing thirty-two people, now lying by the entrance to the port, being made ready for the breaker's yard. We laugh and talk. We drink white wine at

Altura and sit in companionable silence and watch the sun going down behind Montecristo and Corsica beyond, and dine with Gabriella and Francesco and their friends at Tonino's at Campesi, where the rocks slope down to the sea, smooth and curved as whales breaching, the waves sliding over them, breaking, cascading down their sides.

'I am the king because I choose to cook, and you are the slaves because you have to wait,' says Francesco. It's Lois's last night.

'So what's on the menu, chef?'

'Fish roe with apple, zucchini, peas and peperoncino,' he says as we squeeze in around the dining table.

'Apple!?'

'Perche no? I like adding fruit to dishes,' says Francesco. He opens his eyes wide and spreads his hands.

And then?

'Cacciucco di Taranto. Just fish, whatever the fisherman gives me, onions, peperoncino, bay leaves, tomato and water left over from cooking the aragosto.'

And so the waiting, eating, drinking and chatting goes on.

'France-e-e-sco,' coos Gabriella, stretching out the middle vowel, 'Tesoro, do you remember how you seduced me?'

She tells us how she and Francesco had met in Florence, and how they had gone on a romantic tryst to a 'hotel' run by Tonino, proprietor of the trattoria where we'd eaten the night before. She draws a picture of Francesco wooing her with honeyed words and of herself as a wide-eyed ingénue.

'Imagine me, a sweet innocent from Mantua,' she says, eyes wide, daring us to disbelieve her, 'packing my best nightdress to meet this man. And him telling me that we're going to a romantic hotel. The hotel turned out to be a building where factory workers had lived. Tonino had bought it, and was trying to turn it into a hotel. Imagine me, a sweet young girl, with this… this… this satyr.' She dissolves into laughter.

As we eat the roe with zucchini, peas, apple and peperoncino, all delicate tastes and odd accents, Francesco tells us how they organise a concert at Altura every year at the end of July.

'These are serious musicians,' he says, 'from the Nuovo Quartetto Italiano and I Solisti Veneti. They bring their Stradivarius and Amati instruments. Incredible. People say "What about the sun, the humidity, the salt?" But they come. And after the concert, and all the listeners have gone home, we have dinner in the vineyard, just us and the musicians, by candlelight. It's incredible.'

'It sounds magical,' I say.

'It's magic that we're here to do it,' says Gabriella.

'We aren't here because we're told to do this or that,' Francesco says. 'We are here, just here, at this point, because of decisions we've made. And I have made some bad decisions.' For a moment he looks solemn, and then breaks into a great guffaw.

Lois looks on in smiling amusement. We eat. We sleep. The next day she goes back to London.

———

I sit under a nectarine tree, shaded from the sun, catching up with notes and writing, and adjusting to Lois's absence. Having her with me, watching her curiosity, braced by her common sense, seeing her evident pleasure in the place and the people, has added immeasurably to the richness of these days. I haven't been lonely before. How could I be with Francesco and Gabriella? Occasionally, you meet people with whom you feel as if you've been friends for ever. I feel that way about Francesco and Gabriella. There's a warmth, generosity and affection, a sense of being embraced and accepted. But more than that, there's that feeling of connection, of seeing the world from roughly the same perspective, of being able to explore ideas without careful diplomacy, and of sharing humour at the absurdity of life.

A blast of noise announces to the world that the fish truck is on its way to the piazza at Giglio Castello, the modern incarnation of a very old practice linking the port to the inland. A jade beetle crawls across the table on which I'm writing. The light flickers off the sea in chips, a shifting, irregular lace of diamond points, quick, urgent signals, intimate and immense, personal and impersonal, specific and general.

I have the melancholy sense that I'm tracking a vanishing culture through the islands. Of course, life on them has always been harsh and difficult. I'd read some of the great novels of Mediterranean life – *Arturo's Island*, *The House by the Medlar Tree*, *The Law*, *South Wind*, *Graziella* – and they make clear how impoverished, insular, narrow-minded, restrictive, prescriptive these micro-societies were and are.

But, while social change, improved communication and tourism have brought significant benefits, at the same time they've helped erode the communal experience that embraces vines and wines; familiarity of what grows best where and when; seasonal changes; the skills of terracing and wall building; drainage and irrigation; the fabric of communities and their customs; food, songs and language. We're watching knowledge and experience and wisdom built up over millennia vanish.

The natural pattern of life on these islands will, in all probability, vanish altogether in Lois's lifetime. If she were to attempt the same journey when she's my age, the liberal ambitions of Gorgona, the surly insularity of Elba and the unexploited beauties of its coast, the deserted melancholy of Pianosa and its cemetery, the walls that've stood for 1,000 years on Giglio, and the terraced magic of Altura with its remarkable proprietors and their circular house will have gone, and the way of life, the awareness and appreciation, the skills that these extraordinary social outposts need to survive, will have withered away. It's a depressing prospect.

———

Poppies, rock roses, wild chrysanthemums, wild fennel, curry plant, thistle, cornflowers, vetch, honeysuckle, myrtle, mastic, strawberry trees – I stride out along the track from Giglio Castello that leads to Pardini's Hermitage, and to lunch. I can't miss the way Francesco and Gabriella had told me as I set off. Just turn right when you see the sign that reads Cala degli Alberi. The Hermitage is at the end of the track, a hotel and sanctuary, a lovely place. Ghigo will be waiting for you, they say.

The warm air is hazy with spicy, peppery, citric perfumes. Bees buzz. Birds sing. The going's good. Every prospect is gilded. Lizards scutter from my coming. My shoes whisper-crunch on the dusty surface of the path. Dazzling light and pitch shade flicker on its stony surface. A very small, startled rabbit dashes away into the underbrush. An iridescent green scarab beetle settles on the lacy head of wild carrot. A hornet drones past, as large as an Antonov transport plane. Butterflies – brimstones, fritillaries, swallowtails, gatekeepers – dance up and over the surrounding bush. I laugh. I sing. I'm tempted to dance, but decide that would be undignified at my age. Besides, the ground underfoot isn't quite regular enough for that kind of behaviour. This is a path less travelled to judge by the overgrown nature of parts of it.

From time to time I can see the sea through the trees and the headland for which I'm heading, on which a white building, Pardini's Hermitage, stands in an irregular block of trees. I imagine it as Shangri-La-by-the-Sea, a place where a table and a glass of wine are waiting for me. It vanishes behind a screen of scrub as I dip down towards the coast. I'm beginning to feel the familiar flutter of excitement at the approach of lunch.

I have a surge of joy as I scamper the last few steps from the precipitous final stretch of the path onto a tarmac road. A few strides now and—

And I discover that I'm not where I think I am, that I'm a long way from where I thought I was, and to get to where I ought to be, I'll have to retrace my steps up the precipitous path less travelled in order to find the turning that I'd been assured I couldn't miss. My fury at churlish Fate, at my own incompetence, at the world at large, is past describing. I think of Francesco's Cinciut demon as I plod back up the hillside, sweat cascading into my eyes, every muscle in knees, calves and thighs protesting at the effort, all dreams of lunch scattered to the four winds.

I find the turning I should've taken without any difficulty. How I could have missed it in the first place is a mystery. Cinciut has a lot to answer for. But I stride out with renewed hope and vigour, and presently, only two and a half hours later than projected, I descend a well-kept stone track, past a piggery, a donkey enclosure, a chicken run, a place where the goats stand in the shade, past a kitchen garden, olive trees and vines, to a terrace fragrant with the resinous perfume of eucalyptus trees and Corsican pines surrounding The Hermitage.

Scarlet in the face, shirt soaked in sweat, legs bleeding from a thousand scratches, I burst into the calm, orderly world of a well-run hotel. I would've turned myself away, but the greeting from Francesco 'Ghigo' Pardini cannot be more courteous, more kindly, or more soothing. His only concern is that I'm in one piece. He'd been worried when I hadn't arrived on time. He'd rung Francesco. Francesco was worried. But that's all in the past. I'm here, aren't I? That's all that matters. What do I need? A glass of beer? Certainly. A little lunch perhaps? Were I not in such a disgusting state, I'd embrace Ghigo.

Where in England can you walk in at 3 p.m. in an advanced state of sartorial dilapidation and physical distress, be received with courtesy and warmth, and sit down to a late lunch of insalata di farro with cheese and rosemary, melanzane alla parmigiana, a salad of carrot and mint dressed in lemon juice, a brochette of prawns, squid, zucchini and tomatoes, and a glass or two of chilled white wine? I know how a weary traveller struggling through the snow in Alpine passes in the dead of winter must feel when he spies a great St Bernard bearing a barrel of schnapps trundling towards him.

———

'Do you ever think of doing something else?' I ask Francesco. 'Would you like to change your life in any way?'

'No,' he says. 'Why should I? If I did, I'd want the one I have.'

I'm happy with the life I have, too, but it's time to move on. I have to resist the temptation to stay on when time and place are so agreeable. I promise that I'll return as soon as I can.

2

A RICH AND LOVELY
SEA-GIRT LAND

JUNE 2014

Sardinia – Tavolara – Maddalena – Caprera – Asinara –
Sant'Antiocco – San Pietro

Sardinia

The man in charge of parking at Porto Santo Stefano directs me to the area for motorcycles waiting for the ferry to Olbia. Nicoletta and I have the place to ourselves.

Soon two people on a muscle-bound BMW motorcycle turn into the enclave. The machine looks as if it's been sculpted by Jacob Epstein, all angular curves and gleaming black surfaces. More motorcyclists arrive, in groups of two or more. Soon we're hemmed in by thirty or forty monster Ducatis, Kawasakis, more BMWs and Hondas, with butch metal panniers on either side. Nicoletta looks delicate and dainty among them.

At first sight the riders are clones, armoured in black leather or Kevlar, with reflective piping and flashes of silver or white, and plastic-visored bascinets. When they shed their gauntlets and helmets and undo their jackets it's almost a shock to see soft, lumpy, vulnerable human beings emerge from the chrysalises of biker-dude uniforms. They're mostly German and Dutch, and male, of all ages and portliness. Marlon Brando and Lee Marvin in *The Wild Ones* or Jack Nicholson, Peter Fonda and Dennis Hopper in *Easy Rider*, they're not. Neither am I, for that matter.

They eye up each other's bikes with competitive wariness. Then they start exchanging technical data and comparing travel experiences with cheery camaraderie. Big biking's obviously a companionable business. Occasionally someone quickly squints in Nicoletta's direction, and looks away, as if they've spotted some strange and unusual creature at which it'd be rude to look too long.

When it's our turn to board the ferry, they take off, a flock of large, angular, black or silver-grey rooks, engines muttering. I follow them in and find a space to tuck Nicoletta away among them.

Porto Istana is a small, unremarkable resort, more a scattering of holiday homes and chalets among the surrounding dunes and pinewoods, about twelve kilometres from Olbia in northern Sardinia. My base, Casa Anna, is quiet and comfortable and serves splendid, if eccentric, breakfasts cooked by the proprietor, Marzia, or her brother, Jerry. There are airy ricotta pancakes one day, Moroccan bread the next, or a ham and cheese toastie, with random slices of pizza or ham to bulk things up, and superb homemade jams and local honey.

They remind me of the breakfasts at the Hotel Mare e Pineta in Cervia on that first, memorable Italian holiday, where there'd been similar little bowls of honey that attracted wasps. Breakfast in the Mare e Pineta had been a war-with-wasps zone. Like experienced hunters at a waterhole, my brothers and I waited until one settled on the edge of the honey-filled bowl and was sipping the viscous sweetness. Then, with a deft flick of the knife blade, we tipped them over into it. Having watched their struggles in this new medium for a minute or two, we lifted out the unfortunate insect, now stuck firmly to the knife blade, and mashed it on the side of the plate. At the end of breakfast, each plate was ringed with a grisly display of trophy wasps. I don't follow such barbaric practices at Casa Anna, although I'm tempted.

But, before breakfast, I take to slipping down to the nearest beach, a brisk ten minutes' walk away, for a swim in the sea that's still nippy for the time of year. The sand bears the indentations of the day before, but it's clear of any litter. The sunbrellas and sun beds are neatly lined up, the umbrellas erect but furled. A few early arrivals are already staking out their plots, unfolding chairs, putting up sunshades, arranging the support systems for the day. The real pros have trolleys loaded with their gear.

I have an instinctive revulsion of mass humanity. I want pristine beaches and empty seas to myself. Of course, this is simple selfishness and snobbery, and I soon realise that there's more pleasure to be had in watching the movements of people, the comfortable couples, garrulous groups and the self-regarding singletons turning in the sun like sausages under a grill, than simply indulging in solitary introspection.

By the time I get back after breakfast the beach is thoroughly colonised with bodies in irregular ranks, glistening with oil. By 10 a.m., the bay's a glittering mass of multi-coloured sunbrellas and gleaming sun-worshippers laid out like fish on a market slab – an old man as wrinkled and dark as an Egyptian mummy, leaning back, eyes closed, head shielded by a battered stove-pipe hat; a plump wife solicitously slathering sun cream over the mountain of her husband's belly; a father bouncing around his young children, first with a beach ball, then buckets and spades, then wooden racquets and a rubber ball while his wife lies face down nearby, oblivious to all their activity; a solitary man with a fleshy nose and thick scrub of white hair on his chest, reading a book with quiet intensity; one couple stretched out, his head on her back, inert as corpses; a full brown bosom escaping from a bikini in a display of topless daring. Not that I stare.

Not many people seem interested in actually going into the water, except for one young woman in a blue-and-white-striped bikini, frizzy hair in a frizzy ponytail, wading resolutely through thigh-deep sea from one end of the beach to the other and back; and three blokes in their seventies cavorting like boys in their teens, squeezing into wet suits, donning an armoury of masks, flippers and air tanks before kersploshing out into the bay while their wives stand by gossiping, oblivious to their husbands' merriment.

Fifty years ago in Cervia there'd been an old woman who walked up and down the beach shouting 'A-ror-via gelati e vitamine B-B' and selling ice creams and grapes and apple and orange segments covered in clear, friable caramel from a box arrangement she carried. She's given way to a constant progression of African and Indian pedlars selling watches, dark glasses, swathes of brightly coloured clothes. I wonder at their persistence and stoicism as they take rebuff after rebuff. Some sun-worshippers don't even acknowledge their existence. Others engage them in long, and usually pointless, sessions of bartering. Only occasionally does anyone buy anything.

This is the poetry of human variety: shifting, arranging and rearranging, turning over and over, standing, sitting, eating, drinking, wandering up and down within the strict limits of the beach; talking, gossiping, chattering, prattling, yammering, yattering, yapping, jabbering on mobile phones or even to each other, as companionable as nesting seagulls, until it's time to go, to fold up, pack up, load up and move back to their holiday chalets or apartments, just as wildebeest or caribou suddenly form into irregular, yet cohesive, masses for migration.

Tavolara

The sign above the dining terrace reads 'Ristorante da Tonino – Re di Tavolara' (Little Tony's Restaurant – The King of Tavolara). It may lack something of the majesty of the House of Windsor, but once upon a time the House of Bertoleoni had sufficient credibility to be registered by Queen Victoria in her comprehensive catalogue raisonné of European royalty.

The island of Tavolara is a great limestone fin that rears up from the sea just off Porto San Paolo. The rocky upper parts burst free from a mat of trees and vegetation covering the lower slopes. However, that section of the island is off-limits, the realm, not of Tonino it seems, but of the Italian military according to various blood-curdling signs warning the casual visitor to go a step further at their peril. I suspect that this is a cunning ruse to keep the major part of Tavolara in a pristine state for eagles, mountain goats and blue lizards.

So the few dozen seekers after solitude and golden sand who, like me, have made the twenty-minute trip from Porto San Paolo, are restricted to a long, flat foot of low dunes, scrub and reddish outcroppings of rocks that extend from the base of the limestone fin. On this sandy extension sits King Little Tony's restaurant, and another bar next to it, half a dozen houses huddled about, two swimming beaches and a cemetery. Cemeteries are becoming a sub-theme of this journey, but they have their own point and poetry.

The one on Tavolara could take its place in any Sergio Leone spaghetti western. It stands apart amid low, scrub-covered dunes, the cracked and dilapidated tombs stacked among sea grasses, cacti and low shrubs sprouting from the sandy earth within a crumbling wall pierced by a rickety gate of driftwood. It's a spot of melancholy and sweetness, with only the creaking and tonk-tonk from the windmill above a water borehole a couple of hundred metres away to disturb the silence.

Here I find the history of the House of Bertoleoni told on the gravestones, which reach back to the first king, Paolo. That of Carlo Paolo Bertoleoni 'Re di Tavolara 30.11.31 + 6.5.93' bears the subscript 'ti pensano sempre la mamma, e tuoi cari' (they think of you always, your mother and your dear ones). La mamma, Italia Murru, 'Regina Madre di Tavolara' died in 2003, outliving Carlo Paolo by ten years. To the left of these tombs is that of Principe Carlo Ernesto Geremia, Luogotenente Generale del Regno, with a photograph of Principe Carlo Ernesto who bears an uncanny resemblance to the late Omar Sharif.

While Paolo Bertoleoni had been quite serious in his claim to the kingship of Tavolara, it seems that his original high purpose has gradually modified over the years, and now the Bertoleonis accept the humorous side of their family history and acknowledge that it's in the best interests of the family and the island to continue the myth but to change the emphasis. In the end, when it comes to royalty on Tavolara, comedy is king.

Past the cemetery, the foot narrows and slides out into the translucent sea. I slip into it. Fluid, lacy patterns of sunlight, thin bands of white and gold, ripple over the ridged sandy floor. I come across a single boot, toe down, dancing lightly on the sandy floor of the cove, laces floating on either side. I feel the same fascination and revulsion I experienced in Cervia when I'd watched the carapace of a crab slowly swaying over the same kind of sandy bottom to the rhythm of the sea – 'a pair of ragged claws/Scuttling across the floors of silent seas'. I'm relieved to discover there isn't a foot inside the boot.

Back in the court of Little Tony, I sit at a table open to the sea front, looking down the shore where a ramshackle jetty, a long, arthritic wooden finger, stretches out over the barely crinkled surface.

After a while la zuppa di cozze e arselle arrives. Sweet, fat, flubby mussels and taut, meaty arselle clams in a sparkling tomato and white wine broth shot through with lush clam and mussel juices, are heaped up like Tavolara itself.

Across the water a line of pristine white clouds form a fluffy buffer between the lumpy skyline and the ethereal blue sky. Just outside the restaurant a very large man with a red, fleshy face shaded by a peaked military cap, a voluminous blue polo shirt and knee-length khaki shorts, erects a tripod, screws a very small camera to the apex and starts taking photographs. There's something anomalous about his bulk, the thin, spindly legs of the tripod and the diminutive camera. Presently he packs up his gear and moves off down the shoreline, and sets up his tripod and camera all over again, a small, mysterious, inconsequential diversion.

The plate of mussels and clams disappears. Its place is taken by a dry, rustling fritto misto of little fishes I'd seen swimming in the sea an hour before, crunchy prawns of a caramel sweetness and supple squid. After, a few fingers of pecorino cheese. Half a litre of white wine, and I'm in that deeply agreeable state: mind empty of all thought, just staring out across the bay, perfectly happy just being.

Sardinia (again)

'Political satire became obsolete when they awarded Henry Kissinger the Nobel Peace Prize,' said the great satirical American songwriter/mathematician, Tom Lehrer. I feel the same way about Porto Cervo and the Costa Smeralda, the development created by the Aga Khan in the 1950s and 1960s. It's a monument of pristine ghastliness to manufactured taste and all the most meretricious values of commercialised Europe. It's beyond adequate description or comment. I once spent a few days at a wine festival there a number of years back, and have no wish to return. Olbia next door is another matter. Modest, dusty and a bit down at heel Olbia might be, compared to the ersatz glitter of Porto Cervo, but there's La Gallura, I remember.

Olbia is in the province of Gallura, and the eponymous trattoria was one of the finest restaurants I've ever had the pleasure to eat in. Not fine in the sense of spit-and-polish, designer-bred elegance, sophistication of food or any of that conventional palaver, but fine in spirit and style. Great restaurants aren't about breaking boundaries, pushing envelopes, blue-, or any other colour-, sky thinking, although they may well do that as well. They aren't about designer luxury, Bible-sized wine lists, and super subtle service either, although they may have a part to play. They're about feeding people really well irrespective of the style of food; and making sure the customers leave feeling happier than when they arrived. That was La Gallura. It was old style, a bit gloomy, comfortable, time-weathered, confident. It was great because of its rare sense of character and the absolute quality of the dishes it served. I had left it not so much happy as euphoric.

When I last visited it, Rita Denza was La Gallura's chatelaine and presiding spirit. She must have been in her seventies, as small as a sparrow, and even more energetic. Her one objective, it seemed, was to persuade you to eat as much as you possibly could, because by eating as much as you possibly could, you could try an almost unending series of remarkable dishes.

La Signora didn't really deal in menus. She served what was local and in season in overwhelming abundance. I forget how many dishes we ate in the end. Many of them were based around fish. Anchovies, sea urchins, whelks, limpets, prawns of various colours and sizes, raw and cooked, baby crabs, squids and squidlets, variations on octopi, winkles, and other unidentifiable marine creatures, came and went; each curious, individual and above all delicious. Vegetables – fresh tomatoes and dried, olives, zucchini, melanzane – all enjoyed strong supporting roles.

The flavours were precise and pointed. Each dish had its roots in Gallurese traditions, transfigured by La Signora's taste and imagination. It had been a memorable meal, culminating in a brilliant large sea bass cooked in a crust of salt, as theatrical as it was glorious to eat. Thank God I wasn't paying the bill, because none of this came cheap, but then great food, great fish, great imagination, great fun rarely does in my experience.

The lure of another epic meal at La Gallura is one of the main reasons I've come here, so I'm puzzled when I can't find it. I wander across the road and ask a lady running a newsagent's kiosk where it is.

'It's closed,' says the lady.

'Closed!'

She gestures at a building site that had formerly been La Gallura. Men are carrying chairs and other fixtures into it.

'Closed? For ever?!' I reel.

'La Signora, she's very ill,' says a sympathetic bystander.

I'm appalled and devastated. Further enquiry reveals that, indeed, Rita Denza is sick, but that's not the end of the story. It seems there'd also been dubious shenanigans involving landlords and the law behind the closure of La Gallura. How bloody typical. Italy is probably the only country where it's possible to believe that there's a conspiracy rather than a cock-up behind every malign act.

I wander off to nurse my grief and unexpectedly find sanctuary in the Basilica di San Simplicio that stands on a piazza, part of a hinterland of smart, modish examples of modern urban chic set back from it, as if maintaining a respectful distance. The basilica, itself, is a formal statement of Romanesque aesthetics, simplicity and moral strength in keeping with the principles of San Simplicio – Saint Francis of Assisi. It was built in two stages, during the first half of the eleventh century and then at the end of the twelfth.

It takes a little while for my eyes to adjust to the dimness of the intimate interior. It's without a trace of pretence or adornment of any kind. Square columns alternate with stocky round ones to form the central nave, with a narrower nave to either side, rising to a flat, beamed roof. Above the altar is a half cupola. Here and there the narrow windows pierce the walls, shafts of light bursting through them, tunnelling through the shadow. It's a calm, intent, serious space.

A woman comes in, kneels at prayer for a few minutes and goes out without glancing at me. A few minutes later a man enters and busies himself with some maintenance. I stand in front of the plain altar and say a prayer of thanks. As I leave I look around for postcards, leaflets, boxes in which to leave a donation or any of the other delicate commercial activity that you habitually find in any church these days. There's nothing. For a moment I think of taking a photograph, but it seems wrong to disturb the calm of the place, so I imprint it on my memory and go out.

———

That evening I bump into some of my fellow guests from Casa Anna at Est Istana, a café-cum-deli-cum-wine shop on the road between Porto Istana and the main Olbia-Siniscola highway. It's run by Giovannino and Piera, who are as canny as they're charming and energetic. Piera flirts with the customers and doles out the food – prawn, celery and tomato salad; stuffed mussels; octopus salad; lasagna; roast suckling pig; carta di musica-grilled zucchini, peppers, and melanzane – while Giovannino deals with the wine and keeps a beady eye on the profit margin.

I've only gone in for a beer, but I'm spotted by Ian, a charming young American banker taking a few days' refuge from the sturm und drang of City of London life who I'd met the day before. He's with a group of four German TV techies, photographers, sound technicians, a film editor and a political advisor, all in their late twenties or early thirties, who are celebrating the last evening of their holiday. Genial and kindly, they invite me to join them. They've all been boating together that day, visiting both Tavolara and Molara, a small, uninhabited lump of rock hard by Tavolara.

The odd magic of Tavolara that I'd found seems to have passed them by.

'The sea, it was fantastic. It was so clear.'

'But at Molara it was better.'

'That was where Klaus and Alex jumped off the rock. It was so funny.'

They're relaxed and ebullient, with that surging energy of their age. I remember it, vaguely. They ask me what I'm doing there. I explain my mission.

'But that is fantastic. That is a dream,' says Alex.

They finish eating, and move on to more beer, mirto, the sweet, vaguely medicinal liqueur made from myrtle berries, and limoncello, the equally saccharine liqueur flavoured with lemon peel. They insist I drink the same.

'Let's buy a house here,' says Alex.

'And then we can come out whenever we feel like it.'

'It's only a couple of hours from Berlin.'

The world's full of possibilities and potential. It's a pleasure being with them.

'Come on, let's go to the beach,' says Klaus.

'I've got a couple of litres of wine.'

'And I've got a bottle of limoncello.'

'Come on, Matthew. You'll be coming with us, won't you?'

'Yes, you must.'

For a moment I'm tempted, but some small sense of propriety and self-preservation takes me to my bed, thank God.

———

The next day they go home, and I go in search of pompia.

La Pompia is one those numerous citrus mutations you find throughout Southern Italy and Sicily. Blood oranges are one, bergamot another, and cedro a third. But pompia is possibly the grandest of all. As big as a football. As fragrant as an orchid. As yellow as the sun. So runs the legend. And it only grows around Siniscola, a small town south of Olbia.

'And I can't say much for Siniscola,' wrote D. H. Lawrence in *Sea and Sardinia*, the brilliant record of the trip he made to the island in 1921. 'It is just a narrow, crude, stony place, hot in the sun, cold in the shade.' Not much seems to have changed in Siniscola since Lawrence's excursion. There's little by way of antique curiosities, impressive monuments or even civic improvements to lure the curious traveller, unless you're looking for pompia.

Having ridden through the 'narrow, crude, stony place', I turn round and pull into the side of the road in the middle of the town to work out my pompia-locating strategy. I'd assumed that there'd be a sign announcing Siniscola as the pompia capital of the world or signs of a Festa della Pompia, a celebration of some kind that you routinely find in Italy, or even a greengrocer selling them, some sign that this is the home of pompia. There's nothing, not a sign anywhere. I'm puzzled, and baffled as to what to do next.

A woman in glasses the size of window panes appears at the foot of some steps above my head and starts bellowing at me. At first I think she's shouting at me for polluting the air outside her front door. Not a bit of it.

'That's a beautiful new Vespa,' she says. 'Lovely colour.'

I thank her, explain my mission and ask her where I can find the elusive fruit.

'Come on in,' she says. 'I can tell you all about pompia.'

I follow her up the steps, past some boxes of zucchini, French beans and strawberries, and into what's obviously her front room. She says her name is Lina Casu. She checks my spelling when I write it down.

'Would you like a beer?' Lina Casu asks, as if we're old friends. I say I would.

She explains that unfortunately this isn't the season for pompia.

'We start picking them in November and stop at the end of January or the beginning of February.'

'It's a kind of lemon, and huge,' she says. She holds up her hands to indicate the size, roughly as big as an American football. It only grows around Siniscola, she says, and it's candied or turned into liquore or kept in honey. She doesn't have one, but she does have a cedro, which, she says, is similar. I take a picture of her holding a cedro. It looks like a very large, warty lemon. La pompia is even bigger, says Lina Casu.

She sells vegetables and fruits that her husband grows in their vegetable garden, she says.

'And honey, too,' she adds, opening a cupboard and bringing out a box with pots and plastic containers of honey.

'It's very special,' Lina Casu says. 'Cedro honey, from the zagara, the blossom, of the cedro tree. It has a slight touch of bitterness you don't get with pompia honey.'

'Honey is so much better for you than sugar,' she goes on. 'It's a natural product. Full of goodness. People come from Milan and Turin to buy my honey.'

The cedro honey has a rich, brown buttery smell, and is just as full to taste, with, as she said, a slight touch of bitterness at the end.

I ask her where I should eat in Siniscola.

'Il Talismano,' she says without any hesitation. 'Just up the road.'

Unfortunately, Il Talismano is shut that day, but a young man cleaning the dining room suggests I try the Trattoria da Bovore on the other side of the road. It's nondescript to the point of invisibility. Without the young man's advice, I'm not sure I'd go in.

It turns out to be one of a disappearing breed; a modest, family-run trattoria. The walls are white, dotted with photos and pictures in haphazard arrangement. The floor's black and white composite marble, the tablecloths and napkins coral pink. It may be modest and visually undistinguished, but it's obviously a place where people eat regularly.

I have a plate of moscardini alla diavola, tiny octopi braised until they're as soft as kid gloves in a tomato sauce full of their flavour, piquant with chilli. Next, spaghetti con arselle e bottarga. The arselle – clams – are plump and flushed with garlic and fresh with parsley. A generous grating of salty, minerally bottarga seasons the dish.

A young woman brings the dishes and carries away the empty plates. On the other side of the room, her two young children are having lunch with their father. Every now and then the young woman stops to sit by them and make sure they're eating properly. A group of four informally dressed men, a solitary man and a middle-aged couple are all absorbed in the business of lunch. The young woman's mother pops out of the kitchen from time to time to see how things are going. One of the group of men asks her if a particular dish has garlic in it? No, says the cook/mother, just onions. Could she add garlic? asks the customer. No, says the cook/mother, and that's that.

I have room for seadas, or sevada as Lina Casu had written in my notebook, a thin circular tart served hot, filled with molten cheese and with honey poured over it, and dusted with grated lemon peel. The pastry of this seadas is delicate and biscuity, the filling of goat's cheese mild and chewy, and the honey sweet with a hint of citrus from the lemon peel. It's a masterly pudding.

And finally, finally a little plate of pompia sweetmeats, one version cooked in honey that has the texture of warm wax, the other candied with orange and mixed with almonds, which is chewy and crunchy, fruity and nutty.

It's been an ordinary lunch on an ordinary day, just good, simple, brilliant food cooked with precision, assurance and instinctive understanding, without any fuss, any show, any flourishes. I compliment the young woman looking after me on the excellence of the food. She looks surprised and pleased. There are days when you're glad to be alive and thank providence for unexpected joys and this is one of them.

In easy time, Nicoletta and I move to Arzachena, high on the northeast corner of Sardinia. By the scale of recent trips, it's a short haul along busy roads. We arrive at Qui Si Sana, an agriturismo just outside the town, as quiet as a Trappist monastery, but rather more comfortable.

Arzachena has never made much of an impression on history. 'Mildly interesting' is about the best anyone has said about the town, but Qui Si Sana is perfect bolt hole, and only a short hike to Palau, the port from which I'll be catching the ferry to the islands of La Maddalena and Caprera.

Of the two, Caprera is the more interesting as far as I'm

concerned, because it was the home of Giuseppe Garibaldi, about whom I've been curious, half-admiring, half-exasperated, for years.

On the way back from checking the ferry times in Palau, I take a detour along the coast, nibbled and ribbed on one side by the sea, and honed and shaped into rocky spines and quiffs by the wind on the other. At some point I stop to get my bearings, and spot what appears to be a path leading to the sea. It's littered with broken glass, paper and other detritus, but something about it lures me on. After a few metres the rubbish vanishes. The path winds down through rocks, juniper, myrtle in blossom and wild rosemary, to a little sandy cove. I skitter down the last few yards and sit in the sun. A light breeze feathers my skin. The glassy sea slip-slips on the sand. Reflected light moves mazily on the underside of the rocks on either side of the cove.

I take off my shoes and take a couple of steps into the water. It's crystalline and warm. I look down at my white feet. They don't seem to belong to me. A tiny fish comes up and inspects them. I peer round and carefully check the cove. Then I strip completely, and swim naked, with delicious sensations of freedom, surreality and pleasure, heightened by the fear that someone may appear on the little beach at any time.

Many years before a younger me had done the same thing and had the same sensation in a cove near Marina di Maratea in Basilicata. 'And then the pagan spirit of the place took hold and I shed the last vestiges of civilisation and swam naked' I had written afterwards. Had I changed that much in the years between? Physically, certainly. Mentally? Hardly at all, it seemed.

———

Palau. The harbour is a frieze of incidental activities – a blue-and-white fishing boat puttering to the quay; a fisherman hosing down a deck; another sorting out his nets; yachts, masts gently rocking; sleek, identikit ocean cruisers bobbing quietly at their berths. The sea, lapis lazuli here, periwinkle there, cobalt further out, the blues eliding one into the other, sharp points of light flickering off fluid facets. A ripe reek of oil, diesel, fish, brine, iron filings, ammoniac vegetal decay.

Three men stand in animated conversation. Travellers in twos, threes, tribes; people waiting to greet friends or relatives off the arriving ferry; people dragging suitcases on wheels; people just watching. A cream scooter weaves its way between them, its rider shouts greetings to various friends. Trucks line up like elephants to form an orderly queue. Cars sit nose to tail, drivers and passengers tethered to them.

Then there she is, our ferry, white, shaped like a trug, roll-on-roll-off stern and bow, Delcomar, the name of the shipping line, in large letters on her side, turning in, slowing. There's a slight shiver of anticipation. People turn their heads, drivers and their passengers disappear into their cars; two stout men position themselves on the quay to catch the ropes that'll be flung from the deck to tether the ferry during its short stay.

The ferry edges in, closer, closer, hovers a few feet from the quay, towering above us. Shouts between the two stout men and the crew. Foam seethes up on either side of the hull. More shouting from the deck of the ferry and bystanders on the quay. Weighted lengths of twine come looping through the air, unravelling in their parabolas. The two men catch them and haul up the attached heavy mooring ropes, pull them in, loop them over bollards along the quay. The ferry's secure.

Pause. Shouting from inside the hull of the ferry. The bow slowly clanks upwards, like the visor on a giant knightly bascinet. A metal drawbridge descends. A covey of motorcycles scoots out of the bowels of the ship and moves in a phalanx through the small crowd of onlookers, along the quay and away. The first car emerges cautiously followed by another and another, bouncing over the metal drawbridge, which heaves and clatters as each vehicle, and then the trucks and lorries, pass over it.

Now the reverse traffic, foot passengers first, then cars; the tickets are checked and cars beckoned to their appointed positions in the hold. The drivers of trucks and lorries exchange familiar banter with the ferry hands. Nicoletta and I bump up the ramp and into the maw of the ferry. A sailor indicates where I should park her, tucked away to one side. He loops a rope over her handlebars to hold her steady. I pat her saddle in reassurance and make my way up the steep steps to the passenger deck.

Slowly the drawbridge clanks upwards and settles into place; the thick ropes are hauled back inside, choreographed by the orange-jacketed crew; the ferry shudders; a surge in the fume of diesel; water beside us churns; we begin to move; shouting and laughter from the passengers; cameras emerge, poses are struck, loos sought, drinks provided. Children chase each other. Parents look on with indulgent smiles. Couples lean against each other. The port recedes, grows distant. A fine marine breeze tempers the heat of the day. Sunlight winks Morse code from the clipped waves.

My father used to shout 'All aboard the Nancy Lugger,' to encourage his family to get into the car to go anywhere. It transformed each outing into a voyage, an adventure. I remember my father's call each time I line up Nicoletta to slither and bounce up the gangway of a ferry.

Caprera

La Maddalena, the island, is just a shape, low slung, a curved mound silhouette. Maddalena, the town, a blob, a blur, a mound within a mound; now less of a blur; now taking shape; now individual houses, buildings with precise form, crisp-painted in the sun; the quay waiting for us; palm trees; bougainvillea as brilliant as a sari; people; cars lining the quay; our turn to be disgorged in a disorderly queue. Nicoletta judders as we clatter over the lumpy flagstones of the road along the sea front. We follow the signs to Caprera about seven kilometres along the coast. A causeway joins La Maddalena (the island) to Caprera. It hadn't been there in Garibaldi's day.

It turns out that there are quite a lot of other things on Caprera that weren't there in Garibaldi's day, including a German film crew with film trucks and film cars and film catering facilities and numbers of film people standing around doing whatever it is that film people do. It's hard to tell what, exactly. Is there any other activity in which so many people devote so much ingenuity and so much time to produce something so nugatory?

My indignation turns to fury when I discover that the film crew have also taken over Garibaldi's farm buildings. These original structures have been adapted to serve food to visitors like me. Not only could I not soak up the atmosphere of the place, but worse, far, far worse, I can't have lunch there either. A board by the gate promises 'Antipasti verdure al forno, pecorino, salumi; gnocchetti sardi; porchetta al forno; dolce; vino, caffe e digestivo' for a princely twenty-five euros. The apple in the Garden of Eden wouldn't be more tempting than those dishes seem to me. I feel like a small boy with his nose pressed up against the window of the sweet shop with a notice saying 'Closed' hanging on the door.

It's easy to understand, though, why Garibaldi would have wanted to live on this remote craggy, rocky, wooded island. Caprera was far removed from the belligerent world in which he played such a significant part for so long. Even with today's trappings of tourist culture – tarmac roads, signposting, picnic spots and refreshment stalls – Caprera has an austere and elemental tranquillity. It rises through a series of burly hills to a central point that commands an immense view of the surrounding seas and their islands. Much of it is covered with thickets of pine and rough brushwood through which erupt violent humps.

Garibaldi bought half the island in 1855, before his adventures in Sicily and Calabria, the other half being bought by some English admirers and given to him ten years later, and it was here that he retired after ceding his conquests of Sicily and southern Italy to King Victor Emmanuel II.

Count Camillo Benso di Cavour, the Prime Minister of Savoy, may have been the political genius manipulating the political landscape that allowed the unification to become a reality, but Garibaldi was its undoubted hero. His reputation in his own lifetime was prodigious throughout Europe, and it has scarcely diminished since in Northern Italy and Northern Europe.

Garibaldi was particularly lionised in Britain from the beginning of his remarkable career. True, he understood the part that journalism could play in moulding public opinion, but there was something about the directness of his manner, his courage, his actions to promote political freedom, his advocacy of democratic principles that appealed to many in Britain, particularly among the working classes. When he visited Britain in 1864, an estimated half a million people turned out at Nine Elms to greet the 'Hero of Two Worlds' and the dockworkers of Tyneside clubbed together to buy him a sword. More practically, the British navy shepherded him and his little flotilla to allow them to land at Marsala in Sicily in 1860, and begin the decisive war against the Bourbons that led, de facto, to the Unification of Italy. My great-great-great-uncle paid for a platoon of the Thousand.

However, not all contemporary Italians lionise him in this way. For many southerners and Sicilians he was 'il traditore del Sud' (the betrayer of the South, as one Calabrese put it to me once). Until his deal with Victor Emmanuel, Garibaldi had been a staunch, vigorous republican. In the view of many Southern Italians, he abandoned his republican principles and left them at the mercy of exploitative northerners. In place of the tyranny of the Bourbons came the tyranny of the robber bankers and industrialists of Milan and Turin.

My own views on Garibaldi are somewhat ambivalent. I admire his courage and the audacity with which he led men, not simply the Thousand in the invasion of Sicily, but earlier, in the wars of liberation in South America, and subsequently in France during the Franco-Prussian War of 1870, when, at the age of sixty-two and crippled by arthritis, he commanded the Army of the Vosges, the only French army to enjoy any success against the Prussians. There are few self-taught soldiers who enjoyed his level of glory. His energy, resilience and inspirational qualities were remarkable.

But I can't help feeling that he was the most impossible figure to deal with. He was a man of great contradictions, exhilarating and infuriating in equal measure, humane and brutal, generous and implacable, radical and dictatorial, with an utter conviction in the rightness of his cause and an intolerance of others who might disagree. He may have been very good at winning battles, but he was inept at sorting out the peace afterwards. Sicily descended into administrative chaos for a decade after its liberation. Politically he was a radical and a maverick, and he didn't seem to have much of a sense of humour.

So overwhelming is the presence of the public Garibaldi, that the private Garibaldi has all but vanished. The tragedy of his pregnant first wife Anita, who died of malaria in his arms during his hide-and-seek retreat after the failed rising in Rome in 1849 is treated as a footnote to the great man's progress. And what of his other wives and his eight children? There had been two more wives, one of whom he had only been married to for a day. Two of his sons fought alongside him during the Franco-Prussian wars, and one, Ricciotti, married an English woman, Harriet Constance Hopcraft. One of their sons, Giuseppe Garibaldi II, served in the

British Army during the Boer War, carrying the very sword the dockers of Liverpool had given his grandfather.

I know that he kept a hospitable table on Caprera, serving wine to his guests while drinking water himself, but what about the rest of his life at home? How, for heaven's sake, had the Scottish radical, John McAdam, come to Caprera with a plan to set up a salmon hatchery on the island with funds from the Glasgow Ladies Sick and Wounded Fund? The historical hero and the drama of his public life buried the domestic, private man. I hoped that a visit to his house and farm on Caprera would redress that balance and show that he wasn't the monumental, humourless pain in the arse he seems to have been.

A fort, built on the highest part of the island several years after Garibaldi's death, has been converted into the Giuseppe Garibaldi Memorial Museum, with 'interactive multi-media installations' describing the 'pivotal hubs' and 'decisive moments' of the great man's life. I can think of no reason why I should want to spend daylight hours wandering round a 'pivotal hub'. Its contemporary grandiosity seems out of keeping with a man known for his personal austerity.

I head back down to the house he built for himself and his family. I find it delightful, sympathetic in a way I never expected, in spite of the gracelessness of a stone-faced guide, who hurries the group of Italian visitors to whom I attach myself from room to room, reciting the relevant facts about the house and Garibaldi in a robotic monotone, as if we're making her late for an important engagement and she's determined to be shot of us at all possible speed. Any dream of communing quietly with the past at my leisure that I might have seems impossible.

We start with a tour of the outbuildings that show that Garibaldi was a useful carpenter and turned his hand to blacksmithery. He was also an innovatory farmer and a keen vegetable grower, and there's the remains of an extensive vegetable garden. Sadly, it isn't planted with Garibaldi-heritage vegetables.

Garibaldi designed the family home himself. It's pleasingly bourgeois, solid and substantial; a house for living in, comfortable, sensible and practical. The bedrooms of two of his children are next to that of him and his third wife, Francesca Armosino, who he married when she was eighteen, and who survived him by almost forty years. The kitchen is a good size, and, unlike British houses of the same period, next to the dining room.

And clearly he was a sucker for a gadget. The kitchen has an up-to-the-moment butter churner, an automated rotisserie and an ingenious fresh water system. There's a steam-driven threshing machine in a stable and a proto-fridge. He had a number of ingenious chairs in which he could sit and write, and state-of-the-art bath chairs for getting around in when his arthritis got too painful in later life. I think that at least one of these bath chairs was English-made, but I'm dragged away and outside before I can make sure.

Finally, we come to the room where he died aged seventy-four. At his own request, his bed was placed to face a window so that he could look out over Caprera to the sea. It seems natural that that was the direction in which his spirit flew at 6.22 in the evening of 2 June 1882. The clock in the room was stopped at the time of his death. Nothing has been changed. I find it profoundly moving.

His grave lies in the shade of some pines near the house, surrounded by the graves of some of his children and that of his widow, Francesca. It's a monumental piece of craggy granite inscribed simply with the name, Garibaldi.

My view of him has been completely changed by this visit to his house. What a chap! The Hero of Two Worlds, admiral, general, sea captain, revolutionary politician, MP, family man, DIY expert, gadget geek, agricultural radical and a fully paid-up member of the Gardening Club. Although a preternaturally energetic, restless spirit, the domestic Garibaldi was a much more rounded, sympathetic, homely figure than I had imagined.

La Maddalena

I head back across the causeway to La Maddalena, and spend the afternoon cruising the road that runs round the perimeter of the island.

There isn't much to it – some nice swimming spots, and clusters of 'tasteful' developments in the manner of the Costa Smeralda at various points of the dramatic coastline. I stop at one of them, Porto Massimo, for a beer. There's hardly anybody about, aside from the engaging, droll girl manning the bar. It's dinky enough, and chic in a counterfeit way, looking out over a pretty, rock-strewn bay, with a few smart, shark-shaped boats, but nobody to man them. It has the dead, immaculate look of a place that's just been taken out of bubble wrap, waiting for people and money to give it a marionette existence for a few months before being swaddled in bubble wrap once more.

But La Maddalena isn't a vacuous, formless place, like Giannutri. Genoa and Pisa had squabbled over it in the twelfth century. Perhaps on account of frequent depredations by pirates of varied origins, no one seems to have paid it much attention from then until the eighteenth century, when the Piedmontese took control of it. Napoleon took part in an attempt by the French to capture the island in 1793. Later, his naval nemesis, Horatio Nelson, used the island as a base when conducting operations against the French navy during the Napoleonic Wars. In fact, it has been a convenient centre for any number of navies over the years. NATO and the US both maintained a military presence there after World War II. The Americans finally left in 2008, leaving the island open to an annual invasion by northern hordes shod in flip-flops and armed with sun cream and bathing trunks.

Initially, I'm inclined to dismiss the port itself. All clip joints and no civic personality, I think. But I'm wrong. Clean, narrow streets lined with crisply painted houses cascade down to the port. And there's at least one outstanding gelateria, Dolci Distrazione, on the Piazza Matteotti. I sit outside licking a combination of lemon, cassata and nocciola, trying to finish it before it melts down my hand, listening to the swifts shrieking through the thickening light and watching two men dressed in white shirts and blue trousers and waistcoats, arms folded, guns in sleeves slung over their shoulders, eyes hidden behind dark glasses, projecting a grim, pointless masculinity. I can't make out whether they're paramilitaries or simply hunters.

Around them flows la passeggiata, the evening ritual that divides the working day from domestic pleasure in Italy, when, around 6 p.m., everyone slowly perambulates up and down the public spaces. Here on La Maddalena it has a relaxed, looser form than the stately ritual I noted when I first came to the country. It used to be part of the fabric of every Italian town or village, but in recent years it seemed to have gone the way of hole-in-the-wall barbers' shops and family alimentari. Watching the conversations, the groups forming and reforming, the couples pushing buggies, grandmas and grandads, the gossipings, the greetings being tossed around, shopkeepers sharing the day's news, I have the sense of a strong, vigorous community and the pleasing continuation of old ways.

Sardinia (again)

Ian and Henny occupy another room at Qui Si Sana. Ian is English and in his mid-seventies, slightly stooped, tanned, with a long, handsome face, a full head of hair and a trimness that puts me to shame. He speaks in a manner that unites lugubriousness and irony to dry, droll effect. He was born in Scotland and, he says, lived in Italy and Japan before ending up in the Netherlands. He's had a career of singular variety that took him from engineering to rubber and tyre manufacture to industrial belting and finally to the shoe industry before he retired. He makes the progress from one to the other sound inevitable, although, on reflection, it seems pretty remarkable to me.

Henny is Dutch, the same age as Ian, and equally tanned, with a pretty, open face, astute eyes and the quick, crisp, no-nonsense manner of the nurse that she is, 'like her mother'.

How did they meet? I ask. There's a quick, complicit glance, and they smile.

'Computer dating,' says Ian. 'Henny's was the first photograph I saw when I logged on, and that was that. Eight years ago.'

They'd both been divorced before they met, but they don't live together.

'But we talk every day.'

'And we get together two or three times a week.'

'Why don't you live together?'

'Why should we when we are happy as we are?' says Henny.

They both have children about whom they worry, although the children don't worry about them.

'They're very happy we have each other.'

Each year they take a month's holiday together, exploring different parts of Sardinia.

'How do you find it when you spend so much time in each other's company?' I wonder.

They look at each other again.

'We don't fight or squabble, do we?' Ian says to Henny.

'That's one of the advantages of age,' says Henny.

———

I've been wrestling with the Nuraghi Question since I arrived on Sardinia. The Nuraghi dominated Sardinia from the Bronze

Age to around AD 200 and left a string of monumental stone buildings as evidence. Aside from that, almost nothing is known about them. There are no nuragic Rosetta Stones or cuneiform tablets. Indeed, it's not known if they wrote at all. Consequently they left fertile ground for speculation among contemporary archaeologists. Theories about them abound: they were warlike; they weren't warlike; they were pastoral farmers; they weren't pastoral farmers; they traded with other parts of the Mediterranean; they weren't into trade as such, but they were retailers and so on and so on.

What is without question is that they were master builders. They left buildings, villages and temples all over the island, massive, brooding, cone-shaped constructions formed out of great, uncut stones fitted together with extraordinary skill. They might look as if they've been made by a race of giants, but the rooms inside are better suited for a race of gnomes.

Along the way, I've seen any number of signs alerting me to nuragic villages, necropolises and temples. I've studiously avoided them because... because... for no good reason, really. Idleness, possibly, or the thought that everyone visits them and what could I possibly say about them that hasn't been already said more ably by someone else. However, there's one nuragic homestead conveniently at Albucciu not far from Qui Si Sana, and I decide I'd better confront the Nuraghi Question once and for all.

The site stands in an olive grove just off the road, massive, protective, familial, made from colossal stones laid one on top of the other, tapering inwards, in a crude but immensely effective jigsaw tower. Form and function blend with a kind of elephantine grace. There are some similarities to Bronze Age houses I've seen in the Orkneys, but the design and scale is far more sophisticated. There's one door lintel, a single gargantuan stone, lying across two upright irregular columns. It's curious to think it's been resting there, possibly, for three-and-a-half millennia. For all its monumentality, there's something touchingly domestic about it. It's a home, not a fort.

I sit down on a large rock mottled by age and lichens, sitting where a man might well have sat 3,500 years ago, give or take, in a grove of olives spaced for light and shade and dreaming. I sense his presence, quiet and comradely. Herder? Grower? Trader? Warrior? Husband? Father? He doesn't say. I watch ants on the speckled earth at my feet, moving matter with determined energy, fetching and carrying, carrying and fetching, and wonder what he dreams of.

I wave goodbye to Ian and Henny and Qui Si Sana with much regret. They were kindly, generous and interesting company.

I head for Stintino, a small town that's the jumping-off point with the next minor island, Asinara. The road leads westwards from the top right of Sardinia to the top left, through an enchanting landscape, undulating and thoroughly farmed. Parts are more like Sussex than Sardinia. There're fields of toasted gold wheat, some already harvested, leaving straw bricks strewn in abstract patterns across the stubble; blocks of vines; tilled café-au-lait earth; a herd of cream and brown cattle resting in a grassy field. The fields merge into hills covered with holly-green shagpile woods. Signs for Sant' Antonio di Gallura, Luras, famous for its bitter arbutus honey, and Tempio Pausania ease past. The SS672 from Tempio Pausania is so straight and long, the countryside so unchanging, the flicker of trees, of light and shade, shade and light so repetitive that there are moments when I have the hallucinatory sensation that I'm not actually moving at all.

From the moment I clap eyes on it across a flat tongue of land stretching out into the sea, there's something about Stintino that fills me with what my brother, Tom, once referred to as 'les anticipations lugubres'. Once it had been a bustling tuna town. The tonnara, the tuna processing plant, closed in 1974, and it's obvious that Stintino has given itself over, heart and soul, to tourism. Not that I've got any theoretical objection to that, but there's something bogus about the place. The streets are too clean, the houses too recently painted, the shops and bars and eating places clearly streamlined for filleting tourist wallets and purses.

My lugubrious anticipations are amply borne out by my B&B. John had emailed me that it was novel for a B&B to offer B but no B. Not only is there no breakfast, but the bedroom, in a new development on the outskirts of the town, proves to be a dark, windowless box smelling of damp socks and mushrooms.

To cheer myself I go to a bar that looks out over the harbour for a beer. It's a pleasant enough spot to rest and ease the wrinkles of the day's travel out of mind and limb. A woman at a table close by is giving her order to a waitress.

Waitress: Would you like your tuna steak grilled medium or rare?

Woman (who was clearly Northern European): Medium.

Waitress: That's fine. Anything else? Chips?

Woman: Oh, yes, chips please.

Waitress: With ketchup or mayo?

Woman: Ketchup and mayo.

Waitress: Would you like the chips at the same time as the tuna?

Woman: Yes please.

Tuna, chips, ketchup and mayo. Oh, God. This doesn't promise well.

In my experience, it's virtually impossible to find true Italian food outside Italy. The Italian cooking you find in Britain is far removed from the pure version I've been used to finding as a matter of course throughout Italy itself, where salsicce means two or possibly three sausages on a plate, with no gravy or ketchup or seemly vegetables to distract from the qualities of the sausages; and costolette di agnello, lamb chops, come naked to the plate, with, possibly, only a crescent of lemon by way of companionship. The focus was, and still is in many places, entirely on the qualities of the primary ingredient.

Such simplicity doesn't sit easily with the tastes of eaters schooled in the baroque architecture of British food, where no plate is complete without a lump of protein at its heart, and buttressed by vegetables, gravy, sauce and condiments. Consequently, Italian dishes (and not just Italian, incidentally) are remade in a form that we find acceptable, but that would be unthinkable in Piedmont or Calabria or wherever the dish originated. And what is true of Britain, is true of every other European and non-European country as well.

When visitors, like the woman ordering chips with her tuna, habituated to the Italian dishes of London, Berlin, Paris, Madrid, wherever, arrive for their two weeks of sea, sun, sand and spaghetti, they want the stuff they find at home. Increasingly, Italian cooks give it to them. Why not? It's less trouble and more lucrative. They don't need to work so hard or put up with idiotic requests. It makes for an easier, more profitable life. But it debases the relationship between customer and restaurateur, and leads to rip-offs, double charging and the like. It's by no means universal, but I've noticed enough examples – in Livorno, Palau, and Bagnaia on Elba – to get the impression this slippage from the principles of classic cooking, unthinkable fifteen or even ten years ago, is not uncommon. In a reflective mood I make my way to the Ristorante da Antonio, which previous reconnaissance suggested was the place most likely to serve decent food.

Ah, vain hope. Tagliatelle alla Sarda comes with a copious, watery, gutless tomato sauce with nuggets of sausagemeat as gritty as gravel. I'm actually grateful that there aren't many of them. Gloom descends on me.

But then things look up with the next dish, scorfano con patate (scorpion fish with potatoes), which is a cracker, the fish chunky and sweetly juicy in a delicate puddle of tomato, potato and olive broth. There's proper precision in handling the fish and a deep understanding of its qualities in the delicacy of the broth. A sense of pleasure is restored. I call for the bill.

I don't often check bills. I tend to pay them with that casual brio produced by a certain amount of drink, but on this occasion I run my eye over the figures. What's this? A cover charge for two people? But I'm only one. And a euro has been added on the total in an arbitrary manner. Oh, bollocks!

It isn't the amount that bothers me. That's piddling. It's the stupidity and cynicism of the attitude behind it.

I draw my waiter's attention to the anomalies on my bill. He apologises profusely.

'Ah, signor, it was a mistake, an oversight.'

I have the impression that there's a genuine sense of embarrassment, but I'm not sure if it's genuinely for making a mistake or just for being found out. Retiring to my dank cell of a bedroom does nothing to improve my dark mood.

Asinara

There's scholarly debate whether Asinara means 'inhabited by donkeys' or whether the name derives from the Roman word 'sinuris' meaning sinuses, which, so the theory goes, the lanky, lumpy island resembles. No scholar, I vote for the donkey explanation myself, if only because Asinara is home to the mysterious albino donkey, a natural mutation found only on Asinara, a descendant of donkeys abandoned by the farmers or fishermen when they abandoned the island.

Asinara has a rather spotted history in terms of human

habitation. No one seems to have stayed for long. Even Genoese fishermen who colonised it in the nineteenth century were evicted when the island became first a lazzaretto, a leper colony, and then, in 1885, a prison island. The Genoese decamped to Sardinia and established Stintino, where Genoese is still the dialect. In time the prison was enlarged and became famous for housing some of the most brutal Mafia capi, including Toto Riina, the man who waged war on the Italian state during the 1980s and 1990s. The prison closed down in 1997, leaving the island to the albino donkeys.

Although abandoned, the prison still remains a place of curiosity to judge by my fellow travellers on the ferry, mostly sturdy, gnarled retirees. Me, I've had my fill of prisons on islands. Asinara isn't exactly Robben Island and Toto Riina wasn't exactly Nelson Mandela. While the doughty senior citizens head for the prison en masse, I set off around the island in the opposite direction.

I take a path that winds over a flat plain more or less parallel to the sea. I come round the corner of the path, where it runs between an area of marsh and a pool of pungent stagnant water with a rim of dark, viscous mud dotted with the brilliant white of egrets. Suddenly a section of mud heaves into life and takes concrete shape. A wild boar. It must have been having a mud bath. Looking distinctly peevish, it trots across some open ground and vanishes into the marshy space between the path and the shore. I'm relieved it's only been peeved and not cross. There's no convenient tree to climb if it had decided to challenge the interloper.

I continue warily along the path as it follows the contours of the coastline. The landscape reminds me of Carna, a small island that sits in the mouth of Loch Sunart, below the Ardnamurchan peninsula in the Scottish Highlands, where we spent several family holidays when I was a teenager, fishing for mackerel and sea trout when the weather permitted, and playing endless games of blackjack and poker for matchsticks when it didn't. Asinara has the same spare, laconic beauty, the same sweep and profile, a flat, scrubby coastal rim rising abruptly to broad crags of creamy rock. Low-growing, thorny scrub takes the place of heather, and sun takes the place of rain, but both share the same elemental quality; people may come, people may go, but these places will always keep to their own rhythms.

It's easy walking, a broad track cutting its way through bushy and often spiky shrubs. The hot air smells of camomile and myrrh. Grasshoppers fizz away from my feet. It feels as if I have the island to myself. Altogether, it's a good place and a good time, even if there don't appear to be any albino donkeys.

Suddenly there they are, two of them, more cream than white, barley white, perhaps, having an early morning shag to judge by the state of one of them. They give me a long, reproachful stare before wandering off in a leisurely fashion into the scrub. It's something of a shock. I'd begun to think that they were mythical creatures and didn't actually exist. I couldn't be more surprised than if I'd come across a couple of copulating unicorns. There're about 120 of them according to the guidebook, and I've seen two.

In fact, I've seen rather more than I'd expected, and all by 10 a.m. Properly alert now, I keep an eye open for more wildlife adventures, but no further donkeys or wild boar come my way. There's nothing for it but to loaf on the beach, read my book, dawdle in the pellucid waters with mask and snorkel, walk on and find another beach to loaf on, read my book and potter about with mask and snorkel again. I look very hard for the endangered giant limpet that's reputed to live on Asinara's rocky shores but I can't find one.

———

Sardinia (again)

Night's falling over Capo Falcone by the time I find the Ristorante Capo Falcone recommended by one of the crew of the ferry back from Asinara. It's a vast, cavernous place, with a panoramic view over the cape. White water streams through the gap between headlands. Wind buffets the rugged, sombre land beyond. The gathering darkness broods over the waves dashing on the rocks. The scene has an elemental, romantic drama.

The antipasto is insalata di polpo alla stintinesi, the familiar combination of octopus and potato, with tomato, celery and rocket, dressed in just oil and lemon juice. The octopus is very fresh and delicate, and has the firmness of semi-soft cheese. The celery gives each mouthful crunch. Diced tomato adds bulk, dash and density. Then comes a plate of grilled prawns, squid, swordfish and bream, weaving the rich seaweed-and-caramel of the prawns with the swordfish's dry meatiness and the bream's lucent lightness, all set off by a whisper of burnt bitterness. There's nothing novel to it. I've eaten more than my fair share of pesce alla griglia already on this trip, but this version just shines with the casual brilliance of scintillating ingredients and sure cooking.

By the time I finish it's too dark to see anything outside any more. For a while I stare at my own reflection in the glass of the window, a single man sitting alone at a table. Is there a difference between solitude, solitariness and loneliness, I wonder? Am I a natural solitary? I'm happiest in company, and yet I certainly don't mind being on my own. I did feel lonely when Lois went back to England, but then I always feel the pang of her departures.

Travel alone and travel in company are two quite different experiences. A companion always brings a different dimension. They see different things, react to situations in different ways. They broaden the experience of travel. At the same time you have to adjust your own schedule to their needs and take into account their whims. And they're a distraction from the constant observation of the world about. I find it easier to chat than to watch, think about and note what's going on around. All the same...

I turn to watch the wide-screen TV that's inevitably on – are the Italians the only people on earth who can eat, talk and watch TV at the same time? – and while away the time watching a fishing competition of unequalled silliness. It's called *Top Hooker*.

———

Rarely have I left a town with such relief as I leave Stintino, with its dinky pastel houses, its venal restaurateurs, its dark, dank developments, its slovenly cynicism. It seems an odd place for those giants of Australian tennis, John Newcombe and Tony Roche to have once run a tennis club. On the outskirts I pass the old, abandoned fishing stations and tuna processing plants and derelict farm buildings, the crusted, decaying husk of past industry encasing the tawdry contemporary kernel of the town. Soon I'm relieved to be bowling southwards along empty minor roads that wind between hills cloaked with the dark, rough green of cork trees, ilex, myrtle and sessile oak, heading for Alghero.

Old Alghero is romantic to the eye, as the guidebooks said it would be. The port is picturesque. The sea walls are massive. There are battlements, bastions, posterns, ramparts, abutments, old cannons, imposing gates. There are winding streets with cobbles and corbels. There are tasteful buildings with eighteenth-century form and grace. There's an impressive Catalan-Gothic cathedral, La Cattedrale di Santa Maria Immacolata di Alghero. The town is wreathed in history and oddity. The natives speak a variant of Catalan, a legacy from when the town had been under Spanish control, and was resettled by Catalans in 1372. The street names are in Catalan and its classic dishes – cassola de peix, polpo alls catalana, arragosta alls catalana, paella algherese – owe more to Catalonia than they do to Italian tradition.

Above all, Old Alghero has shops. Shops, shops, shops, shops for sandals, 'coral' jewellery, shoes, handbags, dresses, summer clothing, general tat, specific tat, rat-a-tat-tat tat, belts, scarves, 'typical Sardinian foods', souvenirs, knick-knacks of every persuasion. And those shops that aren't shops, are bars, gelaterias, pizzerias, spaghetterias, paninerias, osterias, trattorias, ristoranti. Shoppertunity knocks on every hand.

The streets are full of people walking very slowly up and down, round and round, licking ice creams and apparently mesmerised by the flash of colour, the flutter of fabric, the gleam and glitter of stuff and the music of menus calling them to eat.

It doesn't help that the weather's pretty dreary, wavering between the damp and the downright wet, with only occasional flashes of sunshine. I can only admire the spirit and professionalism of the waiters and waitresses as they attempt to beguile and cajole passers-by, flick out tablecloths, lay the glasses and cutlery on tables set outside, only to whisk everything off a few minutes later as the first drops begin to fall again. Pods of visitors, water dripping off their nylon waterproofs, huddle indoors and douse their gloom with beer, wine and Aperol spritzers.

Just beyond the towering walls of Old Alghero is another Alghero that isn't in thrall to a Catalan cultural makeover or commercial glitz, a more humdrum, everyday, grittier Alghero of chemists, scooter service garages, laundries, bakeries, greengrocers, butchers, a market and mobile phone shops, where people live, many of them in houses of unimpeachable vulgarity; a newer Alghero where the sense of normality, energy and life is palpable compared to the waking dream of Old Alghero.

———

It's Monday and most restaurants are shut, but not I Pronti z Cuocere in Alghero market. There's no market business today, but one waitress and one cook are getting ready for business when

I wander in. It's more of a pop-up caff than a trattoria proper. Moulded plastic garden tables and chairs colonise a corner of the market, with emerald green paper tablecloths, cheap glasses and cutlery. The menu's written with felt tip pen on rough paper splodged and wine stained.

It's grigliata mista di suino for me – a slab of belly pork, a couple of sausages, a thin pork chop, a slice of capocollo, all grilled, slightly shiny with fat, rich and chewy. Oh, what a relief to chew on meat again, after weeks of nonstop fish. There's a crunchy, bitter salad, too. I squeeze a lemon and splash some oil over it, and pour over the meat juices for good measure. Bread with a spring to it, and a whiff of sourness, a litre of perfectly drinkable red wine, water and the bill was twenty euros all in. It may be food reduced to the fundamentals, but each fundamental is very sound, and I'm happy to be there, happy to have eaten well. It's as refreshing as a mountain stream after the relentless sales-pitch-and-polish of old Alghero. It reminds me of the fabulously enjoyable lunch that I had eaten on the platform of the railway station at Villarosa in Sicily about eight years earlier. The view is less intoxicating and the lighting not exactly flattering, but the food and the place have the same sense of unpretentious, unexpected delight.

Fertilia lies just off the road a few kilometres north of Alghero. I'd passed the turning to it on my way, but I'm curious to take a closer look. It's a small town that had been developed in the 1930s to house agricultural labourers as part of a fascist grand scheme of land reclamation.

I expect a seedy, down-at-heel, broken-backed town, but I'm agreeably surprised. It may be struggling – graffiti, crumbling plaster, some rundown corners and sad apartment blocks suggest it might be – but, overlooking the sea, it has the homogeneity and handsome regularity of model town planning. Even on a grey, blustery day, when the sea runs murky and choppy, the arcaded main street lined with palms, copses of pines and exhortatory scenes carved on the square-shouldered public buildings have a sense of serious purpose and human scale unlike the brutal bombast of the Third Reich; and some of the grander seaside villas of the same period have a delicious elegance and playfulness. I can think of a good many developments of the same period, and more recent ones, in my own country that have fared and look worse.

The odd car goes by, but there are few people on the street. It may be the weather or it may be the World Cup. I notice a German flag fluttering from the awning outside a café. Below it an intent group of Germans range around a large television watching their national team.

The scene makes me nostalgic. I spent the summer of 1966 staying with my uncle John and his wife, Brenda, in the Monte Lucretili beyond Tivoli. Because England won the World Cup that year, beating Germany in the final, it was seen to be bella figura to have an Englishman playing in the local football team. On this dubious principle I was selected to play for Licenza. Had my fellow players had any prior knowledge of just how bad I was, I would certainly not have been picked.

However, like Chesterton's ass, I had 'one short hour and sweet', a moment of glory on which I dined, quite literally, for years after. It came in the dying minutes of the needle match of the year, the Married vs the Unmarried men of Licenza. I was selected for the Unmarrieds, and the whole village turned out to watch.

In those days there was not a blade of grass on the pitch, and there were several boulders to contend with, some much the same shape and size as the football itself. I decided to station myself as the penalty area poacher, which meant that I didn't have to run about too much, and stood less chance of making an absolute ass of myself.

We had one or two seriously talented players, men who could tame a bouncing ball with the caress of the inside of their boot, slide through a pass with slide-rule precision, turn on a sixpence, and shoot with explosive power. About two minutes before the end of the game, one of these gifted players, Davide, pounced on a loose clearance, flicked the ball forward and unleashed a ferocious shot.

I stood rooted to the spot, admiring this fabulous piece of football skill. I turned towards the goal just as the Marrieds' goalkeeper performed a feat of aerial acrobatics, diving across the goalmouth to punch the ball away. Unfortunately for him, the punched ball hit my knee and, while he lay on the ground, bounced over his helpless body and into the goal. I was engulfed by my fellow Unmarrieds and carried triumphantly off the pitch. I've rarely felt so fraudulent.

It transpired that this had been the first goal scored in this particular game practically in living memory and for years after I was treated to free pizza and wine in the piazza of Licenza as people told and re-told this moment of football history. 'Ti ricordi, Matteo?' I still do.

———

With some relief I leave Alghero and set off south along the SP105 that runs along the coast. It should be a dramatic ride, but mist, drizzle and intermittent rain rather take the edge off sybaritic travel. In some places the road seems merely tacked onto cliffs that drop sheer to the water, at others it winds its way between craggy hills of khaki. It's as if I've strayed into one of the more spectacular reaches of the Scottish Highlands on a dank summer day rather than meandering along the sun-baked coast of Sardinia.

I turn inland at Bosa, a children's model of a town of houses painted hydrangea pink, blue, yellow, green and cream hunched beneath the squat walls of the twelfth-century Castello Malaspina. I pass through Tinnura where many of the buildings are decorated with neo-realistic paintings of Garibaldi, or sheep shearing and other rustic pursuits. The road climbs up and up the rampart of the Monte Ferru shaggy with cork, chestnut, oak and yew, cold as all Harry, comes down through upland pastures to a dusty, flat agricultural plain, and makes for Paulilatino, a substantial rural village, where a B&B run by Peppino Sanna, a cheesemaker, and his sister Raimonda, is to be my base for the next couple of days.

———

The dogs and cocks wake me. It's 5.45 a.m. I doze in a daze. The church clock sounds 6 a.m. Collared doves begin rurr-rurring. Sparrows chirp. Boots rattle over cobbles. Voices. 'Buongior.' 'Buongior.' Cars, trucks rev, roar, go.

It's 8.30 a.m. Breakfast: trecce, strands of cheese woven like a tress of hair, a pale as alabaster, firm and muscular, the freshest of Peppino Sanna's fresh cheeses, still warm. It squeaks as I break a piece off. It has the same rubbery consistency as mozzarella, but it's tenser, denser, with a breezy airiness, like eating whiteness and flowers misted with lemon. Black coffee. Ciambellone della nonna, a cake of just flour, sugar, a little olive oil, and yeast with a light, fluffy crumb, as delicate as linen.

It's difficult to work out the exact geography of Paulilatino. The village is a complicated knot of short streets of stern, frowning houses. Only one or two are taller than two storeys, their walls of irregular dark stones set in lighter plaster or cement, with big, grey lintels around the doors and windows, and fancy wrought-iron balconies and grilles, reminders of a more prosperous past.

There's no escaping the sense of economic hardship. It has none of the brisk vitality of a thriving community. A dusty listlessness hangs over the place. Few people walk along the pavements. The shops and bars are quiet and spiritless, the pavements empty for the most part. Cars pass through it as if hardly registering its existence. Paulilatino feels as if it's moored at some out-of-the-way quay waiting to be broken up.

It's curious the difference a few kilometres makes. While Paulilatino lies inert in a flat plain, about twelve kilometres away Santu Lussurgiu tumbles down the lower slopes of the Monte Ferru, its streets twisting, following the caprices of geography, perky with prosperity. It's difficult to see why Santu Lussurgiu should have fared better than Paulilatino, but it has an alertness, a vivacity and self-possession that its near neighbour has lost. Perhaps the secret lies in the number of small artisan craft producers – iron-workers, weavers, dyers, cabinetmakers and knife-makers.

I almost miss Vittorio Mura e Figli, set back from the road at a sharp corner behind a metal fence, more a place of manufacture than a snazzy retail opportunity. The workshop is a large open space cluttered with work benches and veteran bits of machinery, all with a dull, gunmetal patina from metal dust and fine oil. Piero Mura rests his forearms on a broad counter of glass-fronted cabinets, knives neatly lined up in them. He must be in his sixties, bespectacled, with waves of dark hair scrolling back from his forehead and the slightly weary expression of someone who has seen a great deal of life.

'This is a pattada,' he explains. 'The knife a contadino uses every day for killing animals, sheep, goats, for cutting and chopping, too. It's a knife you can use for almost anything. It's known as la resolva around here.' The blade's about 10cm long, slender, tapering to a viciously functional point. The handle sits lightly and elegantly in the hand, a brass band marking the point where blade and handle meet. The blade swivels back into the handle. It's an exquisitely practical tool.

'Then this one,' Piero says, 'is an arburesa, with a heavier, rounded blade for skinning. Wild boar, pigs, sheep. And this one is called guspine. It looks like an old fashioned razor, but it's for cutting the bark off cork trees and shaping the corks.'

John Irving once explained to me that you rarely find a knife laid by your plate when you sit down to a meal in the house in rural Sardinia because every self-respecting Sardinian carries his or her own. Knives have an emblematic significance as well as practical uses. However, while they may still have a central part in Sardinian culture, progress being what it is, Vittorio Mura e Figli is one of a diminishing number of traditional Sardinian knife makers. Tradition means forging their own blades by heating up the metal tang in a forge, bashing it with a hammer until it's thin enough and properly shaped to start the process of sharpening and polishing. With that endless refinement of detail in which all Italian artisans that I've ever met take such delight, Piero explains that it was better to heat the forge with charcoal than mere coal, which contains chemical impurities that could affect the final blade.

'Of course, it depends whether you're using stainless or carbon steel. Stainless is OK, but I prefer carbon. It's the traditional material, and takes a better edge. But have a look at this.' He rummages around beneath the counter and brings out a handleless blade with a brilliant sheen. It looks as if threads of oil are moving on its surface. His eyes glow with pleasure at the sight of it.

'Damascene steel, the finest of all.' He runs his fingers up and down the blade. 'We make them by beating layers of stainless and carbon steel together, folding them over and beating them again, many times, the way the Japanese sword makers make katana swords. That's why the blade has these patterns in it. It's beautiful, strong and very sharp. A real knife. It takes a lot of hours to make such a knife.'

When the blade's ready, it's fitted into its handle.

'The best handles are made from muflone,' says Piero.

Mufloni are wild sheep with great curling horns the colour of cigarette smoke that wander the thickly wooded mountains above Santu Lussurgiu.

'You can also use cattle horn and wood, but muflone is best. The cattle horn will flake after a while, and wood will fall apart eventually. But muflone lasts for ever,' says Piero.

He brings out two massive knives. One is 160 years old, and the other 200. The handles are smooth with use, and have turned creamy amber. The blades are heavy and dark, and sharp enough to take off the head of a wild boar.

The Mura family have been making Sardinian knives for generations, says Piero. He began learning his trade when he was a child. 'I'd come here after school. It's a real craft making good knives. It takes discipline and concentration. I am a knife-maker. That's what I am.'

He says he's pleased that his son has joined him and his brothers, although he worries that he may have started too late. 'He went to university. He's got a degree. But there's no work for boys with degrees, so he's come to join me here. But he's old to start learning this craft. You have to know, understand, so many things.' He sighs.

I buy a pattada with a handle made from muflone, enchanted by the beauty of its shape, its heft and balance, the way it feels in my hand.

On the way back to Paulilatino, I take a side road to San Leonardo. I'd picked up the name of a trattoria, Le Sorgenti, from a shiny brochure about the area, and it seems worth investigating.

San Leonardo is tranquil to the point of somnolence, tucked away among the dripping, tree-shrouded slopes of the Monte

Ferru. Le Sorgenti is a sturdy temple to local taste. The walls are a shade of burnt orange, the tiled floor brown, the tables and chairs built to last. At one of them sit four workmen in orange overalls. I'd seen them cutting back the herbage on the roadside earlier. A couple of vigorous village elders chunter away at another table. There's a middle-aged son and his mother, and a young couple over by the window.

Plates of antipasti start arriving: tiny rolls of crisp pancetta, with crunchy fried mushrooms; a plate of chunks of funghi porcini slippery in oil, with a breath of vinegar and slivers of bitter deep purple radicchio; a block of fresh sheep's cheese with the springy texture of sourdough bread, cool and lemony; olives and artichoke hearts in oil; silky slices of pink ham with a dainty frill of white fat; more mushrooms, cold, black and tasting of fallen leaves.

A storm bursts outside. The leaves on the chestnut trees surrounding the trattoria toss agitatedly in the wind, rain dripping from them. The village elders chunter on, demolishing a plate of pane carasau and then a heap of wild boar so fragrant, so potent I can smell it twenty feet away. The workmen pay up and push outside. The son and his mother keep up a desultory conversation and the couple by the window watch each other in silence.

'Tagliatelle con ragù di bue rosso' says la signora bringing the plate. I'm not sure to which breed of cattle bue rosso refers. It could be razza sarda or sarda modicana, but there's the usual confusion over local names that frustrates every questing gastronome in search of literal accuracy. It isn't the first time I've come across bue rosso, and it seems reserved for steak and meat sauces. And, bloody hell, this tagliatelle is good – sinuous, strapping pasta with that faint flavour of malt and toast, slithery with the bonny, big, beefy sauce.

A plate of Casilozu, one of Sardinia's rare cow's milk cheeses, to finish. It's rich, slightly buttery, with a clean tang; not as sharp as ewe's milk cheese, but enough to balance the richness. I wonder if it's made by Peppino Sanna.

This is why we come to Italy, I think. It's for food like this, from just here, potent, unaffected, direct, everyday, in an everyday trattoria in an out-of-the-way village, where they just serve the dishes of this place and this season, mostly to people who know what the food of this place and this season should, and will, be. I admire chefs like Davide Scabin in Turin and Massimo Bottura in Modena, the high priests of Italian high cooking, but I love the food of places like Le Sorgenti, with their simplicity, assurance of long practice, directness, purity, balance and lack of affectation.

'Making the cheese is the easy part,' says Peppino Sanna. Peppino is one of the last cheesemakers to make Casilozu in the same way that his mother made it before him, from the milk of fifty or so dove-grey, suede-hide Sarda cattle, descendants of Modicana cattle brought over from Sicily 300 years ago. Silvery hair and beard frames a broad forehead and smiling eyes. He's dressed in faded jeans, a polo shirt and green wellies; sensible, practical, working clothes rather than the antiseptic white coat and gauzy hairnet of most modern dairies.

'When I am making cheese I am tranquil,' he goes on. 'It's filling in all the forms that makes life difficult.'

Peppino's dairy is down a dusty track, about a kilometre from Paulilatino. Two loose-limbed, brindled dogs sleep in the sun in the yard outside. Beyond them is a vegetable patch with neat rows of tomato plants, frothy lettuces, stumpy beans. The dairy doesn't look much from the outside, but the inside is a clean, shiny working space, with a tiled floor slick with water, stainless steel vats and coils of hose snaking across the floor.

'I don't make many cheeses at this time of year,' he says. 'There isn't much grass for the cattle to eat.'

The milk isn't pasteurised, he explains as he slices yesterday's compacted curd into thick strips. He dumps the slices into a large, blackened pot half filled with milk that's heating over a gas ring. He stirs the cauldron with a wooden paddle until the strips suddenly coalesce into a white, molten mass.

Swiftly Peppino transfers the mass to a terracotta bowl. As it cools, he begins to shape the top, crimping a bit to create a neck, and then allowing the mass of the cheese to drop slightly under its own weight, forming a giant white fruit. He tears off the top of the neck and tosses it into the pot with the hot milk. He moves the Casilozu to a bowl of cold water, makes a slip knot from a plastic tie, and slips it over the remaining neck of the cheese with deft fingers. He moves the fat, pear-shaped cheese to another tub containing salted water and hangs it from a stick resting just above the water, so that the cheese is completely immersed.

It'll stay there for several hours until it's ready to be dropped into a smart red net bag and hung to age 'for as long as you like. Some people like them fresh, after twenty days or so. Others like them aged for seven or eight months. The oldest I've tried was three years old. Very strong and spicy – piccante. The cheese varies through the year, depending on what the cows are eating. The best milk is between November and January, when the grass is richest.'

To begin with it tastes quite mild, but I notice it has an elegant persistence, with shades of fresh grass, eucalyptus and almonds that deepen and harmonise as the cheese ages. Its character moves from initial understatement to subtle definition to rich satisfaction.

Peppino also makes treccia, the fresh cheese I ate at breakfast; and fresa, a true raw milk cheese, flat and round as a curling stone. He sells his cheeses all over Italy, but times are hard. There's La

Crisi. And there are those damn regulations that interfere with the natural order of things.

'You can only make good cheese by working with nature,' Peppino says, twisting the next casilozu over the wooden paddle. 'The bureaucrats work with paper, not nature.'

Casilozu is an endangered species, even with the support of Slow Food. Like many artisanal food products, its producers are squeezed by the effort and hours required to make the cheese, the meagre financial rewards for doing so and bureaucratic interference. Unless we recognise the work, craft and passion that goes into cheeses like Casilozu and other products, and are prepared to pay for them, they and their makers will soon disappear.

Giovani Ruffa pushes una birretta into my hand. Cold beer. The outside of the glass is misted with condensation. The beer evaporates in my throat. Pure bliss.

The ride from Paulilatino had been gruelling. I left the village and the hospitable Sannas early in the morning, taking the pass that led over the Monte Ferru once more. I crossed the rice-growing flat lands around Oristano, passing within hailing distance of Cagliari, before looping southwest through the rugged hills of the Monti di Sulcis and the Monte Linas, where abandoned farmhouses carried graffiti, more polite than menacing, declaring 'Attention Tourist: Sardinia is NOT Italy'. The road finally delivered me to Is Xianas, a tiny speckling of cottages outside Santadi in the bottom left-hand corner of Sardinia, among rolling, golden labrador-coloured, stubble-covered hills. It had been demanding, but full of curiosity and interest and seductive beauty. Several times I'd been tempted to linger along the way, but I promised that I'd be at Is Xianas for lunch and so at Is Xianas for lunch I am.

I have three hosts, Giovanni Ruffa, Bruno Bego and Marco Bianchi, who are known to each other and to the outside world by their surnames, or in the case of Bruno by his nickname, Kibbutz. They all come from Asti in Piedmont, but have fallen in love with this obscure corner of the province of Carbonia-Iglesias, and have each bought a small holiday cottage here, which, little by little, they're restoring between lunches and dinners and trips to the bar in nearby Santadi. They're men of the left, or liberal at the very least, politically engaged, professional, and, while married or with long-term partners, are without their life's companions in Is Xianis.

More guests start arriving at 12.30 or so. Domenico, the baker, is the first to arrive. He's a chap of commanding ebullience, as wide as he is tall and as thick through the chest as he is wide and tall. The porceddu, roast suckling pig, for lunch has been cooked in his wood-fired oven. Shortly after, Alberto Balia, the owlish newsagent in Santadi, arrives with his wife Sabrina, son Andrea and daughter Gloria, carrying guitars, and a friend, Daniel, from Argentina, with his wife.

We begin with little jars of vegetables sott'olio – tiny broad beans; chanterelles and porcini mushrooms; artichoke hearts; olives; and, finest of all, wild asparagus – in oil, all made by Terre Shardana, a local producer. The jars are passed round and round, along with a board stacked with slices of cured pig fillet and bread for mopping up the oil. We eat the porceddu, which has been resting quietly beneath a mantle of myrtle leaves, the skin crunching like the thin caramel topping of crème brulée, the flesh fibrous, sweet, caressingly porky and gloriously greasy and carrying a ghost of astringent myrtle. Finally come cheeses of various levels of pungency and potency, the most gutsy being a sheeps' cheese matured in the stomach of a lamb, like a lactic haggis. Everything eases along on a tide of wines from the co-op at Santadi. It's one of those lunches, fluid in time and personnel. Conversation and laughter rise and fall like waves on the shore. I've only met Ruffa before, but it's easy to sink down onto the billowing hospitality and easygoing warmth, to feel as if I've known these people for years.

Domenico starts making animal and bird imitations – a raven, a crow, a fox – with unnerving accuracy. This leads to a song 'B-B-B-B-Bicorni' that we all end up chanting. God knows what it's about. Antonio's daughter produces launeddas, Sardinian pan pipes made of three single reed pipes. They make a noise that reminds me of the drone and chanter on the Highland bagpipes. Scotland and Sardinia. How odd. Perhaps there are musical links between the two. At about 4 p.m. Alberto and his son, Andrea, begin duetting on their guitars. Sabrina, Alberto's wife, sings cantu a chittera, Sardinian folk songs, mournful and powerful. Daniel borrows Bianchi's guitar and introduces South American rhythms to the jazz riffs and inflections of the other two.

At some point sheep in a field behind the house begin a circular progress around their domain, adding light chimes from the bells around their necks to the fluid music of the guitars. And so it goes on, wine, music, song, more wine. Time slips away. Then I slip away and fall asleep.

I wake up around 6 p.m. Alberto and Daniel are still playing, but the sheep have settled down. As it's beginning to get dark the party dissolves rather than ends. Ruffa, Kibbutz, Bianchi and I sit drinking and talking as the night quietly settles around us.

Ruffa and Kibbutz return to Asti and I go off to explore Santadi and the land around; an abstract canvas of cereals, olive groves and vineyards, with the sea to the west and shaggy hills to the north, south and east. As its name suggests, Carbonia-Iglesias had once been prosperous thanks to coal mining. Mining and prosperity ended some years ago and Carbonia-Iglesias is now poor and times are hard.

Everyone I speak to mentions la crisi, the Crisis. The Crisis, Italy's continuing economic depression, is responsible for markets drying up, restaurants closing, the lack of disposable income to spend on food or consumer products or investment, and so on and so on. Barter has become a means of exchange again. But, after wandering around Santadi, I wonder how many towns in the UK of the same size – about 3,000 people – would support five butchers, five greengrocers, six bakers and God knows how many bars. I lose count.

The nearest point to the sea is Porto Botte, about a forty-minute ride across the close-cropped coastal plain, past a line of beehives painted sun-faded terracotta, umber, yellow and pale sky blue; past orange and olive groves and vineyards and wineries; past the random hulks of old factories, abandoned plant and machinery spiky and stark; past farmyards with old-fashioned bales of hay stacked in teetering towers on trailers; past golden fields shimmering with ripe wheat with ploughed-up strips along their edges, a firebreak against a fag butt tossed carelessly from a passing car; and past the odd flock of sheep sheltering in the shade, cream shadows on the golden-brown fields.

Porto Botte isn't really a port at all, more a cluster of dishevelled buildings with a miscellaneous selection of leisure and fishing boats anchored along the curve of the sandy bay scruffy with stacks of dried Neptune Grass seaweed blown in by a recent storm. The multicoloured triangular sails of kite- and windsurfers whip across the shallow bay, piloted by lean young men in wetsuits leaping high into the air, twisting and turning.

I find an upturned boat with a cracked turquoise bottom among the rough vegetation. It makes an agreeable office. I rest my back against it and jot in my notebook and watch the kite- and windsurfers. Away to my right an abandoned building

– home? boathouse? fishing station? – stands on a spit of sand sticking out into the bay, dark, decrepit, brooding, mysterious, slightly sinister. Behind me is a shallow, brackish lake in which pink flamingos pick their dainty way, as absurd as they're beautiful. Really, there are worse places to be and worse ways in which to spend one's time.

It wouldn't be true to say that my journey so far had exceeded my expectations, because when I set out I didn't have any expectations beyond a generalised hope that I would have a good time. I didn't know what I'd find or what would happen. But serendipity, with the odd nudge from John Irving, has already provided me with an abundance of brilliance. Even soulless Stintino and Alghero have provided food for experience and thought.

When I get back to Is Xianas, Bianchi's partner Nadia has arrived and Bianchi is cooking dinner. Nadia, a teacher from Asti, is Bianchi's partner. She's trim and wiry with short blonde hair and big earrings. She radiates a kind of impatient energy and decisive intelligence. Her green eyes are as expressive as Gabriella Carfagna's, but lean more towards the ironic, sceptical and downright incredulous. She and Bianchi bicker in affectionate habit, a wrestling match of personalities.

Bianchi's cooking prawns in a pan without butter or oil. He explains that any oil or butter would interfere with the flavour of the prawns. Nadia rolls her eyes at such peculiar particularity. He makes a risotto with crayfish broth left over from an earlier feast. After dividing the risotto between three plates, he dribbles a little olive oil over his. Nadia rejects this as heresy, provoking a lively debate. I try it and find that it gives smooth ease to each mouthful.

We talk long into the night, about their lives, how they've known each other since… well… since for ever. Unfortunately, they had both married other people with unhappy results. But they always kept in touch, kept talking to one another.

Finally they'd got together after their respective marriages had ended. Now they seem to have arranged their lives on an equable footing, embracing friendship, mutual support, affection and love, but without the more testing pressures of daily domestic proximity.

———

The next day I walk in the woods of Pantaleo a few kilometres away, among wild olive and cork trees. Tiny starbursts of myrtle flowers, whiter than snow, explode against shiny dark leaves, and oleander as pink as strawberries and cream hangs over the path marked by the sere, brown husks of rock roses and euphorbias, lilies and stonecrop. There's a cool breeze and the vigorous rasping of crickets, and the silent dance of butterflies into sunlight, into shade, out into the sunshine again. The warm air is suffused with myrtle, allspice, camomile, white pepper.

I take a fork in the path, to the left, up the slope, looking for a path that might lead back to the road, and soon take another to the left, up and up. I come to a third fork and pause, sweat sluicing into my eyes. I have a drink and consider. I can remember following similar paths across the Monti Lucretili in other summers long ago.

My uncle John and his wife, Brenda, settled near Licenza, a small village on the borders of Lazio and the Abruzzi some thirty-five kilometres from Rome, in the mid-1960s. At the time, the steep-sided hills around Licenza seemed to have changed little in the preceding 500 years. Electricity was something of a novelty. White oxen were still used to till the smallholdings and turn the soil in the olive groves. Sheep and goats were still driven up the rough tracks that led past John and Brenda's house, to the high pastures in the hills, bells on their necks tinkling in the silence of the early dawn. The local dialect was so impenetrable that even visiting Romans couldn't understand a word. John and Brenda, not to mention the steady flow of brothers, sisters, nephews and nieces, were an exotic addition to the area.

John decided that he could use the waters that flowed liberally from a spring higher up the hill behind the house, which was reputed to be the Fons Bandusia celebrated in the Odes of Horace, to fill tanks in which he could farm trout. The trout tanks, themselves, were built by the indentured labour of various nephews and their friends.

Perhaps unsurprisingly, he discovered that trout farming would not supplement his naval pension to the necessary degree, and he turned with rather more success to smoking salmon instead.

In retrospect, it all seems rather improbable, and indeed it was. However, it meant that each summer, for several years, I went to stay in the spartan accommodation offered by John and Brenda, lured by the prospect of a cheap holiday and the girls of Licenza who were beautiful beyond measure (and beyond reach), and worked on whatever stage John's various schemes had reached at the time, while I ambled paths very like these, exploring the countryside around Licenza and the life that abounded in it.

I think of my younger self, who'd had boundless faith in his physical capabilities. He would've pushed on, propelled by some inner conviction that the path he was following would come out somewhere that would lead to somewhere which would take him to the place he wanted to be.

I remember, too, the occasions when the cheery optimism had slowly evaporated, when the paths simply petered out, and, tired and disconsolate, I would simply push myself downhill through scrub and brambles until I came to a road and returned to the house, bloody, sweaty and streaked with dust.

I wipe the sweat from my eyes. I turn and go back the way I came, glad that I'd got as far as I had, gladder still that I've finally learned that there's nothing to be gained by boyish obstinacy.

Just down the coast from Porto Botte is Porto Pino, a marina where holidaymakers park their yachts and boats and tan themselves on the ten kilometres of caster-sugar beach fringed with pines. There's a campsite and holiday homes that remind me of Chateau Vert in Middleton-on-Sea that my grandmother used to take to house her grandchildren during various summer holidays when I was a child. It isn't the style of the houses so much as their character – sensible, practical, jolie-laide, just a bit scuffed – that remind me of Chateau Vert. It's easy to imagine the same piles of soggy towels, cast-off bathing things, trails of sand, beach bats and balls stacked in random heaps, to hear the shouts of squabbling children and the sharp interventions of parents, the sniggers and muffled laughter.

Before it reaches Porto Pino, the road runs straight for a couple of kilometres between huge, shallow lagoons in which candyfloss flamingos, egrets with the blinding white of sheets in a washing powder commercial, and other wading birds forage with delicate intent, and shoals of grey mullet, sea bass, bream and witch sole breed and grow fat on the abundant feed until they're ready to be harvested.

A canal connects the lagoon to the sea. The stream of seawater is controlled by a sluice gate on a weir. Below it two lines of stakes form a huge V. The sections between the stakes are lined with smaller palings of metal or plastic, in effect forming walls with a narrow channel between them. At the point where the two arms of the V meet is a round kind of chamber. I've come across this system twice before, neither remotely connected to Porto Pino. The fishermen of Lake Comacchio in Northern Italy use exactly the same configuration to trap eels in the lake. Even more remarkably, so do fishermen on a remote island off Korea to catch anchovies. How three such disparate fishing communities have come up with exactly the same method of catching fish is a mystery.

When the fishermen want to harvest the fish, they open the sluice gate on the canal, sending a heavy rush of salt water into the lagoon, oxygenating the water, and maintaining the height and salinity of the lagoons. Fish are naturally attracted to oxygenated water, and so swim towards it and into the trap. The system is beautiful in its simplicity.

The smaller fish escape through the gaps between the palings to grow larger. The larger ones congregate in the round chamber. The fishermen scoop up the trapped fish in a net, load them into large plastic buckets and transport them to a metal table where they're sorted by species and size by Pietro, a man with a bald head, tattoos on his biceps and a singlet speckled with glittering scales like sequins stretched over a magnificent tummy. He throws any undersized fish back. The rest are loaded into polystyrene boxes ready to be sold off to the ready buyers lining up.

It's as efficient, practical, natural and effortless a system as I've ever come across. There are no concerns about stocking density or fish feed because nature takes care of all that. Nor does the fish harvester have to worry about sea lice or fish shit, or any of the other challenges that dog more orthodox forms of fish farming. At Porto Pino they simply harvest at a sustainable level what the environment serves up.

Pietro's a bit cagey as to exactly how much fish he and the other fishermen take out of the lagoon each year, but points out that it's in their interests to keep stocks stable, and that the fishery has been going for forty years.

Does he eat the fish himself? I ask.

He looks sheepish. No, he says, he's more of a meat man.

All the time he's been sorting the fish, a group of regular buyers have been gradually assembling like gulls around the sorting table. While Bianchi, Nadia and I are waiting around for Pietro to finish, we fall to chatting with two ladies also looking for something for supper. One has gold sandals and toenails painted pillar-box red. Her friend is a motherly looking woman with reddish hair and glasses.

'Ah,' says the motherly looking woman with reddish hair and glasses. 'Take fillets of muggine' [grey mullet] of course scaled, and slices of potato cut thinly. In a dish put down a layer of potato and then a layer of fish, parsley, a little garlic, and then more potato, another layer of fish, parsley, garlic and so on, until it's all gone. A little oil, a splash of white wine and then put it into the oven until it's cooked.' She purses her lips to express how delicious the dish is.

'How about basil instead of the parsley?' suggests Bianchi.

The ladies look horrified. He might just as well have suggested devil worship. Basil! Absolutely never! Only parsley.

'But,' concedes the woman with gold sandals and toenails painted pillar-box red, 'you could use tomato sugo with the fish and potatoes, and you could put basil into that.'

'Yes,' agrees the first lady. 'Potatoes, fillets of branzino, potatoes, dried tomatoes, tomato sugo. With basil. And a little Parmesan. And white wine. That's very good, too.'

'Buon appetito,' they call out as we leave.

Sant'Antioco

Both Sant'Antioco and San Pietro, about twenty minutes to the north of it, have close connections with tuna fishing. For millennia tuna have tracked migratory routes across the Mediterranean. Their importance as an icon and a food source goes back to the first settlements on its shores. Images of the fish occur frequently on Greek pottery. The Romans were very fond of tuna, too.

According to John Wilkins, the classical scholar, and Shaun Hill, the chef, in their translation of and commentary on Archestratus's *Hedypatheia* (Life of Luxury), the poet recommends using the tail of a large female tuna from Byzantium. Apicius, with typical Roman restraint, recommends a sauce of lovage seeds, celery seeds, black pepper, fresh mint, fresh rue, date syrup, honey, vinegar, olive oil and sweet wine.

Curiously, not much is known for certain about the migratory and breeding patterns of blue-finned tuna, and yet, for years, their demise in the Mediterranean has been forecast with a kind of gleeful gloom by a whole range of international bodies. The same has been said of the swordfish. Overfishing, fishing piracy, greed, inadequate policing, official corruption, pollution and general mayhem have all been blamed.

I've long been sceptical about the reliability of the data on which the self-appointed guardians of our piscine heritage base their forecasts and strictures. It seems odd to me that no fishermen are listed on the various rosters of experts, advisers and directors. I know that the relationship between fish scientists and fishermen is pretty adversarial, and even two marine biologists to whom I'd spoken on an earlier visit to Sardinia and who had some kind of relationship with local fishermen, admitted that they had to tread warily. Still, it seems odd to omit such an obvious source of information altogether.

In the interests of research, Bianchi and I are on our way to meet Fernando Fois, who runs Solky, a small tuna-canning business in a back street of Sant'Antioco. Like many artisan operations in Italy, if we hadn't known it was there, we'd have missed the small notice 'Solky – Affumicati e Salati' above the door of a narrow-fronted terrace building.

Inside, however, is a small shop-cum-office where we find Signor Fois. He's a trim man in his sixties, with a dapper moustache, canny brown eyes and a thirty-a-day habit. He explains that Solki was the name given to the town by the Phoenicians when they founded it in the eighth century. They were catching tuna back then, and locals have been catching them ever since. He shows us a form that he has to fill in every time he takes delivery of a fish. It runs to several pages detailing where the tuna has come from, carefully documenting and authenticating that it's been line-caught and by whom.

Beyond the shop-cum-office is a tiny, shiny workshop/factory where each tuna is painstakingly steamed in salt water and cut into chunks by hand ready to be packed into cans or pots with olive oil by Signor Fois's niece and a young man, and then sold under the generic brand of Carloforte. Nothing of the fish is wasted. Even the heart is smoked and vac-packed and there's a stack of cured tuna roes (bottarga di tonno) the size of cricket bats.

He leads us to a café on the seafront of Sant'Antioco, and continues his exposition of the tuna industry over a glass of white wine. He hasn't always been involved in the tuna industry, he says. At one time he was an engineer, building all over the region. This experience made him open-minded about the tuna business, sceptical of official statistics and intolerant of officialdom in general. When he retired, he started smoking salmon out of curiosity and to have something to do, and from that branched out into canning tuna.

'There are plenty of tuna,' he says. 'Red tuna – you call them blue fin – yellow fin, bonito, albacore, palamita. Whatever people say, there are plenty. For years, scientists have been telling us that the blue fin tuna is being fished to death, is almost extinct, and yet they come back in good numbers every year.

'The trouble is that the industry isn't properly policed. For example, there's still one mattanza each year. It takes place off San Pietro, the island next door. The mattanza is the annual ritual when migrating tuna are trapped in nets as they swim between Sant'Antioco and San Pietro, and then gaffed and slaughtered, a violent, bloody and curiously inefficient (and so sustainable) method of harvesting fish that's been practised for thousands of years. Aeschylus compared the slaughter of the Persians at the battle of Salamis to the mattanza in Sicily, and the ferocious Mafia wars of the 1960s were known as La Mattanza.

'The number of tuna they can kill in the mattanza is strictly controlled,' Signor Fois goes on. 'But let's say the numbers in the nets are more than the kill quota. The tuna are kept alive, transferred to other nets and slowly taken to Malta, where the controls aren't so strong. They're fattened up off Malta, and then sold to the Japanese market.'

He suggests that this process isn't just restricted to the mattanza surplus. 'There's a strong Black Market, too,' he says. 'What do you expect when taxes are so high and there's so much bureaucracy? The incentive to get around the rules is pretty strong. I'm all in favour of quotas, and properly enforcing them. But they must be based on facts, and only the fishermen really know how many fish are out there.' He waves his hand at the open sea.

San Pietro

A few days later, I go to Carloforte on Sant'Antioco's smaller sibling, San Pietro, on my own. I take the ferry from Calasetta, which looks like a fishing port of fifty years ago, but accommodates tourism without losing its soul.

Once again I settle to the easy content of sitting on the dock of the bay, watching time just rolling away, waiting for the ferry to turn into the quay, the sea slipping and sliding in the sunlight. How wonderful to be spendthrift with minutes and hours, to feel the agreeable anticipation of the unknown.

Carloforte is a dainty, pink-and-white icing-sugar town stretched around the curve of the bay, with a large barracks-like building the colour of ox blood above it. In a process tortuous even by the standards of Mediterranean migration, coral fishers from Pegli, near Genoa settled on Tabarka off the Tunisian coast in the sixteenth century. They lived there for 200 years before moving on to Carloforte in the eighteenth century. The locals still speak a Ligurian variant of Tabarchin.

I make my way to the Osteria della Tonnara at one end of the promenade. The Osteria was once one of the many tuna-processing plants scattered throughout the islands. Now it's a bright, cool dining space looking out on a lagoon to which snowy egrets and blush-pink flamingos again lent elegant decoration.

I've always thought that there are only two ways to eat tuna: completely raw, as in a tartare or ceviche, or completely cooked. On the whole, I prefer the completely cooked version. The seared-on-the-outside-raw-on-the-inside thick steaks favoured by trendy restaurants in London and elsewhere are unspeakable. The taste, temperature and texture are actively unpleasant. As with most protein, cooking brings out the best of the flavour.

The trouble is that, cooked thoroughly and without understanding, tuna becomes alarmingly dry and fibrous. There are two ways of getting round this: you can cut the meat into thin slices and cook them a padella, very fast on a very hot pan; or as they do at the Osteria, alla tabarkina, in homage to Carloforte's past. The fish is sliced quite thickly, dried, and fried briefly in hot olive oil and then gently braised with a few cloves of garlic, a glass of white wine, tomato sauce, a few bay leaves, some capers and a splash of vinegar.

I've already eaten eight fishy antipasti and another Carloforte speciality, bobba, a voluptuous, heavy-gravity soup. It's made, so the chef, Andrea Rosso, says, by cooking a sliced onion in an earthenware dish until soft; adding dried broad beans, marjoram and sliced zucchini; covering them with water and cooking for about three hours over a low heat, stirring occasionally to make sure nothing's sticking; adding a couple of basil leaves when the beans have finished cooking and been pureed; and serving with a splash of olive oil or a dribble of chilli oil and some dried bread. It's something of a miracle that I can still clatter through the braised tuna with such pleasure.

I end with a small pudding, canestrelli, pastries halfway between a bagel and a cake, decorated with hundreds and thousands reminiscent of some of Lois's childhood parties, served with a jug of muscatel. Fully charged, I'm now ready to explore the coast and hinterland of San Pietro.

I follow the road that weaves parallel to the coast, past a number of stylish and impregnable holiday villas along the shore line. The interior of San Pietro is rugged in an unmemorable way. By easy measures I reach the northernmost tip of the island, where the one surviving mattanza still takes place sometime between 15 May and 15 June.

The skeleton of a long, low, abandonned stone-built tonnara stands on the shore: a sturdy, obstinate, ruined temple to fishing and fish processing, roofless, graffiti-murralled in the bright sunlight, and colonised by fig trees bearing bitter figs. It looks out across a stretch of water towards the wind farm of Portoscuso and the chimneys of the chemical works of Portovesme, moth-balled or evacuated, a similar monument to grand industrial ambition, human energy and the passage of time.

Stone columns of forgotten usage stand in line down the scrub-tufted slipway sloping to the chortling, gurgling sea. It's easy to imagine the bustle when the fishing boats brought in their gleaming, gun-metal blue, streamlined, barrel-chested catch; fish hauled up the slipway with brisk practicality, their viscous stench clotting the air; gutting, gilling, trimming, cooking, dissecting, canning. The offices dealing with the paperwork. First the carts, later the lorries pulling in, to be loaded up, the shouts, noise, movement. That had all gone years ago. Now silence and stillness fills the place. Even the wind has died in the heat. It feels remote rather than sad. There's a toughness about the place, a certain bloodymindedness that mitigates the melancholy.

Sardinia (again)

The gates to Terre Shardana are wide open, and appear to have been that way for several years. They stand on the outskirts of Giba, a small, dusty town between Santadi and the coast. I've wanted to track down Terre Shardana ever since eating their remarkable vegetables sott'olio at lunch when I arrived at Santadi. Unlike most commercial products of the kind and my own home-made efforts, they actually tasted and had the crisp texture of the original vegetables, shaped by the lightest touch of vinegar.

I turn in past some apparently abandoned greenhouses, a couple of large wooden boxes piled with the dry leaves of spiny artichokes and a peculiarly loopy hound that circles round and round barking in an interrogative fashion.

It takes me several minutes to locate Signor Orru, the proprietor. He's a genial, smiling, very bald man with heavy black eyebrows. He's surprised, but pleased, to have an English visitor.

I explain my own particular pleasure in his products, and assessment of their characteristics.

'Aha,' says Signor Orru with a broad smile, 'that's because we only use very little vinegar, white wine vinegar.'

'How much?' I asked.

'That depends,' he says. 'My aunt, Graziella, is in charge of production. She used to be a research chemist, and she takes into account the characteristics of the particular vegetable. It depends on their quality and the time of year. She tastes them before deciding how much vinegar to add.'

Production for the season is over, a fact that I'm getting used to. In England we think of summer as the most fecund time of year for vegetables and fruit, but round the Mediterranean, summer is the least productive season, as rainfall is slight and the sun is hot. Signor Orru explains that his business cycle starts with fave (broad beans) in January/February, followed by carciofi (artichokes) in February/March, and so on through asparagi selvatici (wild asparagus), melanzane (aubergine), peperoni (peppers), cipolle (onions) and peperoncini (chillis). The funghi (mushrooms) come in autumn.

'Freshness is the secret. We grow our own vegetables here. They're picked one day and bottled the next. We use a mixture of olive and sunflower oils. If you use just olive oil, it draws the flavour out of the vegetables.'

Improbable though this sounds, I think there might be something other than pure economics in what Signor Orru says. On the rare occasions that I've made flavoured oils, I've used olive oil, and it extracts flavour from basil, rosemary and chilli with remarkable efficiency.

'Our problem,' says Signor Orru, contracting his black brows, 'is that everyone is making vegetables sott'olio these days. 'But...' he pauses for a moment, 'most of it is industrial, done by machine. Here, everything is done by hand; picking, preparing the vegetables, cooking them, bottling them. Even our labels are stuck on by hand. You can only get our quality by taking this care of every stage, and quality costs money. There are too many people using commercial vegetables, commercial oil, commercial vinegar – and too much of it – and industrial processes, and then selling their products at rock-bottom prices. How do you compete with that?' He looks tired.

I buy a jar of broad beans, a jar of funghi porcini and a jar of wild asparagus from him. The loopy dog barks in a loopy way as Nicoletta and I speed off.

The lane that runs past the cottages at Is Xianas leads to Santadi in one direction, and through farmland for a kilometre or two in the other. It passes an old farmhouse that Bianchi is patiently restoring, past another farmhouse that has, oddly, an old-fashioned red British phone box in the garden, and an old nuragic village, Tattinu. Then it turns into a dirt track too rough even for Nicoletta to follow, and winds its way through thick woods to God knows where.

It's difficult to believe that anyone comes along the road to visit Tattinu, spread out between bushes of myrtle and olive trees, very often. At one time, 3,000 years ago, it must have been a thriving community to judge by the range and variety of the buildings, drawn by the waters of the pozzo sacro, a sacred well.

There isn't much to look at now, just some stones protruding from the brown earth, outlining the shapes of homes and buildings, but none of the other nuragic sites that I've visited possessed such a vivid connection to the past. This may be because it's so rarely visited, or the way in which the trees cluster round the sacred well, shading it. It may be the well itself, the narrow steps descending to shadowy shapes. It may be the stillness of the encircling hills. Whatever the reason, there's a sense of quiet community and reverence about the place. I sit on a stone in the shade of a myrtle bush. A buzzard mews plaintively as it circles overhead.

I'm sorely tempted to stay on. I've fallen in love with this corner of this taciturn island, with its fields of biscuit-gold wheat, its woods, its melancholy flop-eared sheep, its remarkable honeys and honey producers, vegetables and growers, breads and bakers, wines and wine makers, its mesas and rolling hills, its fluffy-eared olive trees, its sandy beaches and the absence of grand houses. I love its wild parts and its civility. I love the way it reminds me of the Italy I met and fell for fifty-five years ago, a simpler, more vivid, tumultuous place. Here people go about their lives in the way they always have, governed by seasons and elements, chiselling a living in a difficult world. I love that it's given me memories quite as brilliant and vital as those earlier ones. I love that it makes me wonder again at the inherent goodness of people, at their curious diversity.

But I've impinged on Bianchi and Nadia's holiday enough. There's still a multitude of islands left to explore. Reluctant though I am, I know it's time to pack up, load up Nicoletta and head for Cagliari, and on to the islands of the Bay of Naples, Capri, Ischia and Procida.

My stay at Is Xianas ends in the same way that it began, with food, wine, music and laughter. I cook dinner for Bianchi, Nadia, Antonio Balia and his family. I'm quietly pleased by the sardine fillets, as silvery as chain mail, marinated lightly in lemon juice, with lemon peel and basil; more noisily pleased by the friggitelli – mild, green, grassy peppers the shape of arthritic fingers – fried with prawns; and by the time we get to the shoulders of seven-month lamb braised in white wine, vinegar, anchovies, capers and rosemary, I'm quite carried away.

Antonio plays his guitar. His son gives a virtuoso display on his. Bianchi gives the first, and I suspect the last, performance of his composition, 'Un Ballata di un Uomo Inutile' (The Ballad of a Useless Man). It's a typically humorous, graceful, self-deprecating note of a clever, generous, kindly, ironic, passionate person. It makes us laugh. As the music flows on, I reflect how decent these people are, in the way they've taken time out of their lives to show me things that matter to them, to draw a stranger into the warmth of their own friendships.

Sabrina, Alberto's wife, sings.

> Tenis s'axina prus famosa
> Po su gestu e po sa bellessa
> O Sardinnia prefetosa
> Fais cumbido in donnia mesa
> Famosa ses o terra mia

Po si binu prus preziau
Su sabon de su Cannonau
E su gust'e sa Malvasia
Po sa Monica preferia
Un'esempiu di sinzillesa

O Sardinnia prefetosa
Fais cumbido in donnia mesa

Su Nuragus de Campidanu
Un donu de sa natura
Vernentin de sa Gallura
Sa Vernaccia du Oristanu
in Prus nc'est su Carinnianu
De su Sulcis vera ricchesa.

O Sardinnia prefetosa
Fais Cumbidu in donnia mesa

(Yours are the most famous grapes
For their appearance and beauty.
Our beloved Sardinia
Invites you to her table.
You are famous, homeland of mine
For your most precious wine
For the flavour of Cannonau
And the taste of Malvasia,
For your favourite Monica
A model grape.

Our beloved Sardinia
Invites you to her table.

Nuragus from Campidano,
A gift of nature,
Vermentino from Gallura,
The Vernaccia of Oristano
And Carignano, too,
The real treasure of Sulcis.)
Our beloved Sardinia
Invites you to her table.

Her voice echoes through the olive trees around the house.

The next day I head back along the road on which I'd arrived two weeks before, through Nuxis where Domenico has his bakery, through Aquacalda, on to where the ruined castle of Aquafredda on the top of a vertiginous hill watches over the valley below, to Cagliari where I'll take the overnight ferry to Naples.

It's 7.05 p.m. The ferry, the *Dimonios*, judders, as if straining to be on her way.

The evening sun flattens out the façades of the buildings along the front, crisp shadows delineating each window, pediment and coping. The newer art nouveau buildings, as stately as liners, merge seamlessly with the older town as it mounts up the hill to the cathedral and to the cupola of the old castello, that stands against a gentian sky. Somewhere in Cagliari's narrow streets are a Matthew's Bar, a MacPuddu's Fast Food Emporium and the delicious church of St Michele, its façade a joyful riot of rococo ornamentation and scantily clad young women wearing what appears to be eighteenth-century admiral's cockades on their heads, just three of the marvels I'd stumbled upon as I meandered through the streets earlier in the day.

At 7.20 p.m. we begin to move. The juddering shifts to a smooth surge of power. A wake of arctic ice blue churns up behind us. The Mola Sanità recedes. Cagliari stretches along the seafront, more and more of it, swinging away. Tugs flirt with our bow. The sun's light flares off the sea. A yacht carrying the British ensign drops away to stern, heading for a berth in the port. We swivel on our axis and ease out past the protective arm of the harbour wall. Cagliari dwindles, dusted with the saffron gold of the evening light.

The expanse of sea grows, its surface twitchy but not rough, a touch of steel in its navy blue. Our wake curves behind us like a jet stream. The lumps and bumps of Sardinia become misty silhouettes. We're following the same course that travellers have been following since the Mediterranean became inhabited. Boats may have become larger, but they carry the same cargoes, transport the same people – Phoenicians, Greeks, Romans, Carthaginians, Italians, Spaniards, Germans, Turks, French, Arabs, Africans. The Mediterranean is a highway carrying the freight of history.

The wind turns persistent and chilly. I go inside and buy a Mars Bar, the first piece of processed food I've eaten since I set out. It unleashes an electrifying sweetness and a Proustian gush of nostalgia. I left England on 13 May, exactly forty-nine days, or seven weeks ago.

Outside for one last turn about the deck. There's a man with a battered appearance and an expensive camera capturing the setting sun, a vast, glowing orange tablet sliding down into the sea. The sky shades from peach to dusty peach to dusty peachy yellow to dusty yellow to dusty yellowy blue to chalky blue. The sea is graphite. White ponies dance on the surface. The ship powers on implacably through them.

The man with the battered manner and the expensive camera vanishes. Night closes in, each moment a little bit darker, like Grandmother's Footsteps. I never quite catch the moment of change.

At 9 p.m. it's time to go below decks. I opt for a seat in the dozing lounge. I mean to stay awake for the night, noting anything there is to be noted, reflecting on the nature of journeys and my own thoughts. So I settle into my seat, notebook in hand. The television's on, showing one of those programmes that's so idiotic it could only be Italian. A man sitting in the row in front is talking loudly into his phone, on and on. Is this going to go on all night? Through a porthole the sea is the colour of black figs.

Around 10.30 p.m. I fall into a fitful sleep and then, suddenly, it's 6 a.m. and I feel stiff and bruised, as if I've spent the night in the stocks. The ship vibrates very gently, steaming into the dawn. Outside the sky's light and brightening. Two espressos and a croissant filled with crème patissière restore my spirits. Other passengers begin to disinter themselves from sleep in ones and twos. Most have the stunned look of people who've either slept too well or hardly at all.

Just over an hour to go. The tremulous beauty of Kathleen Ferrier singing 'Down by the Sally Gardens' in my headphones sparks a sharp peck of homesickness, a longing for family and friends. I wonder how the fields and hanging woods of Uley, my home village in Gloucestershire, are looking.

A sudden cheery burst of 'Buongiorno, buongiorno' over the tannoy, and an energetic altercation between two middle-aged blokes at a nearby table, and the gentler patter between their spouses, rescue me from further maudlin introspection.

At 8.30 a.m. on the dot we pull into Naples harbour, easing past towering, silent cruise ships, a bungalow among skyscrapers. They seem oddly vacuous without their passengers, Angkor Wats and Teotihuacans of the high seas. Ferries dash in and out. Pilot boats and barges scoot back and forth, sheepdogs marshalling an unruly flock.

Painstakingly we back into our berth. It's time to go below, mount up and work out what the hell I'm supposed to do next. The sky's blue. The sun's bright. It's hot already.

3

SPORT OF THE GODS

JULY 2014

Ischia

Ischia

'Ischia,' wrote George Berkeley, Bishop of Cloyne, philosopher, and proponent of 'immaterialism', 'is the epitome of the world. It seems like an enormous, singular orchard.'

Enormous, Ischia certainly isn't. It's about five kilometres from east to west and three from north to south and round in a lumpy kind of way. And, at first sight, it's difficult to identify the good bishop's Garden of Eden Ischia through the encrustation of holiday villas, hotels, marinas, gelaterie and pizza joints around the shore. But from there it rises sharply in hills fluffy with woods and patched with vineyards and smallholdings. Things have changed since Lawrence Durrell wrote in a letter to Anne Ridler in 1950, 'So soft and sweet and indolent it lies/Under Naples picture postcard skies'.

Perhaps my first impressions are clouded by the discovery that I've lost one of my notebooks, a natty number with a red leather cover that matched Nicoletta's high colour. This disaster may not rank alongside the loss of such masterpieces as the manuscript of *Seven Pillars of Wisdom* that T. E. Lawrence absent-mindedly dropped at Reading Station, or Hadley Hemingway losing all her husband Ernest's drafts of short stories and their carbon copies on a train, or John Stuart Mill's maid using the manuscript of Thomas Carlyle's great work, *The French Revolution*, to light the fire, but I feel my notebook's absence keenly. It contains much of the material about Sardinia, and those glorious days at Is Xianas in particular.

But I soon warm to Ischia. There's certainly something of Donald McGill about seaside Ischia, but there's also still something of La Primavera about inland Ischia. It morphs from a ring of seaside towns that have much of the jolly vulgarity of Bognor-cum-Blackpool-on-the-Med about them, to the classically wooded slopes of Monte Epomeo, 788 metres high at its centre.

'You see, there are six continents on this island the size of the palm of your hand, zones with their own microclimates and environments,' Riccardo d'Ambra tells me. Riccardo is patriarch of the numerous d'Ambra family, wine makers, restaurateurs, chefs, keepers of the flame of Ischia's traditional produce and cooking culture and passionate proselytiser of all things Ischian. He must be in his seventies, with the imposing face of an Easter Island figure, eyebrows like rampant white hedges above brown eyes that flash with animation behind steel-rimmed glasses, and alarming amounts of hair exploding from ears, nose and even from the end of his nose. Hobbled by arthritis he may be, but that doesn't diminish his vigour or fervour.

'Do you know that tomatoes ripen on one part of the island one month – one month! – before they do in another a few kilometres away?'

He goes on to explain that there are six communes on Ischia, each with its own council, its own policies and its own dialect. There are differences between the mentality of the coastal dwellers and the inlanders, he says. 'These days tourism is the most important economic force on the island, but before agriculture was far more important to life here.'

We're sitting in the family restaurant, Il Focolare, tucked into the woods on the edge of Barano. It's as idiosyncratic as its founder. Oatmeal hessian lines the ceiling in swags. The floor is paved with tiles the colour of biscuits, the tablecloths are orange. A rough-hewn, unpainted bookshelf occupies the middle of the restaurant, loaded with cookery books and pots with drooping peonies. A kind of brown gloaming thickens the light. The walls are covered with faded posters of films part or all of which have been filmed on Ischia – a virile Burt Lancaster in *Il corsaro dell'isola verde*; *Appuntamento a Ischia* with the great singer, Domenico Mondugno; and Richard Burton and Elizabeth Taylor in their Cleopatra phase, looking like waxwork dummies. I'm surprised not to see one of *The Talented Mr Ripley* with Matt

Damon, Gwyneth Paltrow, Jude Law and Cate Blanchett, but perhaps such brash modernism would be out of place in the particular rusticity of the interior, where even the air seems rich with the dust of the past.

Clearly, the food and persona of Il Focolare are rooted in historical Ischia rather than contemporary Ischia. Not for Il Focolare menus in English, German and Russian, which I've noticed outside the restaurants clustered around Ischia Porto. Its menu is as much a manifesto proclaiming the principles and virtues of Ischia's culinary culture as it is a list of dishes, and the dishes themselves celebrate the traditions of the land rather than the sea.

While Riccardo talks, I eat a plate of mezzanelli, a rustic relation of bucatini. The dough has been freshly made and incorporates two different herbs foraged on the hillsides around that give the pasta a slightly bitter note that pierces the amiable fruit of the tomato sauce.

'When you say the name "Ischia" to anyone, they automatically think of the sea, Matthew,' says Riccardo. 'But what about the land of Ischia? The land where we grow the vines and vegetables and fruits?

'If you live by the sea, you look to the sea for your food. It's the catch of the day. It doesn't change a lot through the year and the methods of cooking are quite simple. In the interior of Ischia we look to the land. We cook what it provides by the seasons. We depend on vegetables and herbs more and we use braising and other slow cooking techniques, so the food is quite different.'

After the mezzanelli comes an earthenware bowl of coniglio all'ischitana, rabbit in the Ischian style, braised for about two hours, with tomatoes, white wine, a touch of garlic and, in the case of Il Focolare, a very particular, pungent wild thyme that grows on the Ischian hills. At the end of cooking, much of the cooking juices are strained off to serve as sauce for pasta con salsa di coniglio, another thrifty Italian culinary tradition, before the pot is brought to the table so you can gently prise away the tender flesh from the bones and savour the tomato-infused, thyme-pricked, sweet richness of the rabbit itself.

To be honest, I'm not sure I could pick coniglio all'ischitana out from coniglio alla casanese, coniglio in tegame, coniglio all'astigiana or any of the other innumerable rabbit dishes that employ the same battery of ingredients with slight local variations. However, while the dish is served all over the island, cognoscenti make pilgrimages to Il Focolare for its coniglio all'ischitana.

In an ideal world, Riccardo says, coniglio all'ischitana should be made with coniglio da fossa d'Ischia, Ischia's once famous cave rabbits. In former times, agricultural workers would head off for their fields, smallholdings or vineyards carved out of the vertiginous and cave-pocked hills for days at a time. It was easier to find food on the spot than it was to return home every day for a sustaining lunch or dinner. Rabbits also have an easy knack of providing more rabbits, and so by popping them into convenient caves and feeding them on abundant herbs and greenery, the farmers provided an accessible, renewable and tasty source of protein. The fact that these rabbits tasted better than those kept in cages was another attraction.

'When I was growing up here, we had cave rabbit on Sunday, only on Sunday,' Riccardo goes on. However, as agriculture became mechanised and transport improved, the need to stay out for prolonged periods on the land stopped, and with it the tradition of the cave rabbits of Ischia. It's a tradition Riccardo is enthusiastic, almost to the point of obsession, about re-establishing.

'Young people have forgotten their food heritage,' he says. 'We need to keep these things alive, Matthew.' For Riccardo, and his family, Ischia's food culture is quite as important as any other part of its history. He sees a direct connection between the islanders as they are and the islanders as they were. So, along with two or three other producers, he and his daughter Silvia have started breeding the rabbits again in caves just up the hill from the restaurant.

'When we started our own breeding programme, we had to talk to the old-timers to discover how it was done, create the caves, feed the rabbits and so on and so forth. Now there are three of us doing this, with the backing of Slow Food. The demand for these rabbits is far bigger than the number we can produce, but not many people want the bother of looking after the rabbits. It's far too much trouble. But for us the rabbit is a symbol of the land of Ischia, of our – our! – agricultural and social history.'

It's too late to see the rabbits today, but before I leave Riccardo insists on taking me on a tour of the grotte – a chain of caves – behind the restaurant dining room. They're as idiosyncratic as everything else about Il Focolare. The first once served as a wine cellar, but now it's cluttered with a motley collection of bric-a-brac – a boxing glove, patent corkscrews, odd bits of agricultural equipment looking like pieces of a medieval torturing kit, a plank bench, a table made of a single rock or stone, a couple of disused barrels and ancient bottles festooned with cobwebs. The other grotte are empty, but in one Riccardo shows me where he has excavated some clay with which he proposes to make his own tegame, the classic earthenware pot for serving coniglio all' ischitana. This fusion of practical and culinary processes embodies a holistic totality connecting past and present that gives Riccardo great satisfaction. His eyes gleam in the dim light.

Ischia has always had an attraction for literati. Stendhal chatted to vineyard owners as he rode over Ischia on a donkey. Henryk Ibsen is supposed to have finished off *Peer Gynt* while staying on

Ischia, although there's some dispute about this. Pablo Neruda spent time here. Yet another poet, W. H. Auden wrote about

> sun drenched Parthenopea,
> my thanks are for you, Ischia,

But most holiday-makers come just to have a jolly time, to be beside the seaside, beside the sea, tiddley-om-pom-pom. And Ischians go about making sure you have a good time with cheerful, honest venality. There're buckets and spades and beach balls and cheap fishing rods to be bought, and countless shops selling the usual towels, beach wraps, sandals, bags, totes, caps and hats as multicoloured as a bag of sweets. There isn't any candy floss, to be sure, but there are gelaterie, no pubs but plenty of bars, no caffs but many cafés, no piers but Negombo.

There are a good many Negombos – Cava Scura, Castiglione, Poseidon, Aphrodite Apollon to name a few – thermal spas, where they harness the geyser-heated waters in which the island abounds, to the benefit of your health and their commercial advantage. There's almost nothing, it seems, that can't be treated by the magical thermal waters of Ischia. Pliny and Strabo praised the curative qualities of its waters. Garibaldi came to Casamicciola to treat the injuries he sustained during the Battle of Aspromonte in 1862. He'd been accidentally shot in the ankle by troops in Victor Emmanuel's army sent to stop him storming the Papal States. Garibaldi had become disenchanted with the slow progress of unification, and decided to try to speed things up by leading a campaign to conquer the Papal States. Ironically, he was stopped by the troops of the very man to whom he'd ceded his conquests of Sicily and Southern Italy. Marie Curie came to test the efficacy of the waters in 1918, and apparently found they contained radon, the gaseous form of radium.

My Negombo looks like the kind of place you'd expect

some Hollywood white hunter to turn up suave and natty in a pressed safari suit, treading in a manly way among carefully choreographed lush vegetation, curvaceous plunge pools, blue loungers and raffia umbrellas. Bishop Berkeley would probably have taken a dim view of Negombo, but Busby Berkeley would've immediately appreciated it.

In place of an immaculate white hunter are dozens of Italians and Germans of every age and family grouping, wandering around in a fabulous array of beach wear – briefs and board shorts; bikinis strained to the point of indecency and one-piecers as formal as bondage gear; sensible blue baggies to mid-thigh, to the knee, to the calf; and sporty cherry triangles moulded to the genitals, cerise and paradise blue, bougainvillea and leopard spotted, black (the default colour for women above a certain age) and tiger-striped; even itsy-bitsy, teeny-weeny yellow polka-dot scraps of cloth.

There are hour-glass figures through which sand would pass very slowly and figures with a certain voluminous generosity to them. There are tummies as round as the sun and others as flat as the pampas, wrinkled tummies and taut tummies, tummies concave and convex, tummies drooping with no shame, tummies made magnificent by sheer will power.

A man in a pair of orange and yellow-flamed Speedos clinging on for dear life beneath the curving brown overhang of his belly. A middle-aged daughter guides her blind father down the path to a thermal pool with patient tenderness. Out on the beach the old biddy with an aureola of hair of improbable colour engages her friend with unadorned grey curls in endless chatty discourse. Not far away a pale, solitary woman carefully turns herself onto her front and then, after fifteen minutes, turns herself onto her back again, a shapely, alabaster sausage browning under the grill. A very, very large man in a T-shirt, a baseball cap and five chins occupies most of the small, high-temperature Jacuzzi pool like a baleful hippo. And in Thermal Pool 3, there's a courtly sarabande as elderly folk move and move about, taking it in turns to press their flabby/speckled/drooping/wrinkled tummies/breasts/backs/necks against the nozzles projecting the health-giving, age-reducing, body-toning, geyser-heated waters into the pool.

Who can tell which children belong to which adult as they dash and shout and laugh and shriek, into the sea and out, up the beach and down, pushing and shoving and belabouring each other? They don't care. Why should they? Everything's concentrated into this moment.

There's something utterly disarming about this mass exhibition of human flesh and frailty and self-delusion. Of course, there's pointless optimism and narcissism, but there's also a kind of innocence, a trust that no one's going to sneer or call you Fatty or Spotty or Saggy or Pot-Bellied or Shaggy when there's more hair on your back than on your head, or the hundred other names you would have been called when you were younger.

There's a basic decency about Negombo. Absurdity, yes, comedy, yes, crass commercialism, yes; but there's humanity, too, in all its saggy, baggy, quivery, shivery, wobbly, knobbly, firm and flexible, hirsute and follically challenged, laughing, smiling, tender, caring, thoughtful, loving, material variety. Bishop Berkeley was right. Ischia is a singular orchard – of human shapes, in all their diverting diversity.

———

Silvia d'Ambra, Riccardo d'Ambra's daughter, and I crouch above a pit about two metres deep, which is topped by a wire fence. Silvia is even more dedicated to the cause of Ischian food than her father, if that's possible. A hole – the cave – in the hillside opens into it. Actually, the cave is less of a cave than a hillside burrow, in part man-made and in part rabbit-made. Silvia throws a branch with plenty of green leaves into the pit. We wait. Nothing happens. Silvia explains that rabbit management isn't as straightforward as it might seem. Hazards include high infant mortality, inbreeding, disease, diet and the habit of rabbits to try and escape. Keeping cave rabbits is hard work, she says. Small wonder the practice has all but died out.

I'm beginning to doubt that the rabbits will be tempted by this ad hoc addition to their diet, or, indeed, that they actually exist at all, when there's a slight scuffling at the mouth of the cave, a flicker of movement, and there it is, a real, live cave rabbit, larger than I had expected, with a fine pair of ears and a rich, velvety black fur. Presently out comes a second, equally large, with a rather fine stippled brown coat.

I have a faint sense of disappointment. As with the white asses of Asinara, the notion of a cave rabbit suggests something legendary, rare, exotic, mysterious, but in the end, the cave rabbit is just a rabbit, a handsome rabbit, and no doubt a tasty rabbit, but a rabbit nonetheless. And what is a cave but a burrow spelt differently? In theory, I can understand the importance of the project for the d'Ambra family, but, in truth, it doesn't speak to me in the way that seeing a British lop pig or a Huntingdon fidget pie would.

'Siamo chiusi perché stiamo preparando la cena' (We're closed because we're cooking the dinner) reads the notice by the door to Da Assuntina. It doesn't look much, a nondescript front tucked away on a nondescript side street that runs down to the beach at Ischia Porto. Da Assuntina is about as far removed as it is possible to be from the polish, the sharpness, the discreet good taste in various shades, the insistent waiter/touts, the menus in Italian, German, English and Russian, of the more fancied ristorantes and trattorias, but the notice suggests a decent attention to the business of cooking; and the exterior dares me to go in.

There's a perceptible break in the various conversations around the room. People peer at me and goggle. I feel as if I've wandered into a Bateman cartoon – 'The Unwitting Tourist Who Dared to Enter Assuntina's'. The chatter picks up again.

The inside is as free-spirited as the outside. Moulded plastic tables and chairs; paper tablecloths and napkins; tongue-and-groove walls; barrel-vaulted ceiling; white and all-purpose Med blue paintwork; haphazard decorations and yards of fishermen's netting festooned with bits of various sea creatures, along with a football painted in the Italian colours and a Forza Napoli sign. The lack of design finesse is reassuring. In my experience in Italy, the less polished the external display, the better the food.

It's difficult to tell customers from members of the family. There are a number of matrons at work in the kitchen at the back and a revolving cast of improbably sexy women as well as children of all ages by the bar in front. Papà, a tall, silent man with a certain gravity in spite of a grey T-shirt stretched over a paunch, hair pulled back into a short, grey ponytail and a faraway look in his eyes, does most of the fetching and carrying.

Lunch? Fish, inevitably. There are days when I yearn for a chunk of meat, but there isn't any point in going to somewhere like Assuntina's and asking for the meat option. So fish it is – fat, sweet mussels; nice, chewy octopus; fine marinated anchovies with a hint of chilli; a plate of penne all'arrabbiata, with bright tomatoes just broken and warmed by the heat of the pasta; and finally orata (bream) with green olives.

The bream is obviously cooked to order because it takes about twenty minutes to arrive. I couldn't care less. I'm caught up in the fluid dramas among the cast of family and friends, the conversations in three acts, the jump cuts from comedy to tragedy and back again, the vivid diorama of hand and facial expressions. The tableau has the energy and theatricality of an Eduardo de Filippo play. And when the fish arrives, it's fresh and firm, the cooking juices and the oil thickened to an emulsion, nutty chunks of salty green olives providing weight and seasoning and a nip of chilli for very good measure. It's robust and delicate, luminous and gutsy, and oh yes, worth waiting for.

———

I'd seen a poster for a concert performance of Gaetano Donizetti's opera buffa *L'elisir d'amore* at La Mortella, the garden created by Sir William Walton and his Argentinian wife Susana in the 1950s. Jolly music and an evening ramble through a famous garden – it was irresistible.

Sir William was the distinguished composer of very avant-garde (for its time) *Façade*, the jazzy *Belshazzar's Feast*, and the stirring *Spitfire Prelude and Fugue* for the film *The First of the Few*. He died in 1983 and is buried at La Mortella, but Susana lived on until 2010, tending to this extraordinary creation.

The garden is enchanting and exhilarating. A maze of pathways meander up the precipitous hillside, through a teeming mass of lush, luxuriant, exuberant plants and shrubs; of fleshy leaves and spiky leaves; of geraniums and magnolias and hydrangeas, of ferns, and canopies of palms; and emerald lily pads the size of tea trays and grasses and flowers; grottos and leering satyrs, pools and streams, and a bamboo-clad lavatory with a toilet sign that had formerly been used on the London Underground.

At the top, the garden flattens out around an amphitheatre where the concert performance is due to take place later this evening. It looks out over the Bay of Florio where a twin-masted schooner rides at anchor with theatrical precision in the space behind the amphitheatre. Thyme grows between the steps leading to the seats and its scent fills the evening air. The only place of comparable romance I know is the exquisite Greek theatre at Tindari on Sicily. House lights are beginning to prickle down in Florio and on the facing hillsides.

People make their way up through the garden and shuffle into place around me, a curious mixture of smart, well-to-do Italians and a rag-tag-and-bobtail assembly of Americans, Germans and British.

The night air is warm. The light grows hazy. The twin-masted schooner fades into the gathering gloom. I can hear the occasional hoot of a car and a keening siren. The singers warm up, running through their scales, la-la-la-la-la. Violins begin tuning, their runs broken by the odd toot of a trumpet or cooing of a clarinet. There's the tension of anticipation that precedes any performance, heightened by the noises of the unseen performers. A prolonged pause, and then suddenly there they are, the members of the orchestra taking their places, dressed in rather showy costumes as if they're going to take part in the drama as well as play their instruments. The conductor makes his way to the centre, bows to the audience, bows to the orchestra, raises his hand and we're away.

Gaetano Donizetti wrote *L'elisir d'amore* in six weeks in 1831, and it's been part of the repertoire ever since. It's a banker, an opera the music-loving public never tire of, a masterpiece of bel canto lyricism, a dependable, jolly counterbalance to those heavyweights of the nineteenth century, Verdi and Wagner (who wrote a piano version of the score), and has one really famous aria – 'Una furtiva lagrima' – that really is a tear-jerking show-stopper.

But I don't think that Donizetti had taken into account the effect that extraneous sound effects might have on an outdoor performance of his work. Car horns and sirens punctuate the dancing bars of the overture, with barking dogs, braying donkeys, zithering crickets and fireworks by way of variation. To add to a sense of surreality, the orchestral sound has the same tinniness and frenzy of the Marx Brothers' *A Night at the Opera*, and the tenor playing Dulcamara looks and sounds disconcertingly like the meerkat in a long-running series of TV commercials.

And then there are the frogs. As I'd wandered around

earlier, I'd noticed pools and ponds at almost every level of La Mortella, each of which had a healthy population of small green frogs. It's astonishing how penetrating the co-ax co-ax croak of one small green frog can be. Multiplied by several hundred, there's a remorseless cacophony that would have cut through a crowd singing 'You'll never walk alone' at a Cup Final. Donizetti's lively score seems to encourage the frogs to greater and greater efforts. The choruses become vocal battlegrounds, arias are massacred wholesale. And 'Una furtiva lagrima' sung to the irregular, discordant, antiphonal accompaniment of several hundred frogs –

> Una furtiva lagrima
> negli occhi suoi spuntò:
> (co-ax co-ax)
> Quelle festose (co-ax co-ax) giovani
> (co-ax co-ax) invidiar sembrò.
> Che piu cercando io vò?
> (co-ax co-ax, co-ax co-ax)

– provides a musical treat of a most unexpected nature. I treasure the last quatrain in particular:

> Di più non chiedo, non chiedo
> (co-ax co-ax ax)
> Ah cielo! Si può morir!
> (co-ax co-ax)
> Di più non chiedo, non chiedo
> Ah cielo! Si può morir d'amor!
> (co-ax co-ax, co-ax co-ax, co-ax co-ax, co-ax co-ax)

It's all I can do to stop from adding my own guffaws to the sound effects. But no one else seems to notice. It's a precious memory, full of pleasures that I can never imagine having at Glyndebourne or Garsington, let alone the Royal Opera House or La Scala.

———————

It's a splendid morning. Riccardo d'Ambra introduces me to Gaetano, a potter, who makes the tegami pots in which the rabbits of Ischia regularly end up. These are clearly a small part of Gaetano's output, which consists largely of fauns, shepherdesses and large bowls of unimpeachable vulgarity, but Richard is enthusiastic about Gaetano's contribution to the island's cooking tradition. It takes a couple of weeks to make a pot, he explains, waiting for it to dry out, firing it, glazing it and firing it again. He seems very pleased that he'll soon be able to cook rabbits that he's raised, in a pot made from clay from the same area, an integrated culinary experience.

I come down to Barano in search of swimming and lunch. The water is still a bit murky, as if churned up from some vast storm far out to sea. But the beach is as compelling as ever, a jumble of Liquorice Allsorts, brown bodies swathed in a range of brightly coloured wrappings. I lunch properly, but lightly, pay my bill at the Nettuno bar and make my way back to where I parked Nicoletta.

As I do so, I pass the spot where, earlier, Gaetano the potter had interrupted his sunbathing on the terrace above the beach to advise me where to eat. I want to thank him, but can't see him and move on. But it seems ungrateful not to at least make some kind of effort, so I turn round and retrace my steps.

There's a steepish concrete apron next to the terrace he'd been on. I'll just nip up that, I think, lean over the wall, and say my goodbyes. I don't notice that the concrete apron ends with a steep step. I drive the ball of my right foot down. It hits the edge of the step. As I move forward, my heel drops. There's nothing to stop it. The angle becomes too great. Something snaps with the sound of a gunshot and a searing pain.

The air fills with Anglo-Saxon swear words. I lurch around, looking for somewhere to sit down. The only people who notice anything amiss are two African tat-peddlers, a man and a woman. They help me to sit down on the wall they'd been resting on.

I'm pretty certain that my Achilles tendon has broken. I hope, hope, pray that it isn't as bad as that, but in my heart of hearts I know it is. I feel sick.

After a while the initial agony subsides to a savage throb. I haul myself up to where I'd left Nicoletta, and, with my right foot flapping uselessly, get onto her with some difficulty, and ride back to the hotel.

Francesco, the manager, immediately assesses the gravity of the situation and gives me a bag full of ice on which to rest my ankle. I spend an uneasy and largely sleepless night. At one point I feel something like a rubber band snapping and shrivelling up inside my calf and scream in pain.

'È rotta,' Dr Maio at Ospedale Rizzoli in Lacco Ameno confirms the next day. And then again, with a certain grim satisfaction. 'È rotta. You need an operation, and a long period of treatment. Do you want it here?'

'I think I'd better go home,' I say.

While Dr Maio binds up the wounded ankle, and applies gesso (plaster) with unsentimental efficiency, I lie on my front moaning 'Oh God!' into the thin mattress of the couch on which I'm lying. By nature, I'm quite a resilient sort of chap, but there's no disguising the implications of this news.

I try being philosophical. True, I'm not dead. True, too, that I've seen others in far worse states than myself coming through the swing doors of the hospital. But no amount of philosophising can reduce the crushing sense of disappointment, misery, self-pity and hurt.

I trace and retrace the circumstances leading to that moment, obsessively, running memory's video over and over again. Each step is small and insignificant in itself, related to the next only by the fact that they're part of a sequence that cumulatively ends in disaster; the consequence of inconsequence. I have the delusion that if I can change one detail of the sequence, then I can change the outcome.

Finally, I take a taxi back to the Hotel Villa d'Orta in Casamicciola. With kindness and immense thoughtfulness, Francesco, the manager, moves me to a room on the ground floor to minimise my discomfort. I ring Lois to tell her what's happened, but I can't speak to her.

'Dad, Dad, are you OK?' She sounds as distressed as I feel.

'No,' I choke, and put the phone down and weep.

4

ODYSSEUS REFLECTS

2014–2015

Gloucestershire

Initially, I had a good deal of pain, particularly at night, as if hundreds of white-hot needles were being driven into my heel. I couldn't put any weight on the damaged foot, and so I learned the art of crutch and hop management. When you have to lug your body around the place on your arms, shoulders and chest, you resent every gram of surplus weight. My chest became perfectly formed just as my leg was shrivelling away. If you don't use a muscle, it loses definition very quickly. Above the waist I was Arnold Schwarzenegger; below I was a tadpole.

My right foot, ankle and calf were braced inside a rather natty air boot, which looked like the kind of thing spacemen wear when they walk in space. It was certainly a good deal easier to deal with than the orthodox plaster cast (or, indeed, the iron brace Edward VII had to wear when he did in his Achilles tendon by stepping into a rabbit hole).

'Year succeeded year with placid verisimilitude,' wrote Harold Nicholson to describe years in the life of King George V, when absolutely nothing happened in the monarch's life, beyond sticking stamps into the royal collection and shooting pheasants. That's pretty much how I felt about my days of convalescence. Days were marked by the striking of the church clock, two, three, four o'clock, the sound of wind in the leaves of the infant cherry trees and roses in my garden, the chittering of swallows overhead, iced coffee in the afternoon. I got used to seeing the same views and landscapes every day.

Sometimes it was difficult not to descend into self-pity and a tendency to mope. I had to remind myself frequently that, while a torn Achilles tendon is bloody in its way, and takes an unconscionable amount of time to heal, it really isn't that terrible. No life threatened. No limbs removed. No chemotherapy to endure. All I had to do was sit around a lot. Immobility was dreary.

Hugh Kingsmill once said that your friends were God's

apology for your family. In my case I seemed to have been uniquely blessed with both. I wondered if I would have responded with such big-hearted kindness if any of them were immobilised as I was. I liked to think so, but I wasn't sure. It was tremendously cheering in dark times, and there were some very dark times.

August gave way to September, September to October. It was a remarkable autumn, as perfect in its way as summer had been. The weather was beautiful; classic English days of warm, soft honeyed sunshine, mists and mellow fruitfulness. It was a great year for blackberries and sloes, for mushrooms and hazelnuts. But my own foraging was reduced to scrabbling for hazelnuts that had fallen from the bushes in my garden.

But little by little I became more mobile. I started curing pigs' cheeks for bacon – English guanciale – and baked my first cake in several decades while my mind and imagination wandered over sparkling seas beneath blue skies, along dusty paths that smelt of pepper and pine and juniper, waited on quaysides for ferries to dock and depart, followed roads unspooling beneath Nicoletta's wheels, lingered on plates of seafood vivid with marine brightness and fruit dripping with juices and listened to people whose lives had opened up like the doors into a welcoming house.

One evening in March I sat at home listening to the percussion of rain on the glass roof of my sitting room. It had started as a tropical deluge, dramatic and compelling, before settling down to a steady, professional downpour. At least I won't have to water the pot plants outside, I thought. I felt restless.

Well, I had taken the Adventure and for two months heeded the call that the Seafaring Rat had conjured up so eloquently. Was there any reason why I shouldn't heed it again? Go back and pick up where I had left off? My ankle was healing. Nicoletta was resting on Ischia. I couldn't think of any reason why I shouldn't. I had nothing better to do. Plan A might have been scuppered, but now I had a Plan B.

5

RETURN TO THE ISLANDS

JUNE 2015

Ischia – Procida – Capri – Ponza – Ventotene – Stromboli

Ischia (once more)

'Travel must be an extravagance, a sacrifice to the rules of chance, from daily life to the extraordinary, it must represent the most intimate and original form of our taste. That's why we must defend it against this new fashion for the bureaucratic, automated displacement en masse, the industry of travel,' that indefatigable traveller, Stefan Zweig had written in his essay 'To Travel or Be Travelled' in 1926. 'Let us preserve this modest gap for adventure in a universe of acute regulation. Let us not hand ourselves over to these overly pragmatic agencies who shepherd us around like goods. Let us continue to travel the way our ancestors did, as we wish, towards the goal we, ourselves, have chosen. Only that way can we discover not only the exterior world, but also that which lies within us.'

In theory, I'm going to pick up where I left off at Ischia. In practice, I wonder if it's going to be quite as straightforward as that; whether an interval of almost a year will affect my attitude to the whole odyssey; whether that sense of seamless pleasure and invulnerability that I enjoyed so much will wrap me up once more; in short, whether I'm the same person who set off in May of the year before.

For a start, will it be possible to escape the pressures of mass tourism, 'the industry of travel', as Zweig described it? These are far greater now than they had been in Zweig's day, leaving smaller and smaller margins for the solitary traveller, adventurer and explorer to exploit. But it should be possible to find these margins if you give yourself the luxury of time in which to search them out. You don't need to be constrained by exact schedules and narrow formats.

Of course, you can't exactly have an odyssey without travel of some kind. That means making bookings if I don't want to find myself sleeping on park bench or beach, and being aware of ferry timetables because ferries have to be met and travelled on. I have a notional schedule, but it's flexible and adaptable. I can stop and stay as the mood or circumstance takes me. I can choose to linger somewhere or with someone if that takes my fancy. I can hasten on just as easily. I can accept invitations unconstrained by the need to be somewhere else at a specific date. I feel the joy of being the solitary traveller with an expansive portfolio of time, and a buzz at the prospect of being reunited with Nicoletta and heading off again.

And there she is, parked in the driveway of the inestimable Hotel d'Orta. Some kind soul has washed her clean of the dust of last year's travel. She looks trim as ever, scarlet and glistening as newly painted nails in the bright sunshine. I have a brief frisson of nerves as I fire up her 125cc of throaty power, and bounce off over the cobbled surface of the road down into the town, but I soon feel as if we've never been parted.

Procida
I briefly flirt with the notion of revisiting the scene of last year's catastrophe, but quickly dismiss the idea. The imperative of travel means going forwards not backwards, so I go to Procida, Ischia's neighbour among the Phlegraean Islands that crowd the Bay of Naples.

As I head for the ferry, a ferocious downpour suddenly bursts over the harbour. There's no hiding place on the back of Nicoletta. Buffeted by a gusty wind, blinded by driving rain, it's a miracle I make the ferry at all.

How wet can a man get? On a Vespa, very. I'm wearing an admirable waterproof top and a helmet that keep my top half dryish. But below? Trousers sodden in an instant, and cold and clammy. Shoes filled with water. I look and feel as if I've had a serious urinary disaster. Rain not only falls on the just and unjust alike, but also onto the saddle on which I'm sitting. The force of the wind generated by even my modest forward momentum is enough to drive the rain along the seat cover in waves until it reaches the point where trouser and saddle meet. I creep aboard, not so much dripping as cascading water.

'Procida, the Prochyta of the ancients, like its sister-island Ischia, is of volcano origin being composed of pumice-stone and trachytic tufa,' begins the entry in Karl Baedeker's admirable *Guide to Southern Italy* of 1908. It goes on 'Procida is 2m in length and of varying width; population 14,440, whose occupations are fishing and the cultivation of the vine and other fruit. The surface is somewhat flat compared with that of its more majestic sister-isle … The white glistening houses with their flat roofs present a somewhat Oriental aspect.'

What Germanic thoroughness, what masterly accuracy. The Marina Grande is tiny, ringed by flat-topped, cubed buildings seemingly stacked one on another, like boxes. It's the first time I've really been aware of the influence of Arab architecture that Baedeker had observed. The population has shrunk to about 10,000 and the houses are agreeably dishevelled rather than 'glistening' like those on Elba and Giglio, but few other things have changed since 1908.

Procida was originally inhabited from the sixteenth century BC by settlers from Mycenae in the Greek Peloponnese. After that it was subjected to the usual chequered history of the imperial comings and goings of the Romans, for whom it was a holiday resort, of Vandals, Goths, Saracens and Turkish pirates, who treated it as a source of slaves and booty. At one time or another, it's been a feudal fiefdom, game reserve, centre of political dissent and film set. It's the setting of Elsa Morante's classic novel of island life, *Arturo's Island*, which captures something of the hard life and limited horizons of the island before being liberated by modern transport, communications and film making – Procida has played a starring role in a number of films, *Il Postino* and *The Talented Mr Ripley* among them.

By the time we arrive at the Marina Grande, the sun has come out. I steam gently as I dry. There's something deeply pleasing about pottering along with no fixed purpose or particular agenda. I meander up through the port, heading for the Marina di Chiaiolella at the other end of the island. I pause briefly to fortify myself with lingua di bue (ox tongue) I buy at a natty pasticceria in the high street. The name's a little misleading as lingua di bue turns out to be a splendid pastry roughly the shape of a calf's tongue, with a golden brown crust and plump with crème patissière. It belongs the the class of pastries of which one is not quite enough, but two would be sickening.

There's no building of the slightest aesthetic or architectural interest, except for the Torre Murata at the top of the town. This has sixteenth-century walls, but not much else of note until I spot the most extraordinary collection of life-sized wooden figurines stashed away hugger-mugger in a corner by one of the walls. One seems to be Jesus hanging from two rings set in a wall. There's a bald man in a toga with a whip in his hand (Pontius Pilate?); a brace of stiff Roman centurions; a weird assortment of cherubs and crosses; a kneeling woman in nunnish black with a white wimple; and what looks like a vast wardrobe without doors, inside which loom shadowy figures. It isn't the artefacts themselves that intrigue me, so much as the higgledy-piggledy way they've been dumped, as if discarded. I assume that these are the props for one of the many religious festivals like the Procession of the Apostles of Holy Thursday and the Procession of the Mysteries of Good Friday with which the Procida calendar seems studded, but there's no one to ask.

I wander on, admiring the brilliance and colour range of the bougainvilleas draped like flower boas along garden walls, tumbling down in ruffles. I spot a giant lemon growing in a garden high above my head. Like the pompia of Siniscola, it's roughly the size and shape of an American football, but more bulgy around the middle. Its skin is as puckered and lumpy as that of a rhinoceros, and it glows as if lit by an interior light.

Every now and then I pass women wheeling baby buggies, speeding past on scooters, walking home with shopping, gossiping in the street. Almost without exception, they're beautiful, their looks made all the more striking by the self-possessed ease with which they carry them. None of them give me a second glance.

Generally speaking, Procida doesn't make much effort to put itself out for visitors. There's no glittery dross or visitor centres, no menus in multiple languages, no shops peddling the usual dross. Instead there's a resolute, take-it-or-leave-it air to it that's rather refreshing.

After about an hour's gentle rambling, I slope down into the Marina di Chiaiolella, a smaller, prettier version of the Marina Grande, and head for Vivara, a tiny island nature reserve linked to Procida by a bridge. This lies, so the map says, at the end of a narrow, winding lane leading up a steep slope. When I get to the bridge I feel that the Procidani carry their refusal to engage with tourist comfort a bit far. Gates to the bridge are shut, chained and padlocked and there's no other way to get to Vivara. If someone had had the decency to put a sign up at the beginning of the narrow, winding lane rather than at the end of it, they would have saved me considerable time and effort.

Rather grudgingly I slope back again towards the Marina Grande. There isn't really anywhere else to go. Presently, I pass a sign pointing down some steps to a beach, La Spiaggia di Chiaia, and to a restaurant, La Conchiglia. I want a swim and something to eat, and so down I go, 184 steps in all. La Conchiglia is at the bottom, sitting just above a long curve of black volcanic sand, with clear, azure sea in front and Marina di Corricella down the coast to the left. It seems a perfect place to eat lunch.

It is a perfect place to eat lunch, with totani stuffed with ricotta and breadcrumbs bound with egg and light, deep-fried balls of neonate, tiny fish each the size of the tine of a fork, standing out among the shimmering mix of flavours and textures. The lady in charge sells me stracci, large, floppy pieces of pasta which look like pieces of torn fabric, studded with mussels, pine nuts, broccoli and dried grapes, an idiosyncratic combination that turns out to be unexpectedly seductive, a combination of marine sweetness, sweet and sour fruit, vegetable modulation and nutty density.

I talk to her about food on Procida. The dishes at La Conchiglia are hers, she says. Some are typical of the island, others like the stracci, aren't.

I mention the giant lemon I'd spotted earlier. 'What's so special about them, apart from their size?' I wonder.

'Of course, you only find them on Procida, they're quite different from the lemons of Amalfi, Sorrento or anywhere else,' says la signora. 'We call them limoni pane because they have so much pith. The skins have more oil and the flavour is gentle and full.'

'What do you use them for?'

'Insalata di limone – peeled, sliced lemon, chilli, olive oil and mint,' she says.

Mint – it's curious how that very Arab herb crops up in so many dishes around the Mediterranean, a distant echo of the era of Saracen imperial conquest.

It's time for a snooze on the beach and a swim in the cool linen sea. It may be the sun, the sea or the lunch, but I feel this year's journey melding seamlessly into last year's. The time between exists in another dimension and belongs somewhere else.

Capri

There's always been something rackety about Capri, the island of Augustus and Tiberius, Axel Munthe and Curzio Malaparte, Maxim Gorky and Thomas Mann, Alfred Krupp and Graham

Greene, Norman Douglas and Gracie Fields, who all lived there at one time or another. It epitomises a kind of Mediterranean loucheness and cosmopolitan brilliance to my mind, redolent of licence and abandon.

It's quite difficult to see any of this as my aliscafo queues up with seven others to decant its load onto a quayside already milling with visitors. There's a long line of people waiting for the funicular transporting visitors from the port to the Piazzetta, that 'little theatre of the world' as Norman Douglas called it, in the town of Capri above. It's only 11 a.m., but waiters are already touting for business at the cafés, bars and trattorias along the promenade. Even the sparrows scavenging for titbits have a cheeky, begging air to them.

On the recommendation of my nephew, George, an old Capri hand, I go to the reassuringly ordinary Salumeria da Aldo on the sea front and buy a panino caprese to eat while I wait for the queue for the funicular to shorten. 'You have to leave it in the sun for a couple of hours to soak up the juices,' George had directed. Hunger gets the better of me, and I eat it sitting in the sun and watch the great circus playing along the harbour front. George is right about its crunchy, squidgy, chewy, fruity, gently cheesy excellence.

The Italians have developed a crafty way of dealing with mass tourism, whether in Rome, Florence, Venice or any of the other primary destinations around the country. They shepherd them along well-established routes to well-established cultural targets, just as you might herd flocks of sheep from one pen to the next. As most people come to see one or two well-publicised sites, museums, churches or artefacts that they've been encouraged to see, they are happy. At the same time, the system lets the authorities manage the incessant pressure that the visitors create.

This policy reaches its apogee with Capri. Each day hordes arrive from Naples, Sorrento, Pozzuoli and other points of departure on the Costiera Amalfitana, to scale to the heights of Capri and Anacapri from the landing stages of the Marina Grande, thus drawing tourist fire from Procida and, to a lesser extent, Ischia.

The visitors arrive in squads, units, platoons, even brigades, a foreign legion of all nationalities, hundreds of them, thousands of them, hundreds of thousands, ready to storm Capri's historical bastions and to inspect the Villa Jovis, the Villa Fersen, the Villa San Michele and the several other notable villas that dot the island.

These shock troops of modern tourism are armed with maps marking the key sites, cameras, mobile phones, GoPros, dark glasses, rucksacks and bottles of mineral water, bottles and bottles of mineral water. Usually the squads are led by a father or other would-be dominant male, narrow-eyed and focused, commanding or flustered depending on the attitude of those following. They march or straggle in single file along Capri's narrow lanes, only wide enough to allow the flow of one person in either direction, taking swift evasive action from time to time as one of the numerous electric buggies collecting rubbish or carrying suitcases or supplies glides by.

In short order they take their first objective, the Villa Jovis, pose, snap away, tick it off and move on, to the Villa Lysis, the Villa Malaparte, the Villa San Michele, the Piccola Marina, pose, snap, tick at each. And then, they buy gewgaws, lick ice creams, sip Coke or Aperol spritzers in the Piazzetta before tracking back to the funicular, to the port, to their aliscafi and to the resorts from which they'd set off earlier in the day.

This daily onslaught brings with it obvious logistical challenges. Capri neither produces food nor has the space to deal with rubbish on the scale needed. Everything has to be brought or taken away by boat. Through each night all the detritus of the preceding day is collected and carried off to be dumped on sites in the mainland. At the same time, all the food, water and other supplies needed to keep each day's invading army on the march are landed and distributed by the electric buggies. Given the scale and relentless nature of the invasion, it's a miracle of practical organisation.

'Tourism is a blessing and a bane,' Dr Giuseppe Aprea tells me. Dr Aprea is the chief archivist of Capri. He has a nose like that of Franceso Sforza in the Bonifacio Bembo portrait, lively, expressive eyes and receding grey hair. 'Economically it's vital. We can't survive without it. The trouble is that Capri's true character disappears when the tourists arrive each day. There's just a short time at the beginning and the end of the day when the real Capri shows itself.'

'Do you think living on an island creates a different mentality or sense of identity?' I ask.

Dr Aprea considers for a moment.

'I think so. It all depends on our relationship with the sea. By definition, an island is surrounded by water. The sea is a barrier, our protection. It's also a highway. You came here by sea. Trade comes over it. Also pirates and invaders. And it's what keeps us here. It turns each island into a prison. To get even to Naples requires an effort, to get to London is a major undertaking. So it's easier to stay inside our prison.

'Think about Britain and Europe. You're attracted and repelled at the same time by Europe. So is the Channel a channel of communication, a channel for your protection or a channel to keep you in?'

It's evening and I settle down to a first Campari soda at the Bar Tiberio on the Piazzetta (in reality, the Piazza Umberto), surrounded by a herd of Aperol spritzer drinkers.

At a table just down from mine, a goaty man of middle years, with a face the colour of putty and mycelium hair, is holding court. He's wearing a canary-yellow jacket, an orange pork-pie straw hat and a multicoloured silk scarf. His hand rests lightly and briefly on the bare, brown arm of a very pretty girl perhaps a third his age (and twice as old as he'll ever be). She's smoking, holding her cigarette between long, elegant fingers that taper to long, elegant nails the colour of an English post box. Her skin has the lustre and colour of lovingly tended teak. Another girl walks past my table and joins them. Her thong is clearly visible and her tight, globular buttocks oscillate beneath a dress that has the shifting transparency of water. Her hair cascades in thick, tawny tresses to below her waist.

The man in the canary-yellow jacket plays host to a stream of nymphs and satyrs. He's like Pan, the master of the revels. As each arrives or departs, he lets his hand casually brush the arm of the girl beside him. Presently, the three are joined by a barrel-chested man with steel-grey hair wearing a dazzling white shirt, black trousers, braces like sticks of rock and loafers without socks; and by a stylish woman, a mature version of the figures into which the two younger women will grow. She's wearing a dress, the principal function of which is to show off the magnificence of her breasts. Rather disingenuously, she repeatedly tries to draw the two sides of the revealing V of the dress closer together, with little success. The conversation gushes between the five of them. A few minutes later they're joined by a lanky young man, who pulls up a chair, takes out his mobile phone, and disappears into it.

There's a minor kerfuffle as some mega-millionaire and his entourage noisily settle into the ringside seats at an adjacent bar, while a circus of women of all ages mill about dressed in breaths of clothing shifting back and forth over bras and knickers – sometimes no bras and no knickers – revealing everything and nothing; swaying back and forth over tanned, glazed legs; above manicured feet shod in sandals thonged halfway up the calf; low-slung, glittering, gold and silver and cerise tip-top flip-flops; heels stacked as high as supermarket shelves; trainers never designed for training. And men, too, smooth-cheeked and stubble-shaded, shabby-chic, chicly shabby, whippet-thin, pillow-plump, portly as a barrel, cucumber-cool, manly-cool, just-look-at-me-I'm-so-cool-cool, as cool as ironed shorts, pressed jeans, crisp linen, tasselled loafers, and Ray-ban shades can make them.

It's a joy to sit and watch this parade of sweet narcissism and sex, signifying who is getting it, who isn't getting it, who's up for it, who would like to be up for it, who wants more of it, irrespective of race, colour, creed or gender. It isn't a market. It's too blatant, too vivacious, too innocent to be commercial. It's the mating display of peacocks and peahens.

There's one role that some islands play that Dr Aprea hadn't identified – an island as a refuge. Certainly a significant number of writers, artists and intellectuals settled on Capri for that reason. Largely forgotten figures such as Robert Ross, E. F. Benson, Compton Mackenzie, and Norman Douglas; not-such-forgotten writers such as Graham Greene, Maxim Gorky, Somerset Maugham, Axel Munthe (who welcomed Oscar Wilde to the Villa San Michele in 1897 after Wilde's release from Reading Gaol) and Curzio Malaparte, the nom-de-plume of Kurt Suckert; and such diverse figures as Jacques Fersen, Alfred Krupp, Gracie Fields and Mariah Carey have all sought refuge on Capri, drawn by the dramatic beauty of the landscape, mildness of the climate, easy pace of island life, and relative ease of accessibility.

A good many, although not all, of the famous foreigners also took advantage of what many perceive as Capri's tolerance of idiosyncratic sexual proclivities, a tradition that can be traced back to Tiberius and his 'minnows' as reported by Suetonius, that notoriously unreliable historian of ancient Rome, who never allowed the truth to inhibit a juicy titbit.

'I don't think the Capresi are naturally more inclined to homosexuality or promiscuity than anyone else,' Anna Federica of the Biblioteca del Centro Caprense Ignazio Cerio says gently when I put this point to her. 'I think it had more to do with poverty than anything else. Islanders were very poor in those days. Becoming the lover of a rich foreigner was a way out of the poverty of peasant life.'

The next day I wander down the road that leads from Capri town to the Marina Grande. About 500 metres down the hill is the Cimitero Acattolico, or the cemetery 'for all Non-Catholics irrespective of Race or Religion' as the plaque by the entrance puts it, that had been established by George Heyward, a native of Bury St Edmunds, later living in New York, a curious conjunction of places. It's a shady oasis of peace, full of the graves of foreigners.

In the case of Norman Douglas, the 'irrespective of Race or Religion' embrace is just as well. If Douglas subscribed to any belief, it was a rather personalised hedonism. He was Pagan not Protestant, dedicated to the sins of the flesh rather than aspirations of the spirit. The last words he uttered before he died on Capri in 1952 were, 'Get these fucking nuns away from me.'

He'd been diplomat, campaigner, writer, reporter, husband, father, bi-sexual satyr, culinary guru, and in a long and rackety life – once or twice he had to leave countries in a hurry as a result of his sexual peccadilloes – he spent long periods on Capri. During one he became friends with, and mentor to, Elizabeth David.

'The prospect of a day in Norman's company was exhilarating,' she wrote in a delightful memoir of him in the *Spectator* in 1962. 'In *Alone* the passage in which he describes the authentic pre-1914 macaroni as "those macaroni of a lily-like candour" (enviable phrase – who else could have written it?), have led many people to believe that Norman Douglas was a great epicure in matters gastronomical; and so he was in an uncommon way; in a way few mortals can hope ever again to become. His way was most certainly not the way of the solemn wine-sipper or of the grave debater of recipes ... it was not Norman's way to give lectures. These pieces of information emerged gradually, in the course of walks, sessions at the tavern, apropos in a chance remark. It was up to you to put two and two together if you were sufficiently interested.'

Douglas actually produced a cookery book, *Venus in the Kitchen*. It's an amusing assembly, with recipes for the likes of Athenian Eels, Vulvae Steriles, Pheasant à la Hannibal and Salad Rocket (rather ahead of its time), but he lacks David's gift for glittering, almost epigrammatic, evocation of food and place. As she pointed out in the *Spectator* article, his genius lay in informal allusion, not formal instruction.

More typical of him is *Old Calabria*, a record of various travels he made in Southern Italy in 1915, that deserves to be treasured for the chapter on Father Joseph, the Flying Monk of Copertino, alone: a humorous tour de force. *Old Calabria* also contains one of my favourite sentences in all travel literature – 'in the morning the etymological harvest surpassed my wildest expectations'. Such elegance on the subject of bed-bugs.

Somehow it doesn't surprise me that he has a large, stern gravestone of grey slate. It's inscribed with his name, the place and date of his birth – Thuringen 8:12:1868 – the place and date of his death – Capri 9:2:1952 – and the words 'Omne Eodem Cogimur' – 'We end in the same place' or 'We all are herded to the same place' or 'All on the same ferry', depending on which translation you look up. It's a quotation from Horace's Ode 2.3, a suitably ironic reflection from such a worldly ironist.

His grave is surrounded by less familiar figures, whose names and inscriptions are a testament to Capri's mysterious appeal to writers, artists, dreamers, and mountebanks of every hue. Here Hungarians, Finns, Russians, French, Germans, English, Americans, Jews and Danes lie skeletal cheek by skeletal jowl in the dappled shade, their headstones for the most part crumbling. The German names roll like characters in the *Nibelungenlied*. The English names – Pakenham, Beauclerk, Archibald, Lawson – seem very prosaic by comparison.

In life, Douglas formed an unlikely friendship with another long-time Capri resident, Gracie Fields. Indeed, she came to Capri because she'd read his novel, *South Wind*. Her well-maintained grave in white marble stands above and apart from the genteel decay of the rest of the inmates. 'Gracie Fields In Alperovici 9-1-1898 – 27-9-1979' reads the surprisingly plain inscription. Alperovici was the name of her third and last husband, Boris Alperovici, a Romanian odd-job man. They were married for twenty-seven years and he's buried in the same grave.

Below the headstone is another, independent small slab to 'Our Gracie + 27.9.1979'. That's something that used to annoy Boris. 'She is not your Gracie, she is my Gracie. She is Grace Alperovici,' he used to say. She bought a house on the island in 1933, spent much time here before the war, and lived on Capri permanently after it, until her death. It was a long way from the room above a chippy in Rochdale, where she was born. She would always be Our Gracie, whatever Boris said, homely, touchable, real, one of us. I hum a bit of her theme song, 'Sally'.

One of the shades keeping Our Gracie and Norman Douglas company in the Cimitero Acattolico is Jacques d'Adelswärd Fersen, scion of one of France's steel families and a minor French novelist. Even the keenest students of French Literature might be ignorant of his novel, *Lord Lyllian*, published in 1905, in which the hero, the same Lord Lyllian, 'departs on a wild odyssey of sexual debauchery, is seduced by a character who seems awfully similar to Oscar Wilde, falls in love with girls and boys, and is finally killed by a boy' as the summary on Wikipedia puts it. Racy stuff, clearly, but possibly no more than you might expect from the author of *Musique sur tes lèvres (Ebauches et Débauches)*;

L'Hymnaire d'Adonis: à la façon de M. le marquis de Sade; *Notre-Dame des Mers Mortes*, and *Le Baiser de Narcisse*.

Fersen used his wealth to build the Villa Lysis in 1905 as a home for himself and his lover, Nino Cesarini. It lies at the end of one of Capri's steep and winding paths, high among a grove of pines, right on the edge of a vertiginous cliff that plunges about 600 metres down to the sea. In one direction it looks out through the screen of pines to the Marina Grande, in the other straight out to sea. Incised above the portico leading to the front steps is the inscription 'Amori et Dolori Sacrum' (A Shrine to Love and Sorrow).

The outward structure has the squared-up formality of neo-classicism, but the interior has a wonderful airy fluidity. The largely empty rooms are full of light. Not many of Fersen's possessions or furniture are in evidence, but there's supple decorative plasterwork and a metal banister with the swirl and sweeping elegance of Liberty, while downstairs is the stanza dell opio, a room dedicated to smoking opium (how can you not like a house that has an opium room? So much more interesting than a games room or home gym), where art nouveau flamboyance, art deco regularity and classical ornamentation all combine with improbable grace. I'm also struck by the bathrooms, which are temples to hedonism and the hygiene technology of the period.

Fersen killed himself in 1923, with a cocktail of cocaine and champagne it's said, a rather sybaritic method of suicide. Nino Cesarini went back to Rome. While Fersen's life and death seem in keeping with the motto on the portico, his villa is the antithesis, full of sunshine and gaiety and life.

After the luminous beauty of the Villa Lysis, the Villa Jovis, the Villa of Jupiter further up the headland, exudes the dour efficiency of the Romans. Jupiter, the god of the sky and thunder, was the top god for the Romans, who sacrificed a white ox or lamb to him on the Ides of January. In truth, as gods go, he was quite boring. Tiberius, on the other hand, was a good deal more quirky, even by the standards of Roman emperors.

He'd built the Villa Jovis in AD 27, and from it he governed the Roman Empire until his death in AD 37, admittedly in a somewhat haphazard fashion, amusing himself the while, according to Suetonius, anyway, by swimming with his 'minnows', young men, in the waters around the island. It would have been like running the British Empire from the Isle of Wight.

Next to the villa is a point from which Tiberius had people he didn't care for hurled several hundred metres to the rocks below. Extraordinary engineers, soldiers and administrators though they were, it strikes me that the Romans didn't have much sense of light-hearted fun unless it involved a disembowelling or two or animals rending people to bits. On the other hand, it's possible that Tiberius has been roughly treated by contemporary Roman historians and commentators. Unlike a good many Roman emperors he left a fortune of nearly three billion sesterces, largely because he was sensible enough to avoid costly wars.

To balance the absolutist nature of the Villa Jovis, I head for the Villa Krupp, formerly the Villa Blaesus, which the great Russian writer, Maxim Gorky, rented when he first arrived on Capri in 1906. He lived on the island off and on until 1913. I've been an admirer of Gorky's since I read his three volumes of autobiography, or memoirs rather, *My Childhood*, *In the World* and *My Universities*. The first of these, in particular, is masterly; an affectionate, humane and unsparing portrayal of growing up in poverty in rural nineteenth-century Russia.

On an earlier visit to Capri, I came across an exhibition of photographs of Gorky and his circle taken during his time on Capri, in the Villa Lysis, of all places. They captured the exuberant egocentricity of the man, and included two of him entertaining Lenin, in one of which Lenin was playing chess. Lenin stayed with Gorky in 1908 and 1910. By all accounts, he was a prickly guest and not a good loser at the game (or indeed, at anything, his later life suggests), but he was an energetic tourist, and he took to local food with gusto. He was reported to have enjoyed scialatelli alla ciamurra, a pasta dish made with olives and anchovies, and calamari con patate. There's something beguiling about the idea of the revolutionary plotting the overthrow of the world order while sucking pasta into his mouth and sipping a glass of white wine, his napkin tucked into his shirt collar.

By all accounts, Gorky was a generous host and master of the revels. Improbably, or so it seems to me, he established a School for Revolutionaries in the villa as well. It would be difficult to think of a more bizarre place to teach revolutionary dialectic, develop radical cell structures and practise bomb throwing. It would have been the equivalent of setting up a theological college in Sodom and Gomorrah. Gorky was nothing if not a survivor. He died in Russia in 1938 aged sixty-eight.

The story of his successor at the Villa Blaesus, Friedrich Alfred Krupp, known as Fritz, the German steel and armaments magnate, ended less happily. He committed suicide after he was exposed as a homosexual in a German newspaper.

Subsequently, the villa has been turned into a hotel bearing Krupp's name. It's out of respect for Gorky that I climb the many steps on the seaward side of the hotel, overlooking the Piccola Marina. I pause to enjoy the view and reflect on the piquant conjunction of a great writer, a Russian revolutionary and a capitalist industrialist, all sharing a similar taste in property and dramatic panoramas.

As I step out on the terrace, hot and perspiring, a small man in a white shirt suddenly appears and bars my way. I explain to him the nature of my mission.

'That was a long time ago,' he says without budging. 'You can't come in.'

'At least, please can I have a drink on the terrace?' I say.

'No,' he says. 'This is a private hotel.'

'What!?' I say. 'A private hotel? A hotel that doesn't take guests?'

'No,' he says firmly, and shuts the gate between me and the terrace. I have no choice but to go back down the steps I've just climbed so laboriously. I feel a wave of sympathy with Lenin and his ghastly crew.

Capri, I decide, is an island on which to spend three days is too long and three months too short. I've been here three days. I take the ferry back to Ischia, where I left Nicoletta, and board another ferry for Naples. From Naples I take the road up the coast to Formia to catch a third ferry to Ponza.

Ponza

John Irving, the Sage of Bra, is waiting for me on the quay of Ponza Porto.

John's a friend of many years standing, and is the project manager for my journey. This involves dealing with all the boring admin I can't face – finding and booking hotels, reminding me of the times of ferries, suggesting places to eat, putting me in touch with a remarkable range of friends, acquaintances and people he thinks I might find interesting. He lives in Bra, not far from Turin, the city to which he moved from Carlisle because he fell in love with Juventus football club. He's still a true tifoso after thirty years or so.

There's a natural elegance about John, in spite of being afflicted with peripheral neuropathy, a debilitating condition affecting his hands and feet. While his gestures and movement may be inhibited, his spirit is not. He's a living Curiosity Shop. I have rarely, if ever, come across a mind that ranges so easily over so many topics or that's so well stocked with facts and anecdotes. His knowledge of Italian history, life, society and food is prodigious; his memory for films, footballers, books and cricketers is inexhaustible, and he speaks Italian with grace and professorial precision, and English with a marked Cumbrian accent.

We go to dinner at Gennarino a Mare overlooking the port. As we wait for the antipasto he remarks that Federico Fellini had filmed part of the *Satyricon* on Ponza.

I didn't know that, I say, making a note of it, but did he know that Fellini had once had an affair with Germaine Greer?

He did, he says, and looks faintly irritated that I might've thought that he might not. 'But it wasn't very long-lived, uh.' John has various linguistic habits. One is to inject a meditative 'uh' into a sentence every so often.

The antipasto arrives; a pretty decent salad of octopus, prawns, clams and mussels, and we begin discussing Italy's most famous exports, food and criminal organisations.

'Think of the Ice Cream Wars in Glasgow in the 1980s,' I say.

'But they weren't Italian. Italian,' says John. Repeating the last word or phrase he'd spoken at the end of a sentence is another of John's linguistic idiosyncrasies.

'Yes, they were,' I say firmly.

'I think you'll find they weren't, uh,' he says. 'You're probably thinking of the Bill Forsyth about the wars. You know who Bill Forsyth was.'

'Of course. *Gregory's Girl. Local Hero.*'

'Well, after *Local Hero*, he made a film called *Comfort and Joy*, about a DJ caught up in the rivalry between competing ice cream firms. And they were Italian, in the film, in the film. In real life they were Scots gangsters and the wars were about drugs, protection and prostitution, not ice cream. Although ice cream may have been involved.'

The primo piatto of linguine with prawns, clams and chilli oil arrives.

'Well, what about the Messina family who ran Soho in the thirties? They were Sicilian.'

'Sicilian extraction,' John says. 'In fact they came from Malta, uh. Malta. But before the Messinas there was Charles Sabini. "Derby" Sabini. He was Italian. Or his father was. His mother was English.'

Who remembers Charles Sabini these days? I wonder, aside from John.

We finish dinner with crema catalana and wander back to our respective hotels, his overlooking the port, mine tucked away on a side road. It's full of families and elegant women and men with soft, rounded bodies and slender, knobbly legs, like peeled soft-boiled eggs balanced on bamboos.

Ponza is an elongated, nubbly mass, and just large enough to have two communities, Ponza Porto at one end and Le Forna at the other. The interior is a rocky, scrubby affair, scattered with a remarkable number of ruins – Etruscan, Egyptian, Greek, Roman, Phoenician – that says something about its significance in Mediterranean power politics over the centuries.

Some experts have suggested the island got its name from Pontius Pilate, whose family had property on the island. Well, it's one theory, I suppose. The Romans certainly made full use of the place. There are still Roman fish tanks carved out of the rock in certain grottos where they kept fish ready for shipping off to the market. The fish fared rather better than Nero Caesar, the eldest brother of Caligula, who was exiled to Ponza and then murdered in AD 30. Caligula also dispatched his sisters, Agrippina the Younger and Julia Livilla to Ponza in AD 39. They were lucky and were recalled to Rome in AD 41.

Ponza's isolated position later made it a prime target for Saracen and Turkish 'pirates', and eventually their repeated depredations caused the island to be abandoned in the Middle Ages. Any attractions it might have had as a settlement weren't helped when the Ottoman fleet under the command of Turgut Reis (aka Dragut) defeated the Spanish fleet of Emperor Charles V commanded by Andrea Doria, near Ponza in 1552. The island was finally re-colonised in the eighteenth century as part of the Kingdom of Naples. In 1813 it was taken and briefly held by Charles Napier during the Napoleonic Wars.

As seems to be the case with almost every Italian island, Ponza has served as a prison at one time or another. Mussolini lodged Ras Imiru Haile Selassie, the Ethiopian Prince Regent, there in 1936. A few years later, Mussolini got a taste of his own medicine when he himself spent a few months as a prisoner on Ponza after his overthrow. In view of his subsequent fate, he may have wished he'd stayed there. More recently, Ponza has been a source of bentonite, used in the steel industry and for blocking up drill shafts; and kaolin, used mainly in paper production, but familiar to me in the kaolin and morphine formulation used to treat upset tummies when I was a child.

As well as its fair share of history, Ponza has accumulated an impressive mass of legend as well as history. Some authorities have identified it as Aeaea, the island in Homer's Odyssey where Circe had her cave or grotto. She turned Odysseus's crew into animals and blackmailed him into sleeping with her; not that he put up much resistance, even though he was prone to burst out weeping every time he thought of hearth, home and wife. Circe said she would only release him if he visited Hades, which he duly did, and she was as good as her word.

I've been reading the Odyssey, at a leisurely pace, hoping to learn something from Odysseus about the nature of travel. Although the narrative rattles along, full of incidents and characters, I find Odysseus's reputation for ingenuity and smartness to be a bit overrated. It seems to me that he owes his escapes from imprisonment, drowning, death, enchantment, and his final return to Ithaca, rather more to good luck than his celebrated cunning. And I can't really see how Ponza can be Circe's island. It's a long way from what would have been Odysseus's natural course from Troy to Ithaca, even taking into account the ferocious storms that blow up in the Odyssey every time Homer thinks the action is flagging. Reality hasn't deterred the Ponzesi from playing the Circe and Odysseus cards for all they're worth, what with the Grotta della Maga Circe and a Grotta d'Ulisse, among other imaginatively labelled landmarks.

———

It's 6.30 a.m. Flat-roofed houses in powder blue, dusty terracotta, rose pink, and primrose yellow are stacked up the curve of the hill that rises steeply from the quayside. The sky's an infinite, cloudless lapis lazuli. It's already warm, the sea flat calm, smooth tongues of water slipping easily on the sand around the edge of the bay. Boats rest placidly at their moorings, light flickering on the underside of the hulls. The air smells of heat and salt. The port's beginning to stir in the pearly morning light.

A buzzsaw scooter rasps through the silence; there's the wuhuhuhuhuh of the early morning aliscafo departing; shouted greetings; a young woman setting up tables outside a bar chats to her neighbour. There's a sudden flurry of taxis heading for the far end of the port. Another aliscafo arrives – wuhuhuhuhuh. A man checks the boats for hire.

I stop to talk to a fishmonger in his shop by the quay. He's hacking the cheeks from the head of a substantial monkfish with a curve-ended cleaver. Each time he brings the blade down the whiskery white hair on his head leaps upwards.

'The best bit of the monkfish, the cheeks,' he says.

I inspect the boxes of fish laid out on the slab – scorpion fish, sea bass, tiny whiting, prawns.

'Are there still plenty of fish in the sea around the island?' I ask.

'Not as much as there used to be,' he says. 'Boats from Procida and Ischia help themselves to our fish, too.'

'Where did that come from?' I ask, pointing at the headless, muscular torso of a small swordfish on another slab.

'You'd better ask them,' he says, gesturing at a fishing boat tied up to the quay.

Four large swordfish, two or three metres from tail to bill, are laid out on the deck. Their swords rest on the gunwale of the boat. They have huge round eyes, as if they're surprised by the recent turn of events. I've rarely seen swordfish of this size, and never four of them at once. I think they are two males and two females, as swordfish mate for life. If you catch one, you usually catch two, or so the legend goes, because one mate won't leave the other. They look magnificent and melancholy. I ask if I can take a picture of them. The crew look at me suspiciously. Possibly they think I'm an EU fisheries inspector or a Greenpeace activist. I take a photo anyway.

'Where did you catch them?' I ask one of the men standing in the group.

'A long way out,' he says.

'How did you catch them?'

'On a long line.'

'Where will you sell them?'

'In the market.'

Clearly this isn't a conversation that's going to flourish.

The town is ticking over now, steps washed, shutters opened, deliveries made to bars and restaurants. A column of boxes containing bottles of tomato passata lurches drunkenly against a wall beside a side door of a trattoria, with a stack of mineral water cases to keep it from toppling over. Cheerful young women are beginning to arrange wraps, bags and summer gear outside shops. A few early strollers saunter along the promenade. There's even a jogger looking oddly out of place. A young man straddles a scooter. He's wearing a T-shirt that reads 'I came. I saw. I crawled' in English.

A couple of men are taking down the lights and decorations that had been erected for the festivities celebrating the island's patron saint, San Silverio, one of the Catholic Church's more put-upon prelates. He'd been propelled to the papacy in AD 536 by Theodahad, King of the Ostrogoths, when the Ostrogoths were a power in Central Italy. Unfortunately, Silverio was the victim of some typically murky, labyrinthine shenanigans. At the instigation of another cleric, Virgilius, he was deposed in AD 537 by the Byzantine general, Belisarius, who Silverio had foolishly given permission to enter Rome. Belisarius sent Silverio into exile in Lycia, now Anatolia, and from Lycia to Palamarola, a tiny lump of rock off Ponza, where he starved to death. Virgilius succeeded Silverio as pope and survived in the job until his death in AD 555. Poor San Silverio, he deserves his annual remembrance.

Ponza Porto has a certain smartness. The buildings are well cared-for and freshly painted. The main street is lined with shops, but there are none of the big brand names I've noticed on other islands, no Dolce & Gabbana, Fendi or Max Mara. Nor are there any menus in four languages. Ponza isn't as down-to-earth as Procida or as chic as Capri. It's somewhere in between, with a homelier, friendlier feel to it.

I make my way to the Pasticceria Napoletana and order an aragosta (lobster) a kind of super-sized sfogliatella, a cornucopia of flaky pastry filled with crème patissière and whipped cream. It's monstrously indulgent and impossible to eat tidily. Clots of sweet cream keep oozing out from one end or the other. The front of my shirt is dusted with flakes of pastry. I wash it down with a succession of normale (espressos) from a machine with a hand lever to control the pressure of the water through the coffee, something that only survives in Naples. John joins me. I remark on the Neapolitan connection.

'Ponza was resettled in the eighteenth century with folk from around Naples,' says John. 'From Torre del Greco. That's why the locals still speak with a Neapolitan accent.'

Now that John's pointed it out, it seems obvious. The men serving me speak with distinctive Neapolitan accents, with that sibilant, front-of-mouth enunciation that turns s to schs and vowels barked, rounded and elongated – 'sch-fogli-a-tello', 'norm-a-le'. It seems the islands are full of historical echoes, accents, dialects and dishes cropping up far away from their place of origin, tracing patterns of internal migration, as Tabarchin does on San Pietro.

People come to Ponza for the sea. If you're not interested in being on it, in it or under it, there's not much point in coming to Ponza. Oh, there's a Botanic Garden, the Etruscan, Egyptian, Greek, Roman and Phoenician remains (pretty vestigial in my view), light shopping and some decent eating. There may even be some vibrant night life, although I never came across it. But there are no Norman churches or baroque flourishes or Greek theatres. It's just down to the sea again, to the not-so-lonely sea, to swim, snorkel, dive, mess about in boats, soak in the sun, snooze under a flawless sky and empty your mind. There's a lot to be said in favour of emptying your mind.

In the interests of being on the sea, John and I decide to join a voyage of discovery around the island. It's such a touristic thing to do, but why not? We are tourists.

It's a mark of John's genius how he immediately sets about befriending our fellow trippers. Our captain is Giancarlo, who later incurs John's displeasure by turning out to have Berlusconian political opinions. There's Giuseppe and Aurora with their baby, Massimiliano, who proves a constant and happy distraction to everyone on board, and their friends Marco and Marianna. Quite what the relationship between Marco and Marianna is, we never quite work out. He's protective of her, but not in any way uxorious. They all come from Naples and are on the plump-to-overweight side. John takes a great fancy to Marianna and she to him.

'She reminds me of the girls in Elena Ferrante's Neapolitan novels.'

Then there's lithe, tanned-to-teak Rosella and Domenico from Foggia. Domenico turns out to be a senior warder in a prison, a rather unlikely profession, I can't help feeling, for so cheerful and narcissistic a fellow.

John's only failure is with a handsome, self-absorbed young couple. They keep themselves to themselves although he manages to establish that the man comes from Torre del Greco and she from Sapri on the coast of Basilicata.

Giancarlo rattles off the sights as we slide out of the harbour – the Grotto di Pilato, where the Romans created a vivarium in which to keep fish, eels in particular, until needed; the Punta Fiena; the Chiaia di Luna, where a great curtain of blond tufa drops sheer to a beach; the Grotta della Maga Circe; the Capo Bianco Faraglione di Lucia Rosa.

'Who was Lucia Rosa?'

'An early feminist,' says John. 'She threw herself into the sea just here. Just here. She wanted to marry a poor farmer rather than the wealthy man her family had chosen for her.'

'Seems a bit extreme.'

From the sea, Ponza reminds me of certain of the Shetland Islands, bathed in sunshine. Rugged cliffs rise sheer from the choppy sea, bays are scooped out between headlands, a thin layer of khaki vegetation cover the slopes between.

Not that any of the landscape seems to excite much interest among our fellow trippers, except as a backdrop for an endless series of selfies. I wonder what happens to this monumental catalogue of self? Where do the selfie snaps all go? Are they stored for all eternity in some colossal, labyrinthine, parallel filing cabinet in cyberspace? Maybe this is what dark matter is made of. And why do people take them all the time? What's the point? A form of social narcissism? An iteration of self? A proof of existence? Or are they just aide memoires? But if so, what memoires, if all you're doing is photographing yourself? I'm baffled.

We swim. We natter. Aurora keeps Massimiliano tranquillised with a stream of sweets. We cross to craggy Palmarola where St Silverio starved to death. The only habitation is a fine bar serving drinks and snacks. I munch a plate of crunchy/soft, very fresh fried anchovies, superior fish fingers, and sip a glass of crinkly, green white wine, before heading off again, turning up the west side of Ponza. We swim in the natural pool by the Cala Ferla; pass Le Forna where houses tumble down a steep slope to a tiny harbour; round the end of the island, passing under the lea of a tiny lump of rock, Gavi. Giancarlo points out the remains of a Roman staircase carved into the rockface at the Cala Inferno before crossing the heart-shaped Cala del Core and heading past Frontone and back to the harbour.

We all kiss and wave goodbye and go our separate ways. It's been a cheery, chatty, affable outing, with something of 'All Aboard the Skylark' about it, and something unmistakably, socially Italian. It's a curious process. For a few hours you're a part of someone else's life, a peculiar intimacy. You exchange messages, form temporary relationships that are as real as they are transitory. Then the circumstances that thrust you all together come to an end, and you part, with a mixture of relief and regret.

———

Aqua Pazza, Ponza's Michelin-starred restaurant, looks out over the harbour. It's evening and the lights on the boats and the town flicker over the black, oilskin water.

John and I start with a plate of shaved squid with marinated artichokes, a sophisticated combination that might have been even better had the artichokes been cut as thinly as the squid.

John had been a formidable footballer in his youth, growing up in Carlisle. His hero was Roberto Bottega, the great Juventus and Italy forward.

'Known as Bobby Gol!' John says. 'I was a good header of the ball like him, and I was famous for my backheels. Backheels.' They must have been a novelty in Cumbria in the 1970s. 'I played up to university level, but in truth, I was more of a spectator. I loved watching football, although I went on playing for quite a long time after I knew about my condition.'

He looks back fondly, but expresses no regrets.

'When you start to think about things too much, they spoil your life.'

A plate of octopus and potatoes arrives and staunches the flow of his memories. I get mackerel with zucchini a scapace, fried and then doused in vinegar.

Do I know the story of Carlo Pisacane? John asks.

'No. Why?'

'Well, we're sitting in the Piazza Carlo Pisacane. He's an interesting man, Carlo Pisacane.'

'Well, go on,' I say, by this time occupied by candele con cacio e pepe e ricciola, candle-shaped pasta with Pecorino Romano and cracked black pepper, technically speaking a Roman pasta dish, with chunks of amberjack giving it a local accent, luxurious and austere, creamy and peppery, flubby and firm all at once.

'He tried to provoke a rising in the Kingdom of Naples in 1857. First he came to Ponza and freed hundreds of prisoners held in the gaol here. Ponza. Then he went to Sapri on the mainland, where he was killed by the locals, who thought he was a gypsy who had been stealing their food. Stealing their food. It's all there in Mercantini's poem "La spigolatrice di

Sapri", "The Gleaner of Sapri". Perhaps you've come across Longfellow's translation?'

I haven't, but Pisacane's fate reminds me of the fate of Joachim Murat. Murat was a dashing cavalry general with a penchant for fancy uniforms and he was Napoleon Bonaparte's brother-in-law. At the high tide of his fortunes, Napoleon, who had the provincial French (and Italian) trait of looking after members of his family, put Joachim on the throne of Naples, where he was a decent and reformist monarch. Joachim was deposed in 1815 as a result of the settlements after Waterloo. Desperate to reclaim his throne, he landed at Pizzo to inspire an anti-Bourbon rebellion. Sadly for Murat, the citizens of Pizzo proved too apathetic and failed to rise up. Instead they turned on their would-be liberator. Murat made a run for his boat back on the shore. His outsized spurs got caught in a fisherman's net. Unable to free himself, he was captured. After a short incarceration, he was tried, condemned and shot.

It strikes me that Murat's and Pisacane's stories illustrate the accidental, human nature of history, not subscribing to some grand, unifying theory or the vast movements of political action, but to incidental, mundane, personal quirks. Somehow high-minded endeavour in Italy seems to go hand-in-hand with low farce, with tragic consequences. If Garibaldi had had any sense of the absurd, he would never have set off for Sicily with the Thousand. It's a miracle that Italy was ever unified.

A second bottle slides quietly to rest, and a fine dish of squid stuffed with salt cod with little dabs of olive puree and others of lemon emulsion (meaty muscular squid; soft, pillowy pungent salt cod; sharp lemon; smooth, acrid olive puree) comes and goes.

The lights down in the harbour still wink and oscillate on the slick, black sea. The moon has risen. That's enough for me, but John has a pudding, sfera al cardamomo ripiena di frutto della passione, that has him cooing with pleasure. And now it's time for coffee and grappa. The food, we agree, has been exceptional, cracking, a model of skilful, intelligent cooking.

'The chef has taken traditional forms and reinvented them with understanding, polish and technique, to create sophisticated dishes which still carry the weight of the earthy originals,' I say.

John raises an eyebrow, and I get the feeling that he thinks that I've lurched into gastro-pomposity.

'I couldn't have put it better myself, better myself,' he says drily.

As we make our way back through the quiet town, John says 'Do you know, the last time I was in England I saw a headline in the Carlisle newspaper. It read "Dead Body Found In Graveyard." Well, there would be, wouldn't there?'

Mainland Italy

John leaves early the next day. I feel a bruise of sadness at the loss of his company: warm, ironic, passionate, discursive, droll, opinionated, and informative over an astonishing range of topics, always ready for an 'aperitif' or an adventure. He's a graceful human being, and has illuminated my days on Ponza.

It's time for me to move on, too. Nicoletta and I catch the traghetto back to Formia, where I have to leave her temporarily while I go to Ventotene, where scooters aren't welcome. As I've got several hours to kill before the aliscafo takes off for Ventotene, I go in search of lunch.

Zi Anna is a shock after the quiet civilities of Ponza. It's rammed, jammed and heaving; Babel and Bedlam; a whirl of activity, hubbub and bustle; waiters dashing to serve a hundred or more animated eaters, carrying two, four, and, in one instance, six plates; plates piled with pasta draped in scarlet sugo, heaped with hummocks of blue mussels, hillocks of scarlet strawberries capped with fluffy whipped cream. They greet and dismiss regulars with affection. 'Ciao Bepe.' 'Buongiorno Signora.' Kiss hello, kiss goodbye. 'Ciao Francesco.' 'Uehi, Luciano.' 'Alla prossima.' Everyone seems to know everyone. Children pop up and vanish like rabbits in a warren.

It's a marvel that a mountain of grilled squid, prawns, a langoustine and sea bream should suddenly appear out of this mayhem, each element limpid and perfect, meat-and-butterscotch, with nips of bitter charcoal where the grill has charred the skin or shell, a sharp bite of lemon to set things off. Happy and drowsy I go and sit on a stanchion by the harbour wall to wait for the aliscafo.

The ferry service is one of the minor miracles of island hopping, not simply because these ocean-going buses run pretty much on time, but because they run at all. Their comings and goings impose a certain discipline on my travels, and, inevitably, I spend a good deal of time waiting for them to turn up and sitting on them when they do. It's a form of enforced leisure, almost meditation; not unpleasant, but one which has taken a little time to get used to, gearing down, watching the everyday dramas unfold around, listening to my thoughts. It's in sharp contrast to the way I dealt with time and time dealt with me before I set off. Then, weeks, days, hours, minutes, seconds linked together to create a kind of temporal prison in which, like everyone else, I was confined and by which I was tyrannised. In this more leisurely world, time has become expansive, fluid, imprecise even.

In an essay 'The Two Faces of Time: The City Calendar and the Country Calendar', Piero Camporesi, Professor of Italian History at the University of Bologna, explores our historical interpretation of time. He makes the point that 'The precise measurement of time began with the rise of the urban mercantile society, and from that measurement arose a stern philosophy of time for work and time for death.' He goes on to argue that this was not the case for rural peasants in the Middle Ages, whose whole notion of time was framed by the hours of sunlight and by the seasons, and, possibly, by the disciplines of worship if they lived and worked within earshot of a church.

With the growing ubiquity of clocks from the seventeenth century onwards, particularly in towns, what Camporesi refers to as the 'natural day' was replaced by 'psychological duration'. Our sense of what makes a day 'became abnormal, longer or shorter, the cycle of dawns and sunsets, of longer and shorter seasons, yielded to the exasperating scansion of hours, half-hours, quarter-hours, minutes, hurrying us onward to death. The ever increasing divisions of time have led to a parallel sensitivity to its passing.'

Of course, my time is tempered by certain temporal constraints – ferry schedules, hotel check-ins and check-outs, restaurant and museum or monument opening and closing hours. But by giving myself six months (even if the six months had been involuntarily split into two and four months) in which to travel, explore, watch, wait, sit and think, I've also given myself the rarest of luxuries – time. Time that's not subjugated to the 'exasperating scansion' of seconds, minutes, quarter- and half-hours, hours, days, weeks, and months, but that is fluid and flexible. Already I've lost any sense of the day of the week. Is it Wednesday? Or Friday? Or Sunday? I neither know nor care. I can move or stay as I please. What's the time? Time for a swim. Time for a snooze. Time for a walk. Time to sit and do nothing. Time for lunch. For once in my life I'm the master of time, not mastered by it.

Ventotene

I arrive in the early evening and plod up from the harbour to the mulberry-coloured Hotel Julia. From the window of my room I look down on the black volcanic sand of the Cala Nave, the island's only swimming beach. The last sunbathers and swimmers are packing up, folding up their parakeet-coloured sunbrellas, shaking out towels, pausing for a last chat, climbing up the steps back to their hotels, apartments, B&Bs. The streets are already streaming with family groups in an ad hoc but orderly passeggiata.

Ventotene is a volcanic pimple jutting up out of a shimmering sea; home of winds, birds of passage and prisoners of contrasting types over the millennia. As usual, certain Roman emperors made use of Ventotene's remoteness to get rid of unwanted family members. Augustus banished his daughter, Julia the Elder, here in 2 BC. In AD 29 Tiberius dispatched Augustus's granddaughter, Agrippina the Elder, to Ventotene, where she starved to death. Livilla, Agrippina's youngest daughter, managed to get herself sent to Ventotene twice, first by her brother, Caligula and then by her uncle, Claudius. She also starved to death. Claudia Octavia, Nero's first wife, also ended up on the island in AD 62, where she was put to death on her husband's orders.

Out of this litany of gore and treachery comes one really remarkable figure, Flavia Domitilla, who managed to be both a Christian saint and a Jewish heroine. After her husband, the consul, Flavius Clemens, converted to Judaism, she spoke up in defence of Jews after the Emperor Domitian had ordered all Jews and Christians to be put to death. She was exiled to Pandateria, as Ventotene was known by the Romans, for her pains, where she died.

Just off shore lies the tiny island of Santo Stefano, on which squats yet another prison; stern, abandoned but still sinister. It seems an unlikely place to have played a leading role in the formation of the European Union.

During the war Altiero Spinelli was imprisoned on Santo Stefano, along with 700 other political prisoners, 400 of which were, like Spinelli, communists. While he was there, Spinelli drafted what became known as the Ventotene Manifesto. Spinelli, in common with many on the left wing of European politics, had come to the conclusion that nationalism and national interests had driven Europe into two savage wars. Another had to be avoided at all costs. Spinelli concluded that the creation of a federal Europe was the best way of achieving this, and the Ventotene Manifesto provided the intellectual foundation on which the Common Market, that became the EEC that became the EU, was based.

Ventotene makes Ponza seem like a bustling metropolis. It's one of those places to which, like Ponza, the same families go every year. Parents greet each other with cries of rapture; teenagers compare mobile phones, apps, fashions, music, romances in huddled groups; younger children renew acquaintance, reform groups, engage in ancient games. Their conversation and laughter flutters like the flags in front of the mustard yellow Municipio that occupies one side of the Piazza Castello.

The piazza is full of children, racing about, not an electronic game in sight. Fathers play table football with all the competitive vigour of the real thing, albeit with rather better humour. Mothers sit at tables down one side of the piazza, sipping Proseccos or Aperol spritzers, keeping an eye on husbands and children. A line of elderly men are settled on a bench at the top of the square, nattering like rooks. Astrid Gilberto's dreamy voice drifts up from a speaker, something about saying 'Goodbye'. In the thickening dusk, the faded gold, crinkled cream, dusty pink of the two-storey buildings that frame the square evoke the gentleness of a vanished past.

The next day it takes me about 40 minutes to walk from one end of the island to the other, peering into gardens, pausing by fields in which lentil plants, stripped of their lucrative pulses, are withering away; popping into the bird observatory already colonised by a flock of schoolchildren clutching notebooks and pens; peeking discreetly at the odd villa tucked away among the scrub and the fleshy lobes of prickly pear cactuses.

I have a light lunch of crostone di lenticchie e polpo, and fagiolini dell'orto di Nonnina Vita, or green beans from Granny

Vita's garden, at Un Mare di Sapore, tucked into the shade beneath the cliff by the harbour. The crostone is a fragrant mulch of lentils and capers flecked with parsley and studded with chunks of braised octopus. It's savoury, earthy, primary, sharp, luscious. The beans are French and are dressed in lemon juice, olive oil and mint and have an airy, grassy freshness and verve that remind me of the first time I came across French beans in France as a young teenager.

It's been a brief sojourn on Ventotene, but, in truth, a brief sojourn is all that Ventotene commands. I'd need a lifetime to fold myself into its simplicities, and, while I can go easily, I don't have quite that much time, and so I return to Formia, retrieve Nicoletta and head for Naples.

Mainland Italy (once more)

I love Naples. I love the city itself, its energy, its apparent nihilism and chaos, its passion for food, its many beauties. I love Naples on foot. I do not love it on a scooter.

Some years ago I wrote 'When a man has ridden a scooter in Naples, he does not need to boast. When others drawl about wrestling with crocodiles, killing wild boar with their bare hands and bungee jumping from the top of the Niagara Falls, the man who has ridden a scooter in Naples has only to say, in a quiet voice, "I have ridden a scooter in Naples", and, if they have any sense, these other thrill seekers will fall silent and simply look at him with awe.' I see no reason to alter a word after my latest incursion into the city.

It all starts to go wonky when I leave the ring road to drop down into the city proper. The road from Formia to Naples had been straightforward, enjoyable even. But suddenly it isn't. I enter a turbulent confluence of traffic – the meeting of several rivers of cars, lorries, motorbikes, scooters in full spate. Decisions have to be made at dizzying speed. This way? That way? Which way? Which way is that way? The Neapolitan road system makes Kazuo Nomura's celebrated insoluble maze seem a model of lucid simplicity. The broken road surface and then cobbles set my head juddering. Double vision? Triple, quadruple vision. Sweat courses down my brow and into my eyes. The world becomes a blur. The sun hammers down.

Is that a sign for the city centre? Which direction does it point? Who knows? Who cares? Certainly not the man who carves me up from the left, or the car squeezing past me on the right or whoever it is on the scooter that pulls out in front of me without warning.

We stop suddenly. We start abruptly. The rucksack, the one that's supposed to be firmly wedged between my seat and the steering column and held in place by my knees, threatens to topple sideways, does topple sideways, half on the road. Desperately I haul it back in place. Pip goes a horn. Pip goes another. Paaarp goes a third. Pip. Paaarp. Pip-pip. We head right. But I don't want to go right. I want to go down there. There. But I can't because of the bloody one-way system. Inexorably I'm being forced away from where I think I ought to be going, although I'm not sure any longer. Who can be? Who can be sure of anything in the maelstrom of Neapolitan traffic? And my bloody bag shakes loose and falls into the rushing, pushing, heedless torrent of traffic again. Why, oh why did I ever set out on this trip? On a bloody scooter. I'm too old, too infirm for this malarkey. Why didn't I stay at home? How are the broad beans getting on? And the carrots? Is anyone watering the pots? Haven't I been through this tunnel at least once already?

And then, miraculously I find myself on the seafront, where I want to be, without any clear idea of how I got there. All I have to do now is find a) the Siremar ticket office; and b) the quay from which the boat to Stromboli sails. This turns out to be easier said than done. It takes me four passes along the seafront, and further engagement with the murderous Neapolitan traffic, to locate the ticket office. The man in the ticket office tells me that the ferry sails from quite another part of the port complex. He tells me how to get there. It's possible I've misunderstood his instructions, because I can't find the quay or the ferry. I ask another man. He confidently directs me to quite another part. He's wrong, too. The sun's a golden bludgeon, and my temper is very bad. I've almost lost the will to live. I ask a young woman in the booth of another shipping line. Her instructions are clear, explicit and correct. I love her.

Stromboli

When I wake in the early hours of the next morning, the ferry, the *Lauriana*, is still ploughing a purposeful furrow across liquid silver in cool light. The only sounds are the throb of the engines and the rush of water beneath the hull. A few passengers move about with the stunned expressions of the ill-slept, newly wakened. Others lie stretched out, still wrapped in sleep and clothes, with something – hat, handkerchief, eye shade, sock – covering their eyes.

And then, suddenly, there is Stromboli: a perfect, solid isosceles triangle rising up out of the sea, its summit pearly pink in the closest equivalent I've yet seen of Homer's 'rosy-fingered dawn', artichoke-coloured damask patching the slopes below, stretching down to where neat white houses hem the shore. A few yachts ride at anchor. A tramp coaster swings aft of us. The man standing beside me hawks noisily and spits.

———

I discovered the Aeolian Islands – Vulcano, Lipari, Panarea, Stromboli, Salina, Alicudi and Filicudi – in the late 1970s, when a kindly American friend, who had a house on Salina, invited me to stay there, and I took to escaping to this archipelago. In those days, they seemed to me to be a pre-lapsarian Eden, untouched by the crass commercialism that had corrupted the South of France and the Mediterranean coasts of Spain and Portugal.

In those early island-hopping days, I never visited Stromboli. I heard about Stromboli, read about Stromboli, planned to go to Stromboli, started off for Stromboli, but never quite managed to make it. It's terra incognita as far as I'm concerned.

As I wander up through Ficogrande, the town that climbs up the slope from the quay, I come across what must have been a fair proportion of the island's population of a few hundred people gathered in the square outside the church of San Vincenzo, for a wedding. Of the day? Of the week? Of the month? Of the year? Everyone's glad of the chance to dress up and show off and celebrate.

The piazza is a swirl of white, cerise, cream, stripes, lavender, grey, blue; suits, jeans and jackets and flowing dresses; of stacked heels, winklepickers, Oxford loafers, tasselled loafers, pumps, platforms, wedges, network, slave sandals, gladiator sandals, filigree silver Diana the Huntress sandals with thongs reaching mid-calf. All sorts, shapes, colours; a posing, pausing, jostling, chatting, laughing kaleidoscope of fashion.

Even the church door is decked out, with white roses mounted around the main door and around the smaller doors on either side, and bouquets set at regular intervals on the street leading up to the square.

We outsiders, onlookers, bystanders, gawpers, sit on the wall around the square, viewing and reviewing and snapping. Not everyone's there for wedding-viewing, though. Further along the wall a group of volcano walkers – booted, rucksacked, water-bottled, walking-poled, sensibly hatted – are waiting patiently for their guide.

A band of four young men dressed in white shirts, black trousers, broad red cummerbunds and red neckerchiefs stand in the dappled shade of a towering eucalyptus tree. They're warming up, two casually strumming their guitars, one shaking his tambourine and the fourth squeezing a wheezing run on the accordion.

Just beside me, two old biddies are providing a running commentary as if we're watching the Derby or the Grand National.

'Thick ankles.'

'Thick head.'

'Not her colour.'

'Not his.'

'Well, his mother has a lot to answer for.'

'But his wife's a saint.'

'A saint.'

'A good person.'

'I'm surprised she took him back.'

'I'm surprised he dares to show his face.'

'There must be something in it for her.'

'What about La Ficuzza?'

'She shouldn't wear that.'

'Not at her age.'

People go into the church, people come out, smoke, chat and go back in again. Every now and then I catch the belling note of a baritone, the clarion call of the priest, murmured responses. We hangers-on, voyeurs, wait for the grand exit. 'The time of waiting is short, but the burden of waiting is heavy,' I think.

The volcano walkers rise up as one and head off.

And then, quite suddenly, the doors are flung wide. Out gushes the congregation, faces bright with relief and anticipation. The band strikes up. Selfie after selfie is snapped, selfies of selfies, on smart phones held high, on selfie sticks, snaps of the happy couple, mobbed, kissed, congratulated, patted and hugged, a swirl of colour and excitement and pleasure. It's a beguiling introduction to the island.

———

Dinner at the Ristorante da Zurro, just above the beach. Zurro's real name is Filippo Utano and he looks like an old hippy. His bearded face peers out from a bonfire of wiry grey hair that's kept out of his eyes by a chef's toque that looks like a pancake, brilliantly decorated with tomatoes, chillies and flowers. He wears an orange chef's jacket with the arms ripped off and baggy trousers with flames leaping up them in the manner of Arthur 'Fire' Brown, who skimmed across the pop heavens in the 1980s. He dances around his open-plan kitchen and out of it with a mixture of nervous energy and fierce purpose, both conductor and orchestra.

A shiver of skittishness runs through the place.

'Bread?'

'Yes, bread.'

'Coming up.'

'Water? Fizzy or still? Wine? Of course, sir. Certo, signore. Right away.' The charming waitress frowns and scurries off. A battered menu appears.

'But what's fresh in today?'

'Well, there's tuna and swordfish. Anchovies and gamberetti di nassa.'

'Gamberetti di nassa?'

'Little prawns. Very special. You eat them raw.'

'I'll have some of those, please.' Damn the price.

'With the antipasti?'

'Yes, please.'

Gamberetti di nassa, little fleshy commas, pink as an Englishman who's caught the sun, curl around a filling of paradise blue eggs, red stripes running down their small, headless bodies. I eat them shell and all. The shells are so delicate, a thin rime, and the raw flesh is as soft as Turkish delight. Around them on the plate are small, blue-and-silver anchovies, split and with their backbones removed, lightly cured in vinegar with a touch of chilli; sardines in carpione – fried and then cooked in sugar and vinegar with onions from Tropea and black peppercorns; thin slices of swordfish have been lightly touched with vinegar, too, and then immersed in neutral vegetable oil; and thick fingers of tuna cooked and treated with a different sweet-and-sour marinade with coriander and juniper in it.

It's simple food, the cooking of fishermen, says Zurro as he prances out to deliver the plate personally. Fishermen didn't have fridges in the old days, so they preserved their catch in oil or oil and vinegar or just vinegar, he says. He dashes off again, stops, has a quick word with a group of regular customers, another with two pretty girls. The next moment he's back in his kitchen, flicking a pan of pasta and sauce over and over.

I'm ready for a plate of spaghetti alla strombolana, a mighty mound of pasta slathered with tomato, capers, olives, breadcrumbs, anchovy, chilli, mint – a touch of Zurro here and of the Levant there – all minced up and slithery, sensual, saucy, substantial.

The sun's setting. The sky slips from primrose to pale blue to deeper blue to blue velvet. A few stars stipple the velvet, and out just beyond the compound of the restaurant, the volcanic black beach has all but vanished, the sea darkens, and the lights of fishing boats and cruise boats and yachts and pleasure palaces shiver over it. The restaurant fills with holidaymakers in shorts and deck shoes, dresses with sweaters thrown over the shoulders, with couples leaning together and groups of friends and family, all pantomimes in silhouette. The charming waitress and a young man with tattoos up his arm and a haircut like a peaked cap dash about among the tables.

A candle held firm in black sand in a glass burns with a steady flame on the table. A large plate with two substantial slices of swordfish on roughly chopped chicory. The swordfish is about two centimetres thick and has been grilled so that it's almost cooked through, with only the lightest shading of pinker flesh at the very centre. It breaks easily to my fork, fine curved strata of dense meat, Bovril brown on the outside, milder, more like veal on the inside. The ribands of chicory are crunchy and bitter. There's another plate, too, of caponata, that Sicilian vegetable stew on the sweet-and-sour theme, small chunks of melanzane, zucchini, peperoni, olives and capers.

Now it's completely dark, and I'm completely full. The light from the candles picks out details on the faces at the tables around in dramatic chiaroscuro. Thank heavens da Zurro doesn't take puddings as seriously as it does the other courses. I finish with a plate of biscottini and a glass of Malvasia di Lipari. Some of the biscottini are the colour of sand and some volcanic black, and they both have a crumbly texture, and a sweetness that sits comfortably with the cold, fruity, dry wine.

The bill, please and grazie, grazie mille, I say. Era una cena splendida magnifica. Una per la memoria. I know no Italian would say anything like that, but I want Zurro and my lovely waitress and everyone to know that I've had a really good time.

———

'Why are you eating alone?' asks the man at the next table. He's lunching with a young man.

I explain my mission and tell him about my love affair with Nicoletta. He laughs.

'But my name's Vespa,' he says. 'Carlo Vespa.'

He's a dentist from Milan, he explains, and has a house on Stromboli. He's trim, with close-cropped hair and a droll, ironic manner. He saw I was eating alone, he says, and decided to talk to me. He explains that his father was the same. He would always engage strangers in conversation. The young man is his son and they come to Zurro's pretty regularly.

'Filippo's an artist,' Carlo Vespa says. 'When he's good, he's very good. But he has his off days, like all artists. Today he was on good form.'

We chat some more about our respective lives. He gives off a palpable energy.

'If I've got two things to do, I do three,' he says. 'If I've got three things to do, I do five. I'm sixty-eight. It has its limitations and its pleasures. There's less sex, but I find I enjoy art and food more now that I'm older.'

He stays on Stromboli for several weeks every year, and has many friends on the island. As it happens he's meeting some this evening. Would I care to join him for a drink with them?

'I'd be delighted to,' I say. 'What time?'

'About 7.30. I should warn you that we have to climb 184 steps to their house. It's quite high up.'

I say I think I could manage that. We would go slowly, he says, because he has a heart problem. He's had two heart attacks, he says. He looks remarkably fit for a man who's survived two heart attacks. I get the impression that he's thinking more of me than of himself. He gives me instructions how to find his house and excuses himself and I go to the Gelateria Lapinelli in search of pudding.

The Gelateria Lapinelli is a gem sparkling in the Aeolian Islands. Not since the rose petal and the rice and cinnamon ice cream at the legendary Gelateria Pica in Rome (legendary not least for Signora Pica's refusal to smile at even the most lavish of compliments) have I experienced such ice cream excitement. There's something about the texture of sublime ice creams that marks them out, an exquisite balance between softness and firmness, creaminess and smoothness, substance and airiness, carrying the flavours, not masking them. The Lapinelli gelati have all of these qualities. They evoke the divine confections of Cervia of blessed memory.

The ice creams are made in small batches at the back of the shop by a gelataio who was a cabinet maker in a former incarnation. He brings the same craftsmanship to making ice creams as he used to make furniture. Instead of being decanted into the usual open rectangular tubs, to present a spectrum of often virulent colours – the standard Italian ice-cream display – the Lapinelli ice creams are kept in old-fashioned metal cylinders. For each order, the ice cream in the relevant cylinder is beaten vigorously with a spatula before being draped luxuriously into your tub, cornet, or, in my case, into a split brioche bun. The chocolates – chocolate with cinnamon, fondente or dark chocolate, or just plain chocolate, all subtly different, all exquisite variations on a chocolate theme – are particularly fine, but I've also worked my way through the vanilla, vanilla with caramel, strawberry, almond, coffee and pistachio, and I haven't come across a dud yet.

And the brioche bun brings a whole new dimension to the pleasure of eating ice cream. I start with a few spoons of the ice itself – salted caramel this time, creamy, dreamy, the quiddity of sweetness and indulgence – tearing off the odd bit of the brioche to add springy substance to each mouthful. As I go on, the ice cream slowly melts into the brioche, lubricating its bounciness, soaking into it, melding flavours, turning squidginess into divine squelch, until all is gone, leaving me full, slightly sick and sad that this life-defining pleasure is over.

I go to swim it off. Afterwards, as I lie against a rock to dry in the sun, I notice a man walking along the beach with great deliberation. He's stark naked. I'm not sure whether to be alarmed or amused. Every few paces he pauses and presents himself, first to the sea and then to whoever happens to be lying on the beach where he's standing. He finally stops opposite a young woman lying on the other side of the rock from me. She finds her book more interesting than the naked man, which isn't entirely surprising, given the absurd round pot belly swelling above his genitals. I wondered if he's aware of his absurdity. He turns round and slowly makes his way back down the beach. Really, people are very odd.

———

Carlo Vespa is waiting for me outside his house in Piscita, the smart end of the island. Domenico Dolce and Stefano Gabbana have a summer retreat nearby. Like all the houses on Stromboli, it's painted white, its whiteness made the more dazzling by the darkness of the earth, rocks and sand that's more dusty, greyish charcoal than black. Carlo's house, immaculate with easy-going chic, overlooks a delightful small cove.

'Is this where you swim?' I ask.

'Actually, I piss there every morning,' he replies. 'I feel a real sense of luxury.'

He leads the way along a series of small lanes, and then up the 184 steps to his friend's house perched high up the flank of the volcano, showing no effect from his two heart attacks. Mysteriously, he keeps referring to someone as Iddu.

'Iddu?'

'The volcano. It means "Him" in Sicilian dialect.'

'Him?'

'Oh, yes.'

I think this is very odd.

We eventually make it to the top of the 184 steps. Carlo's greeted warmly and I graciously. Our hosts are a marketing guru from Rome and his wife. The other guests include a banker and his wife, also from Rome, a sound engineer from Milan and a professor of law and his wife from Turin. We help ourselves to frittata, arancini, polpette, mini calzone, pizza, cannoli and other pastries.

Stromboli is an escape for each of them. The banker from

Rome says that he has to come here at least once a month. It helps him deal with the stress of his job.

I ask him about Iddu.

'I come because of Iddu,' he says. 'Iddu inspires respect. You have to develop a relationship with him.'

'A relationship with a volcano?' I ask.

'Of course,' he says. 'Some people can't. They feel intimidated and they leave.'

His wife nods.

'But that's pretty primitive,' I say.

'Possibly,' says the marketing guru. 'But primitive instincts are part of us all. Iddu is the bringer of fire, which is fundamental to society and ourselves.'

He explains that Stromboli is a stratovolcano, in a constant state of eruption, but in a minor key, emitting bubbly volcanic eructations every day, as it has for the last 2,000 years.

'You must climb to the Sciara del Fuoco, the crater, to understand better,' says Carlo. 'Or at least go to the observatory and watch the rocks being hurled into the air.'

While they all adore the island, they never come in August, when Stromboli is invaded by a mass of holidaymakers and sun-seekers, and the character of the island and Strombolani changes completely, says the banker, as if they're suddenly possessed by a collective alien madness.

'All they think of is money, money, money,' says Carlo.

'And then they turn back into normal people in September,' says the marketing guru's wife.

Presently Carlo and I make our way down the 184 steps and go our separate ways. I walk along the winding street to the point where I left Nicoletta. The beams of the full moon on the white painted houses give them a silvery luminescence. The windows and doorways are blocks of solid black from which the occasional shaft of light escapes. It's as if I'm moving through a de Chirico dreamscape, full of the scents of hibiscus and jasmine and the musk of figs.

How odd, I think, that these rational, sceptical, intelligent men and women, who probably don't believe in God or the afterlife, believe in the personality of a volcano. I look up. A faint pink glow emanates from the crater. I remember that Jules Verne's *Journey to the Centre of the Earth* ends on Stromboli. Maybe Carlo and his friends are right. Stromboli is a portal to another world.

———

A couple of days later Nicoletta and I take the ferry to Salina. The streets of Ficogrande around the port are streaming with humanity. Four tour boats have docked in quick succession, discharging their cargo to mingle with that of the regular ferries, the advance wave of the tsunami of tourists and holidaymakers that are about to crash over these islands. It's easy to be appalled by this mass – English, Germans, French, Italians, Norwegians. Inevitably they transform the social and economic structures they submerge, but, I wonder, would any of these islands be inhabited at all were it not for the annual invasion, and the infusion of cash and trade it brings with it? Instinctively, like Stefan Zweig, I revolt against mass tourism, its crassness, its vulgarity, its ubiquity, its insensitivity, but how can I justify denying others the pleasure of such a place?

As we steam away from Stromboli, I can sense Iddu's massive, brooding, quiescent presence. Puffs of smoke or steam suddenly appear above the summit, as if Native Americans are sending smoke signals. The ferry skirts the edge of Iddu and draws into the minuscule harbour of Ginostra, a village of seventeen permanent inhabitants, two alimentari, two restaurants and a handful of sugar-cube houses thrown casually over the surrounding hillsides. It seems there's always another yet more remote outpost to discover. Perhaps here is the Mediterranean haven I'm looking for.

I peer down as the metal drawbridge of the boat drops. A couple and a man and a dog get off. An APE, one of those ubiquitous three-wheeler trucks, zooms on. The metal drawbridge clanks back into place. We draw away.

6

SUN-BRIGHT GODDESSES

JULY 2015

Salina – Filicudi – Alicudi – Sicily – Ustica –
Favignana – Marettimo

Salina

'So there we were,' I wrote in my notebook on the page dated 17.ix.78, 'standing on the quay – a bus strike – on Salina! – one bus island – "You want to go to Leni?" says a well-dressed old man with one silver tooth in his top gum and a full set on the bottom – "I will take you." And so he does in a battered, 1950 vintage Fiat van, chugging along at 20 kph.'

I first came to Salina in that summer to stay with Moyra, an American friend, who had a house on the edge of Leni, the village that peered down on the tiny harbour of Rinella. At the time Salina had an other-worldly beauty and an apparently unchanging pattern of life. It was a summer of delights and the beginning of my affair with the Italian islands.

I had hair on my head in those days, cheekbones and only one chin. I was trim and full of optimism and ignorance. Almost fifty years on I have little hair, no cheekbones, incipient jowls, several chins, and more flesh around my middle than is strictly necessary. I may be marginally less ignorant, but I still feel the sense of possibility.

As I make my way up from Rinella to Leni, through the multiple hairpin bends, I have a growing sense of recognition, almost of familiarity as the landscape unfolds: forbidding hills erupting abruptly from the sea; the thick pelt of holly-green trees cloaking the higher slopes; white, yellow and ochre houses scattered among the vineyards; olive groves and fields that mark the lower slopes in regular shapes.

I have clear memories of Moyra's house. It lay just off a path of volcanic cinder that ran between fields of caper plants on the hill above Leni. The house hadn't looked much from the outside, I remember, just two linked cubes in bad need of repair, but inside it was light and cool, with a decent-sized kitchen, a sitting/dining room and two high-ceilinged bedrooms that looked out over the sea, a terrace on which we used to eat breakfast and, very important, a cistern in which the winter rain was gathered to provide all the fresh water during the summer months.

Now I can't be sure exactly which house it was or even where it had stood. My memory may have blurred over the years, and the neighbourhood seems to be subtly changed. The houses have got bigger and more stylish. It's all a bit smarter and tidier. I'm certain there weren't so many vineyards in those days. And surely there were more capers, weren't there? Is this the path? Or that? Or the one over there? Could it've been that house? Or the one above?

I have flashes of semi-recognition, but no certain identification. All the houses look more substantial than I remember, modified and modernised for holiday use. It's like trying to identify a friend who I haven't seen in years. Frustrated and disappointed, I come to the conclusion that the elegant simplicity of the original has been submerged beneath the accretions of decades. It'd be surprising if it hadn't. Nothing could remain unchanged for so long, but I feel a pang of sadness, and something lost.

I first walked along the path to the black-pebbled, long-curving bay of La Spiaggia di Venezia, with its sparkling, fish-rich waters, that summer. Stone and dust, the track wound unconstrained between terraces set with cactus, capers and olive trees, and smelt of freshly ground pepper. Now the old meandering route is formalised, paved and made orderly between low stone walls. A wooden fence guards approaches to the cliff edge.

At the path's end, Moyra and I would skitter down the steep, uncertain slope, relieved to reach the beach without mishap, and there Moyra would climb up on her rock to read, splayed upon its crest, and I would rummage among the friendly waves, before we scrabbled, laughing, back up the jumbled face hours later.

Now careful, regulated steps lead down the abrupt incline.

I descend them with some deliberation. There's no fear of tumbling now, or the fizz of novelty and freedom.

The beach is empty but for a couple in their middle years sitting on towels just above the water's edge. Their skins are pale. Recent arrivals. We smile and politely say 'Hello', they a shadow on my nostalgia, me an intrusion on their intimacy.

After a swim, I climb back up, sharply aware of breath, sinew, muscle, gravity, pausing at each section of the steps, to admire the ferrous stain of iron in a rock, a face made by chrome-yellow lichens, the heavy roundness of a cactus lobe, a fan of dried lily petals, and ease my panting, and dwell a moment on the unfettered past.

That evening I drink a Campari and soda on the terrace at the Hotel Belvedere, scoffing some stuzzichini and looking out across the scarcely rippling sea. The sun sets behind the neighbouring islands of Alicudi and Filicudi, to which I'll be travelling in a few days' time. They're soft against the hazy, cashmere sky above and beyond them.

'My pen strove in vain to equal this superb creation of divine artifice,' the great Japanese poet and inveterate traveller, Matsuo Basho, wrote of the islands of Matsushima in *The Long Road to the High North*. I've been reading this extraordinary combination of travelogue and haikus as I've been going along, and growing increasingly fond of the troubled, crotchety, kindly poet. I wish I had his ability to distil the essence of a scene, incident or thought into sharp, resonant verses. And if he couldn't 'equal this superb creation of divine artifice', what hope have I? Still, it's deeply agreeable to ramble through my past.

———

'Oh, come on, Dad,' exclaims Lois in exasperation on the phone when I tell her. Sometimes I wonder at my suitability as a traveller, given my tendency to drop vital bits of equipment along the way, in this case both chargers for the various electronic accessories I have with me. They join an ever lengthening list of items that I've left like spoor to mark my passage – notebook, camera, towel, toothpaste and now the chargers. Through the twin marvels of human decency and the island ferry system, I've been reunited with all of them except the towel. After the usual buzz of phone calls, emails and general botheration, yes, they will be delivered to Santa Marina Salina on the afternoon ferry from Stromboli.

As I've got time to kill before I can reclaim my lost technology, I decide to visit Lingua, a few kilometres the other side of Santa Marina Salina. I can't remember visiting it on previous stays on Salina. So I take the shaded, winding road, edged with wild fennel, mullein, acacia trees, purple and blue convolvulus and bamboo. Dozens of goldfinches burst out of the green curtain ahead of me, and vanish back into it again.

The road stops at Lingua, just runs out, as if from lack of interest. There isn't a lot to the place, a modest marina, a cluster of houses and eateries of various kinds, including Da Alfredo, 'world famous' for its granitas, and a stagnant lagoon, once used to make salt, but now abandoned. And the Museo Civico, tucked away on a back street, looking out over the car park beside the salt lagoon.

It doesn't look much from the outside, scruffy and a bit unloved. Inside it's charming and melancholy, a sequence of rooms, each filled with the lovingly displayed artefacts recording ways of life that have vanished from these islands within living memory.

One room houses a baker's oven, the walls decorated with the wooden paddles with which the loaves were once moved in and out. The next contains a granite wheel for crushing olives, and the sisal mats on which the crushed olives were shovelled before being pressed. In a third room is a splendid donkey-driven mill for grinding corn, and a smaller, hand-driven mill for family use.

Behind them are various pieces of fishing equipment – harpoons for tuna and swordfish, tridents for squid and fish, a hemp pot for catching the gamberetti di nassa, so the caption reads, and a large cauldron in which nets were dyed so that they didn't show up in the water. The final room contains a rough-hewn double bed and a cradle. There is a broad shelf above the bed for storage, a water basin and spindles and shuttles for weaving.

All this is shown to me with great patience and grace by a charming, white-haired old gent who limps around, leaning heavily on a stick. I think he's pleased that someone has come in. When I sign the visitors' book, I notice that the last signature was dated four days earlier.

I like the Museo Civico for its modesty, its humanity and its wistful charm. The rooms tell the story of those who have no history, a quiet memorial reflecting the patient endurance that defined those lives.

———

'Decide to walk to circus at Malfa,' one entry in my notebook of 1978 begins. 'At 7 o'clock we set off over the hills, knapsack with picnic supper on back – a lovely walk abt 1 hr – on arrival we discovered we were abt an hour early – it was dark and we had our picnic by the cemetery because that's where there was a light (made more sinister by a total eclipse of the moon).'

I remember that evening with peculiar clarity. The moon had been so bright that it gave the landscape around a luminous, chiaroscuro clarity. I suddenly noticed that it was getting darker and darker. I looked up at what had been a full, brilliant, silver disc, and saw that a perfect semi-circular section appeared to have been bitten out of it. It was then I realised what was happening. Slowly, bit by bit, the moon vanished completely, plunging the world into utter darkness, but for the single inadequate lamp by the entrance to the cemetery. If the dead were ever going to walk, then surely it would be on the night of a total eclipse of the moon. And where were we? Images conjured up by a lifetime of reading H. P. Lovecraft, Algernon Blackwood, W. W. Jacobs, and other Masters of Horror as they used to be called, capered through my imagination. I waited for the rattle of bones, the whisper of the ghost-like figures, but they never came. It's ridiculous how superstitious even the most rational mind can become if the circumstances are right; and my mind isn't always among the most rational. I hadn't admitted my superstitious horror to Moyra, or my relief when the moon emerged whole and perfect after fifteen minutes or so.

'At 9.15,' the notebook continues, 'we made our way into the big top of the Circo Relli – although the show was due to start at 9.30 it actually got off the ground at 10.15 – a motley audience – us, obviously stranieri, in the good seats + a few well-to-do Italians – and then the locals on benches behind us – the first act was a playlet in Neapolitan, Pagliacci-like, but with a happy ending – I slept through most of it and the rest I didn't understand.'

And neither had Moyra, who was a specialist in Italian dialects, so impenetrable was the local patois. I do remember, however, that the audience were obviously so familiar with the dialogue that they were able to say the lines at the same time as the actors, rocking with laughter as they did so.

'… then came a lady in a black chiffon dress that was almost as large as she was, but not quite – her act, if you can call it that, was with pigeons, each mottled and blotched in a different colour, pink, yellow, white; with pale blue eyes – that were picked out of a coffin-like box and hurled at her by an aged crone, whereupon they flapped desperately for a few yards and settled down on their appropriate perches and shat copiously – occasionally one failed to make it and flopped to the ground at the old lady's feet and scuttled away under the benches – the audience joined in capturing them with great enthusiasm – then came a sketch that I couldn't understand but was funny because of an excellent clown – then acrobatic children climbing up a ladder balanced on the feet of a fat girl who took a bow after every trick, brushing her copious hair off her face with a sweep of a pudgy arm, extending the other (arm) sideways, bending stiffly – she walked with the self-confidence of a weightlifter – then came a dance routine that made Cabaret seem straight with three pudgy ladies in black linked to a singing duet of indescribable awfulness; the man with a shock of modishly crinkly grey hair, tight black trousers and black shirt that looked as if it was about to burst although largely undone; the girl with a beaky nose & hair pulled back and black boots and skirt – then extremely straight-forward conjuring tricks done by a lady in a voice more in keeping with a washing machine demonstration – then a blonde contortionist with a dumb face and a nymphomaniacal smile who smoked a cigarette held in her toes as she bent between her own legs – then onto the stage came a chunky young man and a chunkier lady with a boa constrictor wrapped round her, which she shed before shinning up a rope – she dangled from a device he held in his mouth, which says a lot for the strength of his neck, jaw and teeth because she must have weighed 14 or 15 stone – culminating in a neck spin velocissimo – one final humorous sketch and about 12.15 we stumbled out into the night – the mixture of amateurish styles was very enjoyable – its unpretentiousness was like a Fellini evocation of his youth – even the colours were Fellini-like, bold, strong but slightly faded like nostalgia – a hair raising drive back.'

What a clear-eyed observer I'd been then. My memory of the occasion is vivid and precise, but tempered by the affection and nostalgia that my thirty-one-year-old self had presciently identified all those years ago.

I find the cemetery beside which Moyra and I picnicked during the eclipse. It's harmless in the full light of day, devoid of anything remarkable. I search for a spot of flat land nearby, on which the circus tent might have once stood, but all the likely spots have been planted with vines, and so I'm just left with the memory of the big top with the words 'Circo Relli' in lights along the crest.

———

The white houses of Pollara stand on a plateau, the floor of what had once been the crater of a volcano, between a semi-circle of steep hills and the edge of a great, curving curtain of cliff where the sea has taken a semi-circular chunk out of the crater. The cliff falls 200 or 300 metres to a narrow beach. It's another place gilded by the affection of memory.

A path leads from the village down one side of the bay to a promontory of golden sandstone that wind and water have scooped over the years into chambers and terraces with supple, almost fungal, shapes that had reminded me of Gaudi's apartment buildings in Barcelona. Once fishermen hollowed grottos out of the soft rock in which they kept their boats, ready to slide down the slope directly into the amethyst-shaded sea.

Moyra and I had this strange, magical territory virtually to ourselves, to swim, sunbathe and read. One morning, I watched two boys, urchins, making their way along the water's edge, dibbling an olive branch in holes that pockmarked the plateau of sandstone that extended some way out into the bay. Every now and then the boy with the branch would whip it out and his pal would deftly remove a small octopus clinging to it, and slip it into a sack strung over his shoulder. The silver/grey and white leaves of the olive tree fluttering in the water looked uncannily like small fish.

I very much doubt that I'll see that kind of marine harvest again, or, indeed, if there're any octopi to harvest. In the intervening years, the rest of the world has discovered the sandstone cove below the village, no doubt in part because the bay of Pollara featured in the film, *Il Postino*.

The fishing boats have gone, too, and the caves now house kayaks for holidaymakers and a bar of sorts selling Coca-Cola, mineral water and beer. Couples and families with sunbrellas and inflatable mattresses are draped over the curves and contours of the sandpaper sandstone terraces. Buoys linked by a rope mark the limit to which boats can come in to the shore. Beyond it several tourist cruisers ride at anchor, with smaller craft moving around them like waterboatmen.

The only thing that hasn't changed is the water, warm and clear, in which shoals of small fish graze over the rocks mined with spiky black sea urchins, and among weed that swings to and fro to a gentle but insistent rhythm. Beyond the coastal terrace, the bottom falls away steeply, light turning from flickering gold to pale blue to a deeper and deeper blue to the black of an abyss.

Francesca, the serious and gastronomically omniscient young woman who runs the Hotel Belvedere, suggests that I go to the Ristorante da Carla for dinner.

'It's something different,' she says.

She's right, although to call the Ristorante da Carla a restaurant in the conventional sense is misleading. It's Carla's home, where twenty or so people – a young German couple, three gnarled businessmen, a family group of a dozen or so and I – sit at various tables on the terrace, ready to eat the dishes she cooks in her domestic kitchen with the help of her mother, while her husband buttles around handling wine and service. It turns the evening into somewhere between a pop-up trattoria and a dinner party, formally informal or informally formal.

Out of the kitchen comes deep-fried sage leaves, aromatic wafers as crisp as crisps; fried zucchini flowers, vegetable flames trapped in light batter; fluffy potato croquettes; deep-fried balls of dough, intriguingly springy within their crunchy carapace; a slice of grilled melanzana; strips of grilled zucchini; and a caper salad. It isn't sophisticated cooking, but it's masterly in the understanding of the nature and potential of each ingredient.

The same's true of the primo piatto, the pasta dish: ravioli, plump with minced shrimps, the pasta as soft as suede, resting comfortably in a sauce of creamed zucchini crunchy with chips of toasted hazelnut, flavours elegant and airy; and linguine with chunks of scorfano (scorpion fish) and parsley oil, languid, sweet and perfumed.

The secondo piatto is also made up of multiple small dishes on an anchovy theme, one of which, fresh anchovies marinated in lemon juice and then sandwiched in lemon leaves and baked, a whisper of citrus oil infusing the sweet flaking meat, is radiant and bewitching.

And finally ricotta salata al forno, salted ricotta that's been baked in the oven and sliced as thin as a communion wafer, its toasted saltiness matched to a glass of light, layered, sweet Malvasia di Lipari, a strikingly happy combination. It's possible, of course, that I'm inclined to happiness by the pleasures of the foods and the oddity of the circumstances.

———

They don't look much, capers, just little buds of green tucked away among fleshy green leaves of a bushy, low-growing shrub. If the buds are allowed to grow out, they produce a flower of unexpected splendour, about the size of a coffee-cup saucer, pure white except for a tinge of imperial purple around the edge of the petals and a spray of exquisite, long, purple stamens like the tentacles of a particularly beautiful sea anemone, that release the seductive perfume of marshmallow.

To be honest, I've never given much thought to capers before. They have minor, if key, parts in the food with which I grew up – caper sauce with mutton or chicken, or adding dash to brown butter with skate. And then, when I began eating the food of the Mediterranean, there was no getting away from them. That husky, musky, sharp, fruity, pervasive flavour turned up in salads and sauces, on pizzas and bruschettas, with pasta, with fish, tucked away here and there. How odd that something so insignificant in appearance, should be so ubiquitous and so potent in fact. And of all the capers, the capers of Salina are the capers of capers. They have world-heritage status, or should have. Slow Food certainly think so. Caper-lovers seek them out. Caper connoisseurs swear by them. The capers of Pantelleria, Lipari, Spain and other places have their supporters, but the capers of Salina reign supreme in the kitchen of most discerning chefs and cooks.

Roberto Rosello peers at the caper bushes growing outside his small, spotless, gleaming laboratorio-processing unit in the middle of Pollara, with great affection. They're over a hundred years old, he says, and were planted by his great-grandmother. He's known these caper plants all his life.

Roberto is a tall, thin, sunburnt young man. His face is shaded by a few days' dark stubble. He's wearing a 'Sex on the Beach' T-shirt and he's proprietor of I Sapori Eoliani, whose principal products are capers in various forms. He points to a wooden stump that's almost invisible against the dusty volcanic earth from which it just projects.

'That's the secret,' he says. 'Each year the new shoots grow out of that stump. The older the trunk, the more productive and better quality the capers.' He talks as if they are slightly capricious, elderly relatives who need a certain amount of tolerant looking after.

'That's what makes them superior to capers from Lipari or Pantelleria.' He smiles and then looks serious.

'In what way?'

'The flavour; it's fuller, fruitier and more rounded. And our capers keep their texture. They're piu croccanti.'

'Crunchier,' I say.

There are over 120 varieties of caper, he continues, and the ones that grow on Salina are particular to Salina. Their character is due in part to the remarkable fertility of the volcanic humus in which they grow, and in part to the light baptism of salt they receive with evaporation from the sea around. These elements conspire to produce capers of particular quality.

The picking season begins at the end of March and finishes in August, when the heat becomes too great and invasive insects too many. Picking is a delicate business, and has to be done by hand. The secret is to remove just the bud, because that is what a caper is, the bud of the caper flower. And you have to be careful how many buds you pick at any one time, and of which size, because you want each long shoot to go on producing over the picking season. Not all the caper buds are picked. Some are left to flower, and if you look closely at the stamens of a caper flower, explains Roberto, you'll see that one has a tiny green blob at the end of it, like the head of a match. That will grow into cucunci, the fruit or seed-carrying berry, he says.

There are three grades or sizes of caper: tiny ones that are sold to chefs and gourmets, and are largely for decoration, according to Roberto; medium-sized ones, that are mostly used by the Salinesi for cooking purposes; and the largest, fattest ones used to make caponata or insalata di capperi, and which, if you peel back the green, outer sepals, contain within a tiny, perfect flower.

I try a freshly picked bud out of curiosity and spit it out. It's inedibly bitter. So, once picked, the long, slow, silent process of turning the buds into edible capers begins, by covering them in medium coarse salt.

'Sea salt from Trapani,' says Roberto. He points to sacks of the stuff piled against the white-tiled wall. 'That's the best. They stay in that for two months, fermenting. We turn them by hand two or three times a day. They produce a lot of liquid at this stage, and the gas they give off makes you cry as if you're chopping onions.

'The fermentation stops after two months, and we drain off the liquid and transfer the capers to another container where they're covered with finer salt and left for at least six months to develop their flavour. We can leave them for up to eighteen months.'

'And how long should I soak them for before using them?'

'About twelve hours, changing the water two or three times,' he says. 'You can use them right away after that or dry them and cover them with olive oil.'

I Sapori Eoliani produces about forty quintali (forty tonnes) a year, and there are five other producers on the island who adhere to the strict criteria set by Slow Food. The problem isn't selling their capers, it's producing enough to meet demand. Roberto speaks darkly of capers that are labelled as coming from Salina, but don't.

He apologises but he has to dash off to a meeting of his fellow caper producers.

'We have to work out how to deal with the caper producers on Lipari and Pantelleria,' he says.

Kiki, a friend from England, joins me. She's in need, so she says, of a light basting of sun, sea and shellfish.

'What you need,' I say, 'is a course of Dynamic Inertia.'

'Dynamic Inertia?'

'You need to embrace the idea that doing nothing frequently is better than doing something.'

She goggles at me.

'You should always ask if what you're thinking of doing, or

are about to do, is actually useful, beneficial or even necessary. All too often the answer would be "No" if we stopped to think about it. But we don't; we're already committed to the action. We need to cultivate inactivity as a positive force in life. George MacDonald said that "Work is not always required. There is such a thing as sacred idleness."'

'Who's George MacDonald?'

'A Scottish Christian minister. He wrote *At the Back of the North Wind*, *The Princess and the Goblin* and *Lilith*. You were probably read one of them when you were a child.'

'Never heard of him.'

Nevertheless, Dynamic Inertia is going splendidly. Each day hangs like a ripe fruit, full of sweetness. And then we bump into Giuseppe Mascoli, captain, cook, wine maker, philosopher, founder and president of Franco Manca, the chain of pizza restaurants in London.

Why not, Giuseppe suggests over dinner one evening, spend the day on his yacht, *Heather*, drifting down the coast. A bit of a swim. A touch of lunch. A bottle or two. With him and his friend Kristin. How does that sound? We think that sounds pretty fine.

Heather is a thirty-five-foot Bermuda sloop, built of teak and mahogany in Lymington, an exquisite example of English craftsmanship, a trim, elegant and purposeful synthesis of form and function, that Giuseppe keeps in the tiny harbour at Malfa.

We – Giuseppe, Kristin, Kiki and I – skim off down the coast, swimming here and there. It's the kind of day every day in a summer in the islands should be: sunny, hot, clear, easy-paced, indulgent, with that frisson of the unexpected that gives an edge to pleasure and that I always get when sailing. Giuseppe is captain and crew, cook and controversialist. We stop for lunch, pasta all'arrabbiata da Giuseppe, that Giuseppe produces with unostentatious ease. There's much jollity and laughter and serious conversation about the nature of democracy. Giuseppe expresses some heretical views to an increasingly sceptical and then somnolent audience. Kristin has to get back to Malfa, and Kiki decides to keep her company, so Giuseppe summons a cutter on his phone to take the ladies back to Malfa.

I fall asleep on the deck before flopping over the side for a final swim. As I clamber up the hinged mahogany ladder back onto the boat, the brass hinges snap, and the lower section of the steps fall away into the sea, me with them. The remaining steps end, tantalisingly, about a metre or so above the waterline. I'm torn between clinging to the section of the steps that has broken off, and trying to haul myself up onto the remaining section of the steps on the boat. Which I cannot do, no matter how hard I try. I lie in the sea looking up at the side of the boat curving above me. I might as well be contemplating how to scale the side of a skyscraper. I feel completely helpless.

Giuseppe, meanwhile, is pootling around in the water with his mask and snorkel, unaware of the drama unfolding. Eventually I attract his attention. He swims over. I apprise him of the situation, and wait for the recriminations. Instead of upbraiding me, he raises his thigh up and tells me to use it as a kind of platform. I stand on it, and with the help of some shoving from him, manage to grab high enough up the section of ladder still hanging down the side of the boat to haul myself on board. A few seconds later Giuseppe shins up the anchor chain and clambers on board himself. What a man! My panic subsides, but it was a nasty moment.

Giuseppe never says a word of complaint about my breaking the ladder. He just comments that it's as well to know about the design weakness now. We sail back to Malfa without incident and go to dinner.

―――――

I wave goodbye to Kiki and go to meet Federica Tesoriero of the Aeolian Islands Preservation Fund that has been recently set up to 'preserve the exceptional beauty and natural value of the archipelago, to encourage a more sustainable, and responsible tourism, promoting the unique experiences that the local habitat and natural phenomena offer'.

Federica is a chic, smart young woman with a serious passion for the islands. She explains that, beneath the exquisite surface, Salina and the other Aeolian islands face common problems. There's a tension between the economic benefit of tourism and the pressure that it puts on the fragile ecology and social systems of the islands. On the back of their popularity come corruption and criminality that influence such mundane matters as development, rubbish collection and providing fresh water. There are deficiencies in medical services, and problems with pollution, poaching, loss of habitat, loss of biodiversity, loss of identity.

What Federica tells me confirms some things that I suspected, but also points to other issues of which I wasn't aware. She makes me understand just how threatened these islands are. In some ways, it's a miracle they've survived in the condition they presently enjoy, but without awareness and action, many of the reasons why I've found a return to Salina so delightful will be lost.

I spend one last evening on the upper terrace of the Hotel Belvedere, swathed in the aural treacle of country & western muzak, looking across the blue, enamelled sea to the misty silhouettes of Filicudi, my next destination, and to Alicudi beyond. I drift back to other, earlier, dusty, sweet-scented evenings, when my brothers and I spent hours trying to catch humming-bird hawk-moths, as they hovered at the trumpets of creamy oleander flowers, their long tongues uncurling to sip the nectar at the heart of each bloom.

I'm happy that I've come back to Salina, not simply to revisit the past. Certain things have changed. There are new hotels and restaurants, and houses have been repaired, enlarged and painted for holiday lets. The old order of rustic self-sufficiency, of subsistence farming bordering on poverty, has gone, replaced by relative prosperity based on holiday tourism and more commercial agriculture.

But the island is recognisably the same place that I first discovered forty or so years ago. Its inherent characteristics, its confidence and character remain fundamentally unchanged, even in the face of the forces of contemporary travel and tourism. I never feel the need to be on my guard against sharp practice, exploitation or fear of being fleeced. Salina isn't going to be another Stromboli or Capri. There are no mega-boats anchored offshore, no sleek cruisers cluttering up its modest harbours, no squadrons of holiday yachts waiting to crowd on sail. Salina's quietness and purpose and its easy pace are familiar. I've changed more than it has.

Filicudi

There are eight hairpin bends on the road down to Pecorini a Mare on Filicudi. They end where the road narrows sharply and turns into the tiny seaside village.

As I travel through the islands, I have the feeling that I'm running before a flood of tourism that crashes over each island as I leave. The further west I travel, the weaker the flood seems to become. I wonder if the full force will ever reach Filicudi or Pecorini a Mare, where I've rented a flat for a few days. There's something detached about the island. Even more than Salina, it feels removed from the mundane hurly-burly of holiday-making. Those visitors who find their way there soon slip into Pecorini a Mare's agreeable doziness.

There's a smattering of shops and a colony of sun loungers on a headland, and not much else. Nothing much stirs in the village before 9.30 a.m. After that, life progresses in easy stages through the hours, eating sleeping, swimming, reading, watching the comings and goings around the tiny port, staring into space. Each evening, cruise yachts congregate in the shallow bay, like gulls coming in to roost, drawn by the excellence of the one restaurant, La Sirena, and a pop-up bar with the explicit name, Saloon.

There're small, tender moments, too. One morning I meet an elderly fisherman carrying a tin coming up over the stony beach as I'm heading for my morning swim. I ask him what he's caught. He tilts the tin towards me. In it are a few tiny fish and a clutch of elegant pink prawns, each carrying a cushion of familiar blue eggs.

'Ah, gamberetti di nassa,' I say. He looks surprised and pleased.

'Take one,' he says. I look doubtful. There aren't many.

'Go on,' he says, waggling the tin at me. So I take one.

'Molto gentile,' I say. He smiles and trudges off up the shingle. I eat the prawn, relishing the delicacy of the shell crunching between my teeth, and the mild, sweet marine sweetness and the springy jelly of the flesh inside.

It's a mark of the serenity of these days when the most exciting thing is spotting an octopus resting on a rock on one of my daily snorkel patrols. Normally, octopi are shy creatures, given to lurking around in holes or under rocks, and don't often venture out into the open in daylight like this.

I look at it. It looks at me. It flexes its tentacles. They unfurl and curl over the surface of the rock, twitchily fluid. It's weird and beautiful and sinister. Suddenly it resolves into a compact, streamlined whole, and jets off a few feet to another rock. I follow quietly. We eye each other again. Its tentacles do the octopus equivalent of drumming its fingers on a tabletop. Suddenly it becomes fed up with the game, and, collecting itself once more, shoots off into the blue yonder. I feel absurdly pleased by the encounter. For once I think I might like to have one of those underwater GoPro devices that were ubiquitous on Sardinia. There's always one more bit of bloody electronic equipment I don't have.

———

Lisa comes out of the night like a Viking warrior princess, standing in the bow of the boat, profile piercing the dark blonde hair streaming behind her. Any resemblance to a bloodthirsty Norse invader is dispelled by the two vast aluminium suitcases that follow her up onto the jetty. Lisa doesn't believe in travelling light.

I install her in the flat below mine, and we go to dinner at La Sirena and over antipasto misto, spaghetti alle mandorle and gamberoni alla griglia, continue the energetic dialogue we've been having since we met, about colonialism, the origins of pasta alle mandorle, foraging, the state of relationships of various friends, sex, beauty, the preservation of it, the use of pestle and mortars, literary festivals, Angevin history, bringing up children, what we are going to do the next day, and sundry other topics. Lisa brings an energy and sense of purpose to proceedings and I have no option but to acquiesce. It's all rather at odds with the dreamy, 'divine idleness' of the last few days.

———

We head off for Filicudi Porto in a boat piloted by the wrinkled, whiskery, piratical Bartolo with a fez-type, Garibaldian pillbox hat perched atop his head. No one seems to know the origins of Garibaldi's idiosyncratic headgear. Some say it was modelled on one worn by an Italian peasant; others suggest its origins lie in South America where Garibaldi fought in the wars of liberation; and there's a school of thought that holds that it was inspired by the hats worn in Montenegro. Whatever the truth, it became the model for female fashion of the period, although Bartolo wears his with masculine brio.

Lisa has to raid the island's one and only cash machine at Filicudi Porto, and she decides to combine this mission with sailing around the island. Having collected the cash, we putter through the straits of the Filo del Banco, admire the Scoglio Giafante (why does almost every island have a rock that looks like an elephant?), swim in a bay not far from the penile Punta la Zotta, on the glans of which someone has placed a rather incongruous Madonna.

We swim again, through the Punta del Perciato, an arch formed of rocks shaped like organ pipes, and nose our way into the Grotto del Bue, in which, Bartolo assures us, barracuda come to sleep at night. We return to Pecorini a Mare in the pearly light of early evening. Suddenly there are seven cruise yachts anchored in the bay, plus a big Turkish-style caique. The air's filled with the shrieks of children as they jump off the jetty into the sea, the put-put of outboard motors ferrying sailors to dinner at La Sirena and the odd shouted conversation. Perhaps I'm not quite so far ahead of the tsunami of tourism as I'd imagined.

Alicudi

Still further west is Alicudi, an inverted pudding basin of an island, a haven of peace and a model of unchanging ways by comparison with Filicudi. Lisa and I go there for the day and, on arrival, find it difficult to tell if there's life on the island at all. There are a few neat, brightly painted houses just above the waterline. A horse dozes at the side of the one and only street, which runs for a kilometre at most, but of people there isn't a sign outdoors.

We walk back and forth for perhaps twenty minutes, swim, and find refuge in the Bar Airone, where most of the population of Alicudi seem to be congregated. They gape at Lisa, as they might at some visitor from another planet. The modest nature of the Bar Airone belies the excellence of its food – a most unusual caponata, which is more like a delicate vegetable stew than the usual heavy-gravity mulch, with potato in place of the more usual melanzane (potatoes have always been grown extensively throughout the

Aeolian Islands to provide dietary ballast during the weeks when bad weather cuts off the islands from the outside world); and a light, refined variation on parmegiana made with zucchini grown in the garden of our waiter's parents, instead of melanzane.

Heading back to Filicudi with Emilio, our boatman, we pass quite close to one of those let's-go-cruising-round-the-Med yachts, wallowing in the long swells. Several figures on board wave at us, beckoning us to come in close. They turn out to be Russians, and they're in trouble. Their boat has shed its propeller.

Lisa grasps the situation much quicker than I do, and takes command with admirable crispness.

'Do any of you speak English?' she shouts.

'Yes.'

'Good. Anyone speak Italian?'

'No?'

'OK. I do. I'll translate.'

She has a quick consultation with Emilio. He says we'll have to go back to Pecorini a Mare to get a bigger boat to take them under tow. He's obviously dealt with this kind of situation before. I just keep my gob shut. In my experience one admiral and one captain are quite enough in any emergency.

'Can you anchor?' shout Lisa.

'Too deep. It's over a hundred metres here,' the Russians shout back.

Lisa casts an eye over the nearby coastline, which is formidable and rocky. Without motor power, it's possible they might be driven onto it. Luckily, we work out that the wind and current are taking the stricken yacht away from immediate danger, towards the equally formidable and rocky coastline of Alicudi.

'Right,' snaps Lisa, 'we'll take on a couple of you. Bring a phone so we can keep in touch with you while we go back and get a larger boat.'

Emilio swoops our boat in under the stern of the stricken

yacht, and two of the Russians hop aboard, one of whom speaks serviceable English. We roar off to get a bigger boat.

'O, gosh,' says Lisa, her face alight with dash and derring-do. 'This is so Swallows and Amazons. "Better drowned than duffers, if not duffers won't drown",' she quotes.

By the time we return about twenty minutes later in a larger vessel, the yacht's some way west of where we'd left her, heading for Alicudi. Emilio says something to Lisa. Lisa speaks to the Russian on our boat, a young computer programmer from Moscow. The Russian speaks to his mates on the yacht via his phone. A rope is thrown. Emilio fastens it to the thwarts, and begins to cajole the wallowing yacht into turning round.

The measure of the challenge is immediately obvious. Our larger boat may have a more powerful motor, but it isn't that large or that powerful. It's as if a terrier were trying to tow an elephant. It would be easier if the fellow in charge of the yacht had some idea about seamanship. As it is, the yacht has an alarming tendency to veer off to one side or another, yawing heavily in the long swell.

Little by little we get her bow round and begin to ease her back to Filicudi. It soon becomes apparent that the towrope is too short. Only Emilio's expert boatmanship keeps the yacht from careering into our stern. A second rope is thrown. Emilio splices the two together and ties them around the thwarts. This makes things better and safer. Even so, it needs precise speed management, and every now and then the thwart gives a nasty crack when the towrope tightens with a snap.

Word has obviously got out, because one of the large caiques taking holidaymakers on romantic cruises around the islands heaves into view. A rubber rib scoots over. After a brief discussion it's decided that the larger boat will take the stricken yacht in tow. This is clearly the sensible thing to do. We head back to Pecorini a Mare with a warm sense that we've behaved sensibly, practically and honourably. That doesn't happen as often as I would like in my life. I still wonder how you lose a propeller?

Lisa and I celebrate our part in the international sea rescue mission over another dinner at La Sirena. In the course of it, she's attacked by an earwig, or so she says. It turns her as close to hysterical as I've ever seen her. How curious people are, cool in action one moment, reduced to a quivering wreck by a small, harmless insect the next.

———

Lisa leaves for Panarea, with her two vast aluminium cases and yet another love-struck boatman at the helm of her water taxi, and life goes back to its easy pace once more. There's a steady build-up of jellyfish, which means keeping a wary eye open whenever I go into the sea. Someone once told me that the best antidote for jellyfish stings is urine, but it's a bit difficult to administer to your back, say, if you're on your own.

Giuseppe Mascoli turns up on his yacht with his daughter, Heather, and a school friend, and we all have a merry dinner. Come to Panarea, says Giuseppe. Very interesting, Panarea. Very good restaurants. But there's more to investigate on Filicudi. Besides, I'd rather enjoy the placidity of my life at Pecorini a Mare. I don't feel that Giuseppe's approach to life can be reconciled with Dynamic Inertia, so I stay on.

During the circumnavigation of the island with Lisa and the whiskery Bartolo, I'd been struck by the extent and magnificence of the terraces that stretch across most hillsides in wavering horizontal lines. Even the steepest slopes had once been put to agricultural production. I skim up the eight hairpin bends, and go to explore Filicudi's hinterland accessible from its few kilometres of road. In odd corners I come across forlorn stands of apricot, peach, almond, pear and olive trees and straggly vines.

At one time Filicudi must've been a vast orchard, but those days are clearly long gone. Almost all the terraces are abandoned, sad evidence of migration and emigration, settlement and abandonment, forced and otherwise, that have been one of the constant threads of history throughout Italy's islands.

A pattern of desertion and re-population has dominated Mediterranean islands for centuries, and left traces of differing cultures in curious places. Lipari was resettled by Sicilians and Spaniards. Migrants from Lipari itself re-colonised Ustica. There was the Catalan connection in Alghero, the Genoese in Stintino and Carloforte, and the Neapolitans in Ponza.

The case of Filicudi is slightly different. In 1911 the island supported over 1,500 people. By 1961 the number had shrunk to 447. Now the permanent population amounts to 235 according to 2001 figures. In spite of abundant fish and obviously productive growing conditions, the fragmentation of land ownership and the complexities of inheritance, one of the unintended consequences of the adoption of the Code Napoleon in the nineteenth century; the phylloxera that decimated the island's vines; over-population leading to poverty and starvation; and the desire to escape the constrictions of island life and familial conformity, drove the Filicudari to abandon their homes in waves, some to look for employment on Lipari and Salina, and many more for Australia, to settle in Sidney and Melbourne. 'Cu nesci, arrinesci' – he who emigrates, succeeds as the Sicilian saying goes.

One who succeeded was John Bonica, the anaesthesiologist and founding father of the study of pain management. He was born Giovanni Bonica on Filicudi in 1917 and emigrated to America with his family in 1927. He funded his studies at medical school by wrestling professionally under the names of the Masked Marvel and Johnny 'Bull' Walker. His interest in pain management was triggered by the chronic pain he suffered as a result of his earlier profession. He's probably the only President of the American Society of Anaesthesiology to be inducted into the Professional Wrestling Hall of Fame.

Now Filicudi, like most of the islands, is kept alive by tourism. They may come like the corsairs of old, but it's an uncomfortable fact that without the income generated by the cruise ships, touring yachts, the day trippers and holidaymakers, without all the ghastly tat and detritus and conformity of modern tourism, life on these islands will die completely. It's an irony that the very forces that are gradually crushing the individual identity of each island, undermining their traditions and culture, as Federica Tesoriero pointed out, also provides the means of survival for the few people who choose to remain on the island all the year round.

It's easy to sentimentalise and romanticise island life as it was, and deplore the tourist barbarians at the gate, but in reality it isn't so very different from the way in which weekend villagers and second-home owners have given a kind of life to a good many villages in England, after their original occupants – agricultural labourers – had left them as agriculture industrialised, and cities became the focus of employment.

Of course, I lament the disappearance of the old ways, but it seems little short of a miracle that anyone lives on these islands at all.

———

All agreeable idylls end. One last drink at Saloon. One last dinner – sweet, pillowy mussels; tonno alla trapanesi, a pyrotechnic of tuna with wild fennel, mint, parsley, sultanas, pine nuts, white wine and tomato passata; and semifreddo alla mandarla – at La Sirena. One last walk down to the jetty, and one last peer at the stars and the black velvet night sky. The sea glugs and chuckles around the stanchions.

The next morning I ride up the eight hairpin bends from Pecorini a Mare and down a whole lot more to Filicudi Porto in time for a cornetto con crema, espresso and spremuta d'arancia for breakfast, and join the few passengers also waiting for the big, car-carrying ferry to Milazzo on mainland Sicily. Filicudi Porto has something of the 'last service station before the motorway' about it. It's stoking hot by the time we board.

The ferry to Milazzo on the Sicilian mainland is scheduled to take three hours. It takes five, making a leisurely progress from Filicudi to Salina; from Salina to Lipari Porto; from Lipari to Vulcano; and from Vulcano to Milazzo. In theory, the only Aeolian island I haven't visited is Panarea. Even with my generous timetable I can't spend time on them all. I want to spend a summer in the islands, not write a guidebook.

Sicily

'Matthew. Matthew Fort. It is Matthew, isn't it?' As I'm checking out a restaurant, Odeon, in Capo d'Orlando, a handsome woman with white hair hails me.

I've ridden from Milazzo to Capo d'Orlando and am looking for somewhere to dine. It's obvious that the holiday invasion is much further advanced here than it is on Filicudi. The beach is barely visible beneath the mass of multicoloured sunbrellas. The air's bright with the squeals of children and shouts of encouragement of their parents. Traffic trawls up and down the sea front in an unbroken stream. Shoals of holidaymakers browse on the shop fronts, and most of the trattorias are packed.

'It's Anna Venturi. Do you remember me?'

Of course, I remember Anna. Who wouldn't? She set up one of the first Italian cookery schools in the UK, in Beaconsfield and then in London, way back in the early nineties. Originally from Milan, she taught a generation of neophyte Italian food lovers the principles of Italian cookery. She was, and obviously still is, a woman of formidable energy and drive. She sold the school, she tells me, and now splits her time between London and Capo d'Orlando, where she has a house. Would I like to join her and her husband, Bill?

And so I sit down to a classic spaghetti con le sarde that prompts a discussion about the nature of Sicilian cooking, the changing food in Italy (for the worse, according to Anna), Italian food in the UK (never very authentic, according to Anna), the developments in modern gastronomy (Anna doesn't approve of many of them), the pleasure of children and grandchildren, the joys of the prosciutto from the black pigs of the Nebrodi, how she and Bill met and a dozen other topics. Between us we demolish a titanic plate of grilled swordfish, totani and prawns. Around us the Odeon fills up. The warm evening air thrums with cheery conversations.

Eventually Anna says she and Bill had better be getting home as one of her daughters with several grandchildren will be arriving at any moment. We say goodnight and goodbye. Dinner with them has been an unexpected, unlooked-for blessing.

The next day is a real belter. I take the coastal road to Palermo, a hundred or so kilometres away. I must have ridden the same route in the other direction in 2006, when exploring Sicily for *Sweet Honey, Bitter Lemons*. Or was it 2007? I'm damned if I can remember, but I keep getting flashbacks – this valley, this bridge, this section by the sea; they seem vaguely familiar. The sun is searing, the heat's like a hammer as Nicoletta and I buzz through dusty, dirt-scrabble towns, where papers sent billowing by passing traffic are the only signs of life and where the road surface tests nerves and balance; through other towns handsome in form and feature, with confident, four-square nineteenth-century villas with knobs on. God, this must have been a beautiful island 150 years ago. Still is, in many ways.

Now a bridge over a dried river bed with orchards of oranges, lemons, peaches, olives and figs neat on either bank; and tomatoes, melanzane and zucchini, too. Now beside the sea, russet rock wall to the left, cream-laced water below to the right, drifting to left or right according to the road, sweeping through the corners, in, out, never fast, a steady 40 kph, 50 max, cars stacked up behind me. Sensibly they keep a respectful distance. The drivers can tell I'm not your average Vespista.

I stop for lunch at Cefalù, not smart Cefalù, but roadside, pit-stop Cefalù, a caff, all plastic, veneer-thin smartness, but jolly and buzzy, with a startling display of pastries and puds. First, a beer, a very cold bottle of Birra Messina, brewed on the island. Is there a better drink when you're properly hot and sweaty and tired and dehydrated? The shock of coldness, the prickle of fizz bursting around the tongue, throat, against the roof of my mouth, the light, persistent bitterness, the touch of malt for body. Nectar, a life-saver, on the button. Gone. Even here I get a lunch I never get at the equivalent in the UK – pasta with meat sauce; caponata; coffee and strawberry ice cream. Nothing special, but properly flavoured and properly done, all for fourteen euros. I'm primed, ready to go again.

The first time I came into Palermo, I followed the road from the hills to the south, via Monreale, dropping down into the commercial, grungier part of the city. This time I come from the east, through the rings of urban dross you get with all Italian towns or cities, no matter how beautiful, but then into the nineteenth-century city along the seafront, the surviving gardens, palazzi and villas, with elegance, luxury and space; a celebration of money and the opulence it can buy, statements of faith that the future will never change within the Conca d'Oro, the Golden Conch. How utterly captivating it must have been before war, criminality, redevelopment and the twentieth century generally trashed its pristine loveliness. Maybe this beauty was based on exploitation, power and corruption, but exploitation, power and corruption are still part of city life without the concomitant aesthetic standards.

JULY 2015

Within the shell of the Conca d'Oro, there's a sense of a city unfavoured by the people who run it, whether the official or unofficial government, unloved and decaying. Vast graffiti paintings deface some of the buildings. Some are of octopi and turtle, which symbolise the Mafia. Other areas are dominated by graffiti of the Ultràs, the violent supporters of Palermo football club and a minor political force. But there's one graffito quite unlike all the others: a delicate, lifelike painting of a young woman bending over as if washing her hair. The top of her head is missing, exposing her brain. 'Wash your mind tonight,' read the words above it. It's more disturbing than all the others.

I wander around to see if I can find the night market between the via Archimede and the via Ettore Ximenes, where I'd once eaten mackerel and chicory grilled over a vast barbecue by Michele with the stump of a Toscano cigar clamped firmly in his teeth, and watched the circus of Palermitan night life and smoke from the barbecue rising up past the surrounding houses into the night sky.

I find the area looking a bit threadbare and devoid of life. There's no sign of the fishmongers or grocers I remember so clearly. Miraculously, though, I come across Michele, as ebullient as ever, the stump of a Toscano still clamped firmly in his teeth.

'It's all changed a bit,' I say.

'A bit,' he says. 'It's quiet because it's Sunday.'

'Are the fish shops still here, and the fruit and veg shops?'

'Some,' he says, with a slight downturn of the mouth.

'I remember the mackerel and the chicory you grilled for me on the big barbecue, and the wine your boy fetched from the enoteca.'

'The enoteca's still here,' he says. 'And we still have a barbecue.' He gestures to a small grill about the size of a domestic one, where a young man is grilling meat on skewers. 'And I have this spaghetteria. Would you like spaghetti alle vongole? Or with cozze?'

222

I say I'm not hungry just yet and continue my wandering. Maybe Sunday evening isn't the best time for nostalgia.

Ustica

Ustica is something like six hours from London, if you get your timing right. A three-hour flight to Palermo, two or three hours by ferry depending on whether you take the zippy aliscafo or the larger, plodding, car-bearing ferries. Add on a bit of time here and there, call it nine hours to be on the safe side. Or a world, or even a planet, away.

Ustica has seen its fair share of settlement, emigration and resettlement over the centuries. The depredations of the Turkish corsairs kept anyone from staying there for very long until the eighteenth century, when ninety migrants from even more impoverished Lipari settled there.

Ustica has very little fresh water, but very fertile soil. With ingenuity and hard work the settlers flourished to the point that the island could no longer support the numbers, and between the early nineteenth century and the early twentieth century successive waves of Usticani headed for America, for the South and New Orleans in particular. An Italian battalion, including a good many Usticani, fought for the Confederacy during the American Civil War. Today something like 30,000 people in New Orleans trace their origins to Ustica, while the island's population stands at around 1,300.

At first sight, Ustica lacks the drama of the Aeolian Islands, but it has a sweet, understated prettiness. It takes me about forty minutes to ride round it. There's the only conurbation of any significance, Ustica Porto, but nowhere is far from anywhere else.

A crest of hills runs down the centre of the island, sloping down to a broad plain that ends in cliffs that drop sheer to the periwinkle sea. The highest point of the crest is crowned by a vast, white intelligence listening dome, like a colossal golf ball waiting for

Zeus, Jupiter or some other deity to tee off. Around it a mixture of scrub and carefully tended smallholdings, shot with the brilliance of bougainvillea, hibiscus and plumbago, patch the slopes.

The Usticani live modestly, tending their almonds, nectarines, lemons, fig trees and vines, growing tomatoes, melanzane, zucchini, onions, pumpkins and lentils. Visitors are welcomed, accommodated and looked after, but in truth we're peripheral to the real life of the island and the business of survival, which goes on day in, day out. It seems to have escaped the consequences of mass tourism, indeed, to have largely escaped tourism altogether. I can't see any large villas, abandoned palazzi of departed aristocrats or hefty mansions of wealthy merchants, no flash holiday homes, tasteful developments or mega-hotels. Every building is modest and practical.

Antonio Gramsci described the clutter of houses above Ustica Porto as 'a small village of a Saracen type, picturesque and colourful'. Gramsci was the great pre-war leader and leading theorist of the Italian Communist party. He was sentenced to a five-year term on Ustica by a Fascist court. Although he was on the island for only six weeks, he set up a school to teach both locals and fellow exiles, and by all accounts enjoyed his stay.

The house just off the Piazza Umberto he occupied with his colleague and one-time rival, Amadeo Bordiga, has a plaque beside the door. It reads 'Confinati dalla tirranide fascista vissero in questa casa Antonio Gramsci e Amadeo Bordiga operando per il bene e il progresso dell'umana convivenza. Nel cinquantesimo anniversario della morte di Antonio Gramsci L'Amministrazione Communale Ustica 1987' (Confined by fascist tyranny Antonio Gramsci and Amadeo Bordiga lived in this house, working for the good and progress of human society. On the fiftieth anniversary of the death of Antonio Gramsci. The administration of the commune of Ustica 1987).

I wonder how many communist thinkers in the UK are similarly celebrated on, say, the Isle of Man? Or left such a legacy? Everyone on the island I ask about Gramsci speaks of him with respect and affection, irrespective of their political leanings. He isn't simply the most famous person associated with the island, perhaps the only reason Ustica registers on the wider consciousness at all. He represents something, a point of view, a kind of intellectual force and moral courage that Italians admire, maybe because they see so little of it among their contemporary politicians.

Ustica's tranquillity would've seemed remote from the hurly-burly of political change, and yet, as Gramsci found, there's much pleasure to be found in the decency and humdrum rhythm of island life.

One morning a large crowd gathers down by the harbour quay. Apparently a van has inadvertently backed off the quay and into the sea, and half the population of the town has turned up to witness its recovery. 'It's the most exciting thing that's happened in Ustica for months,' says one bystander. A cheer goes up when the vehicle, water pouring out of it, is finally lifted out by a crane.

The Azienda Hibiscus, where I'm staying, is a working farm and winery, the only one on the island. Each morning donkeys greet the dawn with a ragged chorus of hoarse brays. Sometime later, just after seven, I rise and sneak off down the path through the fields that leads to the road that leads to a track that leads to the steps that lead to the sea. The world is mine. Bees and vast mosconi – shiny blue-black beetles – drowse on the faces of sunflowers lining part of the path. The sun's just beginning to turn the sea to a sheet of beaten gold. The sky is dusty blue and ineffable.

I walk along the road for a few hundred metres and then turn onto the track that skirts the excavated skeleton of a prehistoric village. Grasshoppers burst from my footfall like shrapnel, swallowtail butterflies and painted ladies loop from yellow thistle to yellow thistle. The path ends at the top of some steps carved into the face of a cliff. At the bottom the water is slurping and sloshing in a lazy fashion, mazily refracting the sunlight on the rock outcrops just beneath the surface. A few blood-red sea anemones lie closed; plump, fleshy poufs, along the waterline.

I slip on my flippers and mask, adjust my snorkel and slip into a liquid medium not much different in temperature from my blood, where colours and textures and tone are fresh and strange. It isn't a silent world, but full of clicks and scratches. Everything sways in this shallow water – weed, long tentacles of pink-grey anemones, fish, me, suspended, floating over hills, valleys, woods, gardens, outcrops, cliffs.

A nimbus of small fish – baby grey mullet? – glitter just below the quicksilver surface. A pack of larger specimens fossick over a rock below, twisting and turning like beagles. A plump fish the size of a pudding plate in a tight-fitting jersey of yellow-green with narrow horizontal blue stripes eases away between the weeds. Another in vertical emerald green, paradise blue and buttercup yellow stripes, a gaudy parrot of a fish, seems undisturbed by my presence. I drift further from the shore. Suddenly the solid topography dissolves. The shafts of sunlight dim, diffuse into blue and then vanish into blackness that is mysterious, silent, a bit frightening. Not for me to investigate and find – what? Grendel? The Kraken? Some other monster? I'm content with my curious, chattering, beautiful, light-flooded shallow sea world.

Until I spot a medusa, a jellyfish, candy-floss pink, pulsating and sinister, a short fringe of tentacles waving below; and then another and another. It's time to go, time for breakfast.

Red seems to belong elsewhere, or possibly to the future. It's a restaurant with a bar brilliantly situated overlooking a strikingly lovely, craggy bay at Punta Faro. It has the hallmarks of contemporary Scandinavian design, all wood and wire cables, 'environmentally aware', ruthlessly contemporary. On one hand, it's quite shocking, on the other I can't help but admire the astuteness of the execution. It's commercial in a way that nothing else I've seen on Ustica is, a great place to come for cocktails or, like me, for dinner, and watch the sun go down into the sea. The voice of Astrid Gilberto once again, with Gilberto Gil this time, blends with the calls of children and their parents.

The food I've eaten on Ustica has been decent enough, although little has been memorable, bar one dish of voluptuous, rank and rich, slippery, oily, creamy, velvety spaghetti con ricci – spaghetti with sea urchin roe. It tasted as if it was a distillation of marine life, meaty, with mineral traces and notes of iodine and seaweed, an intricate soup of flavours that permeated every crevice and corner of my mouth.

The food at Red isn't quite in the same league, but it's far better than I expected in such a place – gamberetti usticesi, fat prawns with cherry tomatoes, small pulpy balloons, with onions and the tang of vinegar; and then zuppetta di lenticchie usticesi con totani, an intense, taste-bud-drubbing mouthful that combines the earthy gravity of the lentils with the opulence of the squid. I feel full, almost overwhelmed, by the time I dab my chin with my napkin, run a finger round the plate to scoop up the last of the sauce. It's dark, and the stars are high in the heavens as I mount Nicoletta and head back to the Azienda Hibiscus.

———

I ask Margharita Longo, the proprietress of the Azienda Hibiscus, about the lentils I'd eaten at Red. Do Ustica's lentils differ from those of Ventotene, also highly prized? With disappointing, if admirable, pragmatism, she replies that there's no difference because the Ustica lentils are descended from those brought by settlers from Ventotene.

She shows me round the azienda. It looks more like the higgledy-piggledy barn of a working farm, complete with a poster supporting Antonio Gramsci and the Communist Party of Italy. She and her husband grow vegetables, like other Usticani, but, explains Signora Longo, it's also the island's only winery. We taste the wines. The mainstream ones are good, a fine standard as Francesco Carfagna would say, especially the Grotta dell'Oro, made from zibibbo grapes. The Zhabib, a vino passito made from the same variety, is another matter altogether.

A very long time ago, my mother used to buy particular dried apricots at Christmas. I think they came from Australia. They were enormous and fleshy and squidgy and gooey. They had been sweetened so that the sharpness of the original fruit was tempered by a fudge-like richness that sent wave after wave of apricot flavour surging through my mouth. Or so my memory says, because it's many years since I saw one, let alone ate it.

The Zhabib has the same exquisite sweetness, elegance, refinement and voluptuousness as those apricots. Half the grapes are dried in the sun, and half are left undried, Signora Longo tells me. The fresh acidity of the one calms the honeyed concentration of the other. Its silky opulence fuses peach, almond, fig, apricot and light. It fills me with fresh nostalgia.

Sicily (again)

As I come off the ferry from Ustica to Palermo, the heavens open in a tempest of King Lear intensity. Thunder booms. Lightning snaps. Water cascades. I'm utterly soaked within seconds.

Under normal conditions Palermo is second only to Naples as a test of nerve, will and the instinct to survive for the Vespa rider. These are not normal conditions. Streets have turned to rivers.

Crossroads have become lakes. I can scarcely see. Traffic looms through the watery haze. Decisions have to be made instantly and followed through with nerveless courage. In the midst of this storm I discover reserves of concentration, discipline and balance that I thought I'd lost forty years ago. I find the route to Castellamare del Golfo more by roulette than reason. The storm follows me for some way down the highway. Eventually I escape its clutches, and by the time I get to Castellamare del Golfo, I'm quite dry but knackered.

I stay the night with Anders Schønnemann, a photographer friend, and his family on holiday there. Their kindness and good humour restore my pleasure in the world. The next day I head on to Trapani to catch the ferry to Favignana, the largest of the three Egadi islands that lie just off Trapani at the western end of Sicily.

Favignana

Once upon a time Favignana was the capital of the Southern Italian tuna industry. Now the holiday industry has taken its place, with holiday activities, holiday homes, holiday villages, holiday jollity of every shape and hue. There are holiday bikes and holiday scooters and holiday yachts and holiday motorboats, everything and anything that brings amusement, cheer and entertainment, to be hired or rented or bought.

The winding roads are cluttered by jolly folk in twos and fours and sixes on cycles moving in stately formation, and on scooters buzzing like the space fighters in *Star Wars*, to and from the town or to and from one of the beaches or coves. The beaches are crowded with sunbrellas and sunbeds and sun worshippers. The sea's festooned with sails and dotted with kayaks, streaked with motorboats and cruisers. People are there to have a Good Time and a Good Time they will have. 'È un paradiso,' says one beaming cyclist to me, his shaven head pink with sunburn, a handkerchief wrapped around his neck.

It's the world of the short trouser – long shorts, mid shorts, short shorts, hot and inappropriate shorts; shorts plain, shorts decorated with Snow White's seven dwarfs, shorts fun and shorts funky, with a lot of smooth, gleaming brown arms and legs. And everyone sports a rucksack, tote, shoulder bag or pouch.

The locals are veterans of holiday campaigns. They know exactly how to handle us without losing their self-respect. There's a cheerful normality about the service they give, something the English have never learned because we can't separate service from servility. We see nothing noble about bringing someone a cup of tea or a plate of food. Yet it can, like all things, be well done or badly done, carried out with grace and pride or with surly incompetence. The second is easy, the first difficult. The Favignanesi look after all-comers with efficiency and charm.

Il Villaggio L'Oasi is typical of holidaymaking Favignana. It's difficult to know how to classify it. It's not really a village, and it certainly isn't an oasis. It feels like a holiday settlement in the form of a maze. The road to the parking area is bumpy and dusty. To one side there's a children's playground, sad and desolate. It'd be a brave child who used the slide or climbing frame, and clearly there aren't many brave children at L'Oasi. There's also a model train for taking people from L'Oasi to the town parked in another dusty patch to one side of the track at the end of which there's a dusty parking space lined with dusty bicycles and scooters.

A glass-fronted wooden cabin, a kind of holiday customs post or passport control, guards the entrance. It's manned by two delightful, efficient and bouncy young women: Giusy, who has short-cropped hair, a charming smile and a black front tooth; and Anna, who has a rather disconcerting habit of ending every sentence she speaks with a wink.

'Where can I fill up my Vespa with petrol?'

'Left out of the gate. Left at the crossroads and then straight on about 500 metres.' (Wink).

'Can I have some shirts washed?'

'Of course. Three euros an item.' (Wink).

'When will they be ready?'

'Tomorrow morning.' (Wink).

They're both very efficient and deal with all manner of oddity and mischief with brusque good humour. I get the feeling that there aren't many forms of human behaviour they haven't come across.

Beyond the passport control, the maze begins, a marvellous labyrinth created in one of the abandoned tufa quarries that pockmark the island. Odd bits of glittery pottery add random splashes of colour to serpentine, concrete-grey paths that merge into other paths that divide into other paths, up, down, this way and that, between short terraces of holiday cabins or cottages, painted white, with blue shutters. The paths themselves are shaded by a thick canopy of oleander, olive, vines, pomegranate and plumbago, among which statues and pots, that might have been lifted as a job lot from some cheap garden centre, stand in incidental order. The pots have plants in them, some of which are dead. There are also many cacti and geraniums and uplifting messages incised on pieces of wood that hang from the branches of the trees. One of them reads:

PUNTA LUNGA

SERENO È IL TUO VISO RIVOLTO VERSO IL MARE. PUNTA LUNGA TU TI FAI CHIAMARE, IL VENTO DI SCIROCCO SI FA SENTIRE SUONANDO MUSICA PER VOI IN CASA DOVETE UDIRE, IL MARE BALLA E ANCHE LE BARCHETTE TUTTI CANTANO IN CORO PER TE O PORTICCIOLO. DI COLPO TI RISVEGLI AD ASCOLTARE TU CHE GELOSO SEI DEL TUO MARE. SEI BELLO E SEDUCENTE DA GUARDARE, POI LA SERA TI TRASFORMI COME PER INCANTO E DIVENTI UNA STELLA IN MEZZO AL MARE.

L'ARTE NON DORME RINO LI CAUSI 2008

Roughly translated this means:

> Punta Lunga (Long Cape)
> Serene is your face as it turns to the sea,
> 'Punta lunga' is what you like to be called.
> The scirocco wind makes itself felt,
> Playing music for you.
> You have to hear it in your home.
> The sea is dancing and the boats are, too.
> Everyone is singing in chorus for you, oh little harbour.
> Suddenly you wake to listen,
> You, who are jealous of your sea.
> You are beautiful and alluring to look at,
> Then at night you are transformed as if by magic,
> And become a star in the middle of the sea.

It turns out to be a poem from *Art Doesn't Sleep* by Rino Li Causi. It seems a touch cheesy to me, but there's a cheerful random quality to it all.

My cabin is a bit on the cramped side. To open the door properly, I have to move the bed towards the clothes cupboard and away from the reading light. If I want to get at the clothes cupboard or read in bed, I have to move the bed back, and then it isn't possible to open the door properly. The bed is draped in a mosquito net of virulent orange. It's almost impossible to get in and out of bed, let alone sit up and read, without getting tangled up in the net.

The bathroom is surprisingly large and the shower powerful. From time to time the water system shrieks like a wounded animal, and between those times it gurgles not unlike my lower intestine after a particularly demanding meal. Finally the loo seat and cover are made of transparent plastic set with tacks with brightly coloured heads, like Smarties only with sharp points attached. Of course, I can't feel the sharp points, but the idea of sharp points is not a good one to associate with loo seats.

Whatever my misgivings might be, there are plenty of people who come to L'Oasi for their holidays and who are evidently having a Very Good Time Indeed. They come in all shapes and sizes – couples, families with 2.4 children, three generations of families, mothers and daughters, but not, I think, fathers and sons or single men apart from me. I may be wrong about the single men. It's difficult to tell.

———

The Florio family obviously enjoyed enjoying themselves. Here they are in black-and-white photos, lounging around for the camera at their palatial mansion on Favignana, in immaculate suiting and moustaches of various styles, and ankle-length crinolines with carefully constructed hair, looking cheerful and rich. Here one Florio ruffles the hair of another. And here they are in natty swimming costumes, diving off their steam yacht into the sea. Once the Florios were Sicilian royalty, the richest family on the island, one of the richest in Europe.

At one time or another, they were winemakers, shipping line owners, newspaper proprietors, art patrons, motor racing enthusiasts, tuna canners and, above all, colossally wealthy, wealthy beyond counting, wealthy beyond the dreams of avarice. These days their name survives on a brand of marsala, the Targa Florio (if anyone remembers that once famous car race any more), and the tonnare, those palaces of industry dedicated to tuna-canning, that they set up in Sicily and on Favignana.

The scale of the Stabilimento Florio, the tonnara on Favignana, is prodigious, a succession of canning rooms, cooking areas, boat-houses, offices and storage facilities. But even more impressive, to my way of thinking, is the handsome style of the place. This may have been an industrial unit of its day, but, like Brunel's Paddington

Station, it'd been designed with an eye to aesthetics as well as efficiency. Built of local creamy-white tufa blocks, it combines classical proportion with contemporary convenience, laid out on impeccable assembly line principles to accommodate the natural flow of the process. Here's the boathouse where the old fishing boats are still poised, ready to slide down ramps straight into the sea below. Here's the quay where the tuna were landed next to the dissection area where they were cut up before being loaded into vast metal tureens in which they were cooked. Behind these are the canning rooms with ranks of old tuna tins, all neatly laid out, as if ready for processing. The cans were topped up with olive oil here; sealed here; stored here; distributed here. It has the elegance of form and function in perfect harmony.

It's difficult to imagine in the pristine present that these practical, handsome, high-ceilinged rooms with their linking neo-Gothic arches and paved floors would have reeked of slime and blood and fishiness. It's all neat, clean and tidy now, of course, a model of tasteful restoration, a multi-purpose cultural space. Nostalgic black-and-white photographs evoke vanished people and processes.

In one room a black-and-white film celebrates la mattanza, the annual round-up and slaughter of migrating tuna that used to happen each year off Favignana, producing at least some of the raw material for the Florio production line. It was shot in the 1930s, a hymn to the fishermen, their community and their fish, a moving, conscious tribute to the rhythms of the past. Everyone on Favignana depended on this harvest, and most of the community were involved in la mattanza in one way or another. The nets were mended communally, prepared communally, loaded communally. The boats were launched and rowed, eight oars per side, into position. The fishermen waited. The sun went down. The sun came up. The fishermen still waited. And then the tuna arrived and the slaughter began. It was operatic, cruel and noble.

But la mattanza no longer takes place off Favignana. All that ended some years ago, and with it the industry it supported. Tuna made this community in the same way that coal and steel made communities in Britain, and, like them, the community and its culture has vanished, destroyed by ineluctable economic forces.

Its place has been taken by a mattanza of a different kind. Instead of the migrating tuna come migrating holidaymakers, just as predictably. The seas may not flow with blood any more, but the streets flow with money. The whole community is united as it had been formerly, serving together, servicing together, feeding, managing, entertaining together, and unlike the schools of blue fin tuna, the schools of holidaymakers are only likely to grow.

Giusy, the young woman with the black tooth, tells me that there's going to be a concert held in a natural theatre between the bar and the wall of the quarry. The singer is a friend of hers, 'a star from Broadway' she says emphatically.

By the time I settle at a table at the back, with a mojito for company, the Broadway star is well into 'Killing Me Softly' in a voice that ranges over a wide dramatic landscape. She follows this up with 'As Long as He Needs Me', from *Oliver*, in which, she announces, she'd starred on Broadway. The singer gives it some welly, milking it for all it's worth. There's a storm of applause at the end. Lionel Bart, who wrote the musical, ended up living above a laundromat in Acton. I think how pleased he would've been. Time for a second mojito.

Soon 'Wherever You Are' soars out over L'Oasi. Many people talk right through it, sipping their own White Ladies, Margaritas and Aperol spritzers, clapping vigorously at the end, although not as enthusiastically, I'm pleased to note, as they had after the Lionel Bart aria. Then comes 'Questo è Mio', a very theatrical chanson that has something of Mercedes Sosa's great anthem

'Gracias A La Vida' about it. The nattering and chattering continue unabated.

Behind me, some kids start playing in an open-air Jacuzzi. The dusk's coming on as the singer gets stuck into Claudio Baglioni's great 'Piccolo Grande Amore'. Another mojito. It may be cheesy, but there's something fabulous about people basking in collective pleasure. This is the essence of L'Oasi. It hovers on the edge of the seedy, an amateur Butlin's in an exotic location. I feel a great warmth for my fellow humans. Perhaps it's the mojitos.

And yet, even as I revel in the corn of another Bart classic, 'A New Day', I know that I don't really share the experience that everyone else here is feeling. It's a form of communication conducted in a language to which I don't have access. My pleasure is personal and selfish, and at the opposite pole to the collective emotion sweeping through the bar.

Of course, it would be impossible for everyone to travel as I am. More, the people around me wouldn't want to, any more than I would as they are. Being a part of the collective, being with folk like themselves, is a great component of their pleasure. For me, travelling, alone for the most part, is the delight.

We arrive at the finale, 'Don't Cry for Me, Argentina'. What else could it possibly be? The cantante gives it the full treatment. We join in. The collective heart is put through the collective wringer. I can't help a still small voice in my head murmuring 'Oh, for heaven's sake', but, in truth, I'm very happy to be there, to see it all, even if I'm not swept away.

There's a storm of applause and whistles and cries of 'Bis'. 'Bis.' A man in a woolly cap, who bears an uncanny resemblance to Compo in *Last of the Summer Wine*, dashes up and embraces her. The Broadway star looks very pleased.

Marettimo

Marettimo is the smallest and most remote of the three Egadi

Islands, about thirty minutes by aliscafo from Favignana; a rugged, uncompromising scrap of rock stuck in a topaz sea. The port's a cluster of square-topped, white and blue cubes. Around 300 people live here full-time, all fishermen and their families.

The fishermen of Marettimo are famous. However, for a few short weeks, a good many of them desert their traditional vocation for the more productive catch of tourists, who come over to ooh and aah over the island's many grottos and swim in its unspoiled waters.

Pietro, an urbane, Toscano-puffing Sicilian I met while swimming one afternoon on Favignana, had told me a round-the-island cruise was the best way to see Marettimo, so I'm quite happy to be snared by an elderly boat tout almost as soon as I set foot in the tiny harbour, along with a young couple, she from Liguria, he from Pisa; a couple of handsome, silver-haired silver surfers from Milan; and two sets of cheerily chatty middle-aged women. We're bundled on board with little ceremony, and, after a certain amount of careering about the harbour, head for the choppy open sea.

Our captain, Salvatore, explains that it's too rough to go all the way round the island. He does an eloquent mime with his hands. However, he's determined to give us our money's worth, and that means taking us to the two nearest grottos at a cut rate. The practicality of this becomes questionable as we hit open water, alongside several other former fishing boats all heading in the same direction. It's a powerboat race without the power, and Salvatore is going to win it.

The sea rolls in long, slow surges, interspersed with a lot of short, sharp furrows. It makes for exhilarating, if not exactly comfortable, travel, not appreciated by all my fellow sailors. We don't really have time to assess the situation properly before we're actually inside the first grotto. Salvatore has out-manoeuvred his rivals in a ruthless manner that would have suited a cut-throat skipper in an America's Cup race, and the other boats have to sit outside, pitching and rolling, while we have first dibs.

A section of the ceiling has fallen in, so that sunlight lights up the inside of the grotto, casting liquid, shifting webs on the sides. Salvatore is eloquent in his appreciation of this marvel of nature. We are suitably impressed and snap away. And then Salvatore begins a multiple-point turn inside the grotto to get us out. This brings us within millimetres of the rocky sides, and involves a good deal of pushing off – 'Look out for your hands,' 'Not too hard,' 'Careful,' Salvatore roars at intervals – before we're pitching and yawing outside once more.

We head up the coast. The sea becomes increasingly choppy. One of the middle-aged ladies is clearly not a happy traveller.

'I don't want to go into the grotto,' she says.

'No, no, Signora, we have to,' says Salvatore. 'You've paid for it.'

'I'll pay not to go there,' says the lady.

'But the others have paid, too, and they want go.' We look at each other blankly. No one says anything. We're all terrified of Salvatore.

By the time we actually get to the grotto, we're bouncing around. The grotto is quite small and impressively dark. I can't actually believe that Salvatore is really going to take us into it, but he does. It's a tight fit, but it's calm and we can admire the various side grottos and the darkness undistracted by fear of capsizing. And then it's time to back out from the calm of the grotto into the, well, not exactly pounding, but agitated sea. I might have questioned Salvatore's sanity in taking us into the grotto in the first place, but, to his credit, he gets us out again with aplomb and a stream of reassurance. The eyes of the lady who didn't want to go to the grotto in the first place are firmly shut throughout, and most of my fellow passengers look apprehensive.

There's relief all round when Salvatore announces that we're going to a nice quiet cove where we can swim to our hearts' content. Which we do, along with the human cargo of some fifteen other boats.

While lying on the rocks in the sun, I fall into conversation with Marco, a marine biologist with a ring through his nose. He's come from Trapani that morning, and walked from the village, about one and a half hours. I'm suitably impressed.

He was born in Naples, he says, but now works in the Netherlands. He specialises in phytoplankton.

'Phytoplankton?'

'Very small organisms, even smaller than plankton. They're very important because they form the beginning of the food chain in the sea.'

He's studied in Southampton, Australia, France and now the Netherlands.

'It's very difficult to get a permanent job,' he mourns. 'The problem is funding. The best centres attract the most funding and they're all in Northern Europe and Scandinavia. It's very competitive to get a position in any of them.'

He's pessimistic about the future of the oceans.

'The levels of pollution are better than they were, but not as good as they need to be. Towns and rivers are discharging too much pollution into the sea. We need to invest more money in pollution control. It's always a question of money, and that's the problem.'

'So are fish stocks being seriously threatened?' I ask.

'In some places, of course they are,' he says. 'But the balance in the sea is very complex. We don't really understand it yet.'

He's as pessimistic about the political situation in Italy as he is about the future of the oceans. He's pessimistic about the economy, about the future, about life. He doesn't seem cheerful about much. He gets up to walk back to the village in time to catch the ferry back to Trapani. The one thing that would make him happy, he says, would be a permanent job. 'It doesn't matter where.'

Favignana (again)

The heat is penal. The early part of the morning, every morning, 6.30, 7.00 or so, has a delicious cool to it. From about 8 a.m. the heat begins to quicken, seeping into the skin and through the flesh beneath, remorselessly building up and up, as if some invisible furnace is being stoked. Pavements, roads, earth and sand become too hot to walk on barefoot. By midday the heat reaches 30°C and higher, and becomes palpable, wringing energy out of people, cars, dogs, cats, me. People move in a curious torpor. Small shadows become sanctuaries of relative cool.

It's the last morning of this leg of my summer in the islands. The character and fragile beauties of the islands are already vanishing beneath a mass of holidaymakers and tourists. They're a jolly lot, but I can't see the point of hanging around for a month observing inadvertent pillage by the marauding hordes, and the consequences, good and bad, that I've already observed. I'm going to head for the Monti Lucretili north of Rome to spend August in the cheery company of my brother, Johnny, and his wife, Emma. It was here I spent so many agreeable summers in my youth, enjoying the relative cool of the hills and the well-fed simplicity of life.

There's still time for one last breakfast of croissant filled with pistachio cream, coffee and fresh orange juice. A stiff scirocco flaps the awning of the café in the town square. People are revving up for the beach. Delivery vans arrive with supplies to restock the shops, bars and eateries. Bicycles glide back and forth. Wheeled suitcases rattle over the paving. Someone's sound system goes hiphophiphiphiphop. The sounds of the morning, the greetings and chat, burble like water over the rocks.

I decide to make the steep walk to the Castello di Santa Caterina, the highest point of the island, which was used as a strategic watchtower by the Allies during the war, and subsequently as a radar listening post by the Italian Army. It takes me just over an hour with frequent stops, and I'm blinded by sweat by the time I finally clamber up to the crumbling ruin and the junk yard of radar equipment that looks like an installation sculpture.

From this eyrie, I can see a rather different Favignana, one that's difficult to appreciate from the bicycle- and scooter-clotted roads and holiday hokum of the seaside. Away from the immediate coastline are fields of wheat, dotted with bales of hay, cows grazing, blocks of vegetables, vines and olives. It's an agricultural Favignana, a more permanent Favignana, that'll be ticking over when the holiday season is finished, and life returns to normality once more.

I think about my journey so far and how far I have travelled physically and emotionally, and how much further I have yet to go, and remember the poem by C. P. Cavafy that a wiser and far more literate friend sent me earlier.

> Do not hurry the journey at all.
> Better that it should last many years;
> Be quite old when you anchor at the island,
> Rich with all you have gained along the way,
> Not expecting Ithaca to give you riches.
> Ithaca has given you a lovely journey.
> Without Ithaca you would not have set out.

I walk back down to where I left Nicoletta, and ride her back to the town, turning onto a track behind the Stabilimento Florio that runs along one side of the bay. I park Nicoletta and walk down to the sea's edge, take off my shoes and stand in the gently roiling, rushing waves. The sounds of aliscafi and motorboats and the voices of the new arrivals calling out to each other, echo across the water. It's very hot, and the soupy smells of the sea and its shore are pungent in the heat.

7

SWEET BANQUET OF THE MIND

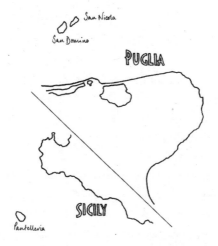

San Nicola

San Domino

PUGLIA

SICILY

Pantelleria

Lampedusa

SEPTEMBER 2015

Sicily – Pantelleria – Lampedusa – San Domino –
San Nicola

Mainland Italy

August. Weeks of reading, Scrabble, cooking and pottering in the cool, upland beauty of the Monti Lucretili. I've spent so many happy summers here, hunting crayfish in the clear streams that run down from the mountains with Adamo, a half-wild shepherd boy; sitting lovelorn in the village piazza watching whichever of the Licenza lassies caught my vulnerable heart that year; basking in the glory of my improbable footballing success; gazing at a pair of golden eagles drifting effortlessly down the valley; cooking for eighteen, twenty, twenty-four on family holidays and bathing in the cataract of sound that accompanied lunch and dinner. I walked many of the paths that wind up through the vertiginous, heavily wooded hills; started at the snort of a wild boar; and stopped, perplexed, at the sight of a porcupine, so odd and unexpected in this place; picked wild cornelian cherries that grow in a stand in the middle of the woods so that my brother, Johnny, could turn them into intense, jewelled jelly. It's a place of marvellous beauty and tender memories.

But now I'm ready for the last part of my odyssey. Away in the islands the ranks of holidaymakers are thinning, the steaming heat of high summer is tempered. It's time to go back. I look forward to being reunited with Nicoletta, who I left in a cosy garage in Trapani, and to the joys of the high seas and open roads.

Sicily (again)

Trapani has changed quite a bit since I first wandered through it in 2007. It's been cleaned and smartened up. It feels and looks prosperous. Salvatore, my taxi driver, told me that it's flourishing thanks to its ship-handling yards, salt, wine, olive oil, marble and tourism. There are berths along the quay for the racing yacht circus that moves from friendly port to friendly port, taking part in a kind of seagoing Formula 1, each marked by sponsor logo.

On earlier visits, I hadn't really appreciated how handsome Trapani is. A town of a thousand balconies, I'd called it, and so it is, but there's rather more to it than that. Much had been destroyed by Allied bombing during the last war, but a number of sixteenth- and seventeenth-century churches and eighteenth- and nineteenth-century palazzi and bourgeois town houses survive and line the Corso Umberto and the via Roma at the heart of the old town, reminders of Trapani's prosperous trading past. Between and around the Corso Umberto and the via Roma are knots of narrow, winding streets, the remains of the old souk that harks back to an earlier, Arab Trapani, an affiliation that finds a contemporary echo in the flat-topped buildings along the sea road.

There's an even more ancient association with the past just outside the town. The salt pans of Nubia lie on the sea side of the road that runs between Trapani and Marsala. The Phoenicians harvested salt from the sea in the same manner on the island of Mozia down the coast 5,000 years ago.

Seawater flows into the shallow pans the size of a large swimming pool through a series of channels. The wind and sun combine to slowly evaporate the water, moving every so often from pan to pan until all that's left is a crust of salt that looks like a rime of ice. The few remaining salinai (salt farmers) take away the salt. It's beautiful in its simplicity. Aside from the chug of the small digger and rumble of the conveyor belt taking the salt to the salt hillocks along the edge of the pans as it's harvested, there's just the riffle of wind, the slip of water against the tufa sides of the pans and far-off bird cries. It's a landscape with a strange, spare beauty. Rectangular mirrors of water stretch away to Trapani on the horizon, with the occasional stump of a deserted windmill that used to pump the water around the pans breaking the flatness of the landscape.

Of course, the salt pans of Trapani can't meet the world's salt needs, or match the financial advantages of more highly geared production. Modern techniques, international competition, the methodical nature of production have all whittled away at the number of salinai. Only a handful remain. But is there a quieter, more tranquil, sustainable, environmentally sensitive form of farming? How long will it be before these salt pans, like the windmills, stand derelict and abandoned?

'After you,' says a tall man with a bushy beard and a bushy pony-tail, as I stand in the queue waiting to collect my ticket for the ferry to Pantelleria.

'But you're ahead of me,' I say.

'And you've been waiting longer,' he says.

Such consideration is unheard-of in Italy, where queuing is treated as a blood sport in which the ruthless self-interest is reminiscent of gladiatorial combat in ancient Rome.

I thank the man for his graciousness. He's clutching a motorcycle helmet, and so we start chatting about the joys of two-wheel travel.

His name is Mariano Brischetto, and it turns out that he's a tenor at the Teatro Massimo Vincenzo Bellini in Catania. Catania has been a centre of opera since its most celebrated operatic son, Vincenzo Bellini, the Swan of Catania, genius of bel canto opera, became one of the most famous composers in nineteenth-century Europe. Mariano has just spent two weeks travelling around Sardinia, the first time he's used his bike, he tells me, for anything other than going to and from work. It's been a liberating experience for him, and he's keen to enjoy the experience again. We exchange phone numbers and promise to meet up on Pantelleria.

Pantelleria
The harbour of Pantelleria is a working port not a posing port, a berth for tramp steamers and beaten-up coasters and the odd

ramshackle trawler rather than scenic, decorative fishing boats and what Lisa on Filicudi referred to as Tupperware yachts, aside from a sleek, black number that belongs to Giorgio Armani, who has a house on the island. The buildings around the harbour are 1950s utilitarian, put up in place of those destroyed by Allied bombing during the war. Not much thought was given to their design at the time, and not much thought has been given to their maintenance since, by the look of things. The sea front strikes a slightly grungy note, beyond a few bright bars and the odd beachwear shop. Perhaps the constant flow of traffic along the lungomare is a deterrent to serious development. It's a busy town. It has a sense of purpose about it.

I meet up with Mariano by the filling station, as arranged, and we set off to explore the hinterland, he on his monster black and orange Kawasaki Versys and I on dainty Nicoletta.

We follow the coastal road to Tracino. The shore is a long, winding, volcanic crust the colour and texture of elephant skin. Here and there it slopes down from precipitous cliffs to exquisite, crystalline waters. Then we turn inland, passing close to a number of peaks with pine and cork tree cladding, through scrubby land and scattered villages. In some ways Pantelleria feels closer to the Maghreb than Europe. There's an unmistakably Arabic cast to the names – Kuddia, Khaggiar, Rekhale, Khamma – and many of the houses, known as dammusi, which are like boxes with a distinctive dome at the centre and painted white to deflect the sun, could have been lifted from Tunisia or Morocco.

We pass through the Piana Ghirlanda, a long, flat valley of irregular fields in capricious shapes and sizes – straggly triangles, hexagons, rectangles, squares and some of geometric designs that defy precise description – shaped by dark, forbidding walls and terracing of volcanic rocks the colour of anthracite. Within these enclosures huddle diminutive olive trees, crouching caper bushes and lines of vines creeping over the ground, each designed to flourish in a landscape scoured by wind virtually every day of the year.

There are various theories as to why Pantelleria is called Pantelleria, but one suggests that the name is the Italianised version of the Arabic Bint al-Riyah, meaning Daughter of Winds. Life on Pantelleria is shaped by wind. It was no more than a breeze when I arrived, but it isn't always as gentle, and growing anything depends on mitigating its effects. Who knows who started the tradition of building walls to protect crops growing in the island's rich volcanic soil? The original Iberians? The Carthaginians? Romans? Most probably the Arabs from Tunisia and Egypt, who occupied the island from AD 700 to AD 1123. They were supreme agriculturists. They created sophisticated and flourishing agricultural systems throughout Sicily, in Southern Italy and Spain, wherever the caliphate of Baghdad held sway. Even the terraces that mount the surrounding hills are structured in such a way as to reduce the effect of the wind, and every now and then we pass topless towers built by the Arabs, with fruit trees growing within their sheltering embrace.

It's claimed that the vines on Pantelleria are descended from the muscat of Alexandria introduced by the Romans. They're known as zibbibo these days – zibib meaning raisin in Arabic – and twenty or so producers turn them into Moscato di Pantelleria and Passito di Pantelleria, famous for their luscious sweetness. So luscious, indeed, that Passito di Pantelleria has been designated as a Masterpiece of Oral and Intangible Heritage of Humanity, whatever that may mean, by the Director of UNESCO.

The harvest is just beginning. Here and there we pass groups of pickers bent over the rows of squat vines. Nearby APEs, those distinctive three-wheeled agricultural workhorses you still see all over Italy, and small trailers are parked nose to tail, stacked with small boxes of grapes. We stop to talk to one group of pickers.

'All the grapes have to be picked by hand because the grapes grow so close to the ground,' explains Michele, the wine maker, trimming out the dodgy grapes from among the healthy ones, before placing the perfect bunch carefully in a crate.

'It's bloody hard on the back because we have to bend down all the time,' he says.

According to Michele, the combination of the volcanic earth, the hot sun, the dry wind and the salt from the sea is responsible for the unique qualities of the wine. Some of the grapes will be dried (passito) for two to four weeks to concentrate the juices still further, before being pressed and added to the juice of undried grapes to create that special combination of intensity, harmony and balance between sweetness and acidity.

'But this isn't a good year,' he adds glumly.

'Why not?'

'Rain in August. Too much rain in August. It's diluted the concentration of the juice. And a lot of the bunches lay on the wet ground, which isn't good for them.'

Mariano and I leave Michele and his crew to their back-breaking labour, and take the road that climbs up out of the Piano Ghirlanda. We stop to inspect some Byzantine tombs tucked away in a grove of ilex, cork trees and holm oak on a spur of rock overlooking the Piano. They're just two elongated, coffin-shaped stones, but there's a certain gentle sweetness to them in the scented air, light and shadow flickering over them.

We end our ride at Scauri down on the coast, where what purports to be a 'Punic-Romano Village' turns out to be rather less interesting than it sounds. It's a pity the remains don't match the view. I can almost hear some Punic estate agent waxing lyrical about the 'fine sea aspect', but in reality it's just a series of holes in the ground running along the shore. We have an agreeable and much needed swim, and a reasonable lunch including dentice alla pantesca, a kind of sea bream in raw tomatoes, garlic, capers and almonds at La Vela at the water's edge.

There's something rather dour and self-absorbed about Pantelleria. It's a little like Elba in some respects, insular and self-absorbed. The agriculture is fascinating, the sea is beautiful, the wines are intoxicating, but there's some kind of invisible, impermeable barrier that I can't penetrate. I don't feel drawn to stay on and head back to Trapani.

Sicily (once more)

Porto Empedocle, the port for Lampedusa, lies on its southern coast, over a hundred kilometres from Trapani. As I have plenty of time in hand, I make a small detour to Segesta, a Greek temple of extraordinary beauty that I've long wanted to see. Unfortunately when I get there, Segesta is closed. Wild fires are leaping and gambolling along the surrounding valleys, and the temple, itself, is threatened.

Leaving a large number of puzzled and disgruntled tourists wandering around outside the locked gates, I head off again, passing several fire engines deploying firemen. It's dramatic and exciting watching stands of trees suddenly bursting into flame, dying down, leaping up again, sometimes several metres away from the last blaze. There's a sinister, random malevolence to their movement. From time to time lumbering fire-fighting planes turn in just over the tops of surrounding hills on water-bombing runs.

Thwarted in my attempts to see Segesta, I decide to pay homage to the battlefield of Calatafimi, where the crucial battle of Garibaldi's Sicilian campaign was fought, not far away. The grand warrior led his rag-tag-and-bobtail assembly of volunteer troops up against the nominally superior force of Bourbon army regulars in a series of bayonet charges uphill with the cry 'Qui si fa l'Italia o si muore' (Here we make Italy, or we die). The battle won, the way to Palermo was open, and Garibaldi's reputation as a leader of genius, somewhere between a guerrilla leader and a conventional military commander, was made.

Oddly, while there're plenty of signs to Segesta, I can find none to the battlefield. I search high and low, along main road and side road, but I search in vain. Then I get lost – a not infrequent occurrence – in the town of Calatafimi itself, come out on the wrong side, and set off in the wrong direction. It takes me time to realise my mistake, and a little longer to rectify it. However, I'm quite happy, pottering along the empty roads through the austere, abstract beauty of the undulating land, a vast, rolling inland sea, sere brown where wheat's been gathered in, and café au lait where the earth's been tilled, broken from time to time by brilliant green blocks of tousled vines and plots of silvery green olives, as bushy as shaving brushes.

I finally chunter into Porto Empedocle at about 6 p.m. very hot, very sweaty, very smelly and very tired. As I register in a hotel right by the port, an elderly white-haired woman sitting in the reception area with her husband obviously overhears that I'm English. With no preamble the old biddy addresses me.

'You English are very clever.'

'Sorry?'

'You're just letting the Syrians in.'

'Um. Oh. Ah. Yes. I –'

'We're getting Africans. Blacks.' There's a whip of contempt in her tone. Her husband looks visibly embarrassed. I open my mouth to tell her that I would rather them than her, but the lift doors close.

I'm surprised because it's the only time I've heard a racist remark on this journey. Everyone else I've spoken to on the subject of emigration has been sympathetic to the situation of refugees, if baffled by the scale of the problem.

———

The ferry doesn't leave until the evening, so I go out to explore the delights of Porto Empedocle, named after Empedocles, the Greek philosopher who threw himself into the crater of Etna to prove he was immortal. He must have had a nasty surprise. The town also lays claim to Luigi Pirandello, although, in fact, he was actually born up the road in the small village of the admirably named Kaos on the outskirts of Girgenti, or Agrigento as it's called now. Porto Empedocle's most famous authentic son is the writer, Andrea Camillieri, author of the thrillers featuring Commissario Montalbano. Although he's lived in Rome for much of his life, he affectionately evokes Porto Empedocle in the fictional form of Vigata. I struggle to reconcile Camillieri's nostalgic evocation with the reality of contemporary Porto Empedocle.

It is a serious test of character. As far as I can see, there's absolutely nothing of note in town, not one remotely beautiful or even interesting building. Somehow you have to come to terms with the disintegrating pavements, the crumbling houses, the weeds sprouting at random, the accumulations of rubbish, the absence of civic pride or investment, the unloved, unlovable nature of a town that simply exists, as it does now, under a sullen sky and humid, heavy heat. Of all the places in which I've had to idle away an hour or even a day or two, Porto Empedocle emphatically takes the biscuit in the Crap Ports department. The smell of fish hangs heavy over the port. None of this has prevented locals from leaping aboard the Montalbano bandwagon with vigour. There are no end of Vigata bars, Montalbano gelaterias and Il Commissario trattorias. Time hangs heavy on my hands.

And then comes the miracle of San Calogero.

Tatty and depressing in the bright light of day, by night Porto Empedocle undergoes a mysterious transformation, not into a place of beauty exactly, but into one of idiosyncratic enchantment. Shadows mask the decaying buildings and general dilapidation. The street lamps light the town in a mellow, theatrical glow. Young, old, very old, families, couples, singletons throng the via Roma. Suddenly there's a buzz about the place.

It turns out that it's the Feast of San Calogero, the local patron saint. His image suddenly appears at the top of the steps from the church in the via Roma, accompanied by a furious, synchronised rattle from five drums, a blast from the local brass band and a peal of church bells, all at once. It's a splendid cacophony. At the same time there's a general sharp intake of breath, many cross themselves, a few applaud.

I can just make out St C. through a forest of smart phones and tablets lifted like votive offerings. Raised up on a kind of wooden raft borne on the shoulders of willing bearers, he's carried through the sea of packed humanity, lurching to one side and then the other as he comes down the steps of the church. Every now and then the procession pauses while puzzled or fearful babies are held up to touch St C., or be touched by him. Other devotees shove mysterious bits of paper into a hole in his middle, below his robes which are dotted with gold. Art nouveau lights frame each corner of the palanquin, and a halo of Christmas tree lights illuminate the saint's austere and unmistakably black face.

Information about St Calogero is pretty thin, and there seems to be a certain vagueness about his origins. Was he a second-century saint from North Africa? Or was he a fifth-century saint from Armenia? Was he a hermit? Or an officer in the Roman army? Or both? He pops up all over the place in Sicily – in Agrigento, Naro, Sciacca as well as Porto Empedocle – and, for whatever reason, he's usually black.

Of course his effigy is kitsch, magnificently so. That's the point. If the image was in the best possible taste, it would be both vulgar and unapproachable. It's the kitschness of St Calogero that gives his image its force. It's direct and immediate. It appeals to our sentimental side. and makes it approachable. The massed ranks of drummers, the band and a phalanx of followers led by a man with a bell, set off around the town, stopping every now and then to allow more puzzled babies to be held aloft.

The streets are awash with folk, eating, drinking, chatting, laughing. I wonder how many towns in Britain in Porto Empedocle's apparently woeful state can boast at least fifteen trattorias, as many bars, not to mention pizzerias, paninoteche and gelaterias. The people of Porto Empedocle may not care a fig for the physical state of their town, but they like to eat well. On a street corner I come across a stall selling pani ca meusa, a bun stuffed with beef spleen and other interior oddities I see bubbling away in a cauldron. It's gloriously greasy, with a delicate, slightly livery flavour and a whiff of drains.

Greatly cheered, I go down to the dock to wait for the ferry to Lampedusa to arrive. An old man sitting on a bollard with a guitar asks where I'm from. What am I doing? Where am I going? I tell him. What a dream, he says, what a wonderful thing to do. Pantelleria is so beautiful, he says. I ask him why he's playing the guitar on the dock. He's waiting to catch the ferry, too, and it helps pass the time, he says. And music's beautiful, isn't it? I agree. He begins strumming. 'I love you, Pantelleria,' he sings in English. 'You're so beautiful.' Beyond him someone is cooking sausages and onions on a barbecue outside the quayside bar. A golden plume of smoke rises up into the night.

Presently the ferry comes in. After the regular passengers have disembarked, 200 or more immigrants, Africans, quietly file down onto the quay. Each carries an identical bag containing their possessions. No one shouts abuse. No one says anything. The first bus pulls away when it's full. Another takes its place. Four buses in all fill up and drive away, taking the occupants to centres in Trapani, Catania, Palermo, Agrigento. It's a smooth, well-practised operation, and there's no enmity among the Sicilians on the quayside as far as I can tell.

As we're about to sail, a sparkling firework display marking the end of the Feast of San Calogero suddenly glitters in the night sky. I wonder if the immigrants have seen the fireworks, and if so, what they make of them.

Lampedusa

Lampedusa looks as if someone has left a slice of tart floating on the sea. This is the final frontier, the last outpost of Europe, 113 kilometres from Tunisia and 205 kilometres from Sicily, a scrubby, dusty, stony tump of sandstone rock, with one town and no villages, between 5,000 and 6,000 inhabitants, a few dips but no elevated spots, and scarcely a tree worthy of the name.

Its position made it a useful naval base for the usual succession of ancient Mediterranean superpowers, the Phoenicians, Carthaginians, Greeks and Romans (who rated the island's garum – that pungent, potent, fishy HP sauce of the Roman world made from fermented fish – very highly). At one time the British considered using it for the same purpose, but chose Malta instead because Malta has deep-water ports. And it gave a title to one of the greatest of all Italian writers, Giuseppe Tomasi di Lampedusa, author of the immortal *The Leopard*, although I don't believe he ever set foot on the island. Aside from that, Lampedusa doesn't have a lot of official history, until recently. It's impossible to escape the refugee 'phenomenon', as one person I met called it.

At first sight, Lampedusa is an unlikely Promised Land. There's little agriculture of any kind because the earth is so thin. All basic supplies have to be ferried over, and even though its waters are rich in fish, the survival of the community has always been fragile. But it's been the principal point of arrival for refugees from North Africa for over twenty years, or more. In recent years the numbers of those who have made it or been rescued, and those who have died trying to make it to the island, have been a constant theme in the news.

Italians have some reason to understand the forces that drive people to move from their homes in their millions. Italy has had its own experience of internal and external emigration. Some of the islands were largely depopulated in the eighteenth, nineteenth and twentieth centuries as a result of repeated pirate raids and economic hardship. The nineteenth century and early twentieth century saw hundreds of thousands of Italians head for America, Australia and the UK. The 'economic miracle' of Northern Italy of the 1960s was built on the muscle of millions of Southern Italians moving north for work.

Of course that doesn't necessarily mean that Italy is better equipped to deal with mass immigration, so how does Lampedusa cope, I wonder?

20 GUIGNO 2015 LAMPEDUSA CELEBRA LA GIORNATA DEL REFUGIATO 365 GIORNI L'ANNO (20 JUNE 2015 LAMPEDUSA CELEBRATES THE DAY OF THE REFUGEE 365 DAYS A YEAR) says the banner outside the school library on Lampedusa. I remember what Salvatore, the taxi driver who drove me from the airport to Trapani, had said. 'You won't see many rifugiati on Lampedusa. They spend a couple of days there to check their health and papers and then they're moved to camps here, at Trapani, or Palermo and Catania. There are three or four camps here.'

'How do you feel about them?' I asked him.

'For myself,' he said, 'I'm very sympathetic. I think it's fine for them to come here, as long as they have papers and they can find jobs. There's plenty of room in Sicily. But if they don't have papers, there's a problem. It's difficult to keep track of them. And some of them may be ISIS jihadists. That's a worry.'

I'd first seen rifugiati that night in Porto Empedocle, disembarking from the ferry that runs every day between Sicily and Lampedusa, a column of men and women snaking out of the boat and across the quay to a waiting bus in the sulphurous glow of port lights.

I spend an hour or so watching the other end of the operations, a few hundred rifugiati being put aboard the ferry. They line up, quiet and orderly, tall and elegant, each clutching a sports bag and wearing obviously new trainers. They're roughly one-third women and two-thirds men. The Carabinieri handle them without any bossiness or force. There're one or two representatives of NGOs standing by. The whole process looks humane and well practised. It's the only time I'm actually aware of their presence on the island.

'Lampedusa is a fishing community,' explains Damiano Sferlazzo, the vice sindaco (deputy mayor) of Lampedusa. He's a trim, tanned figure in jeans, polo shirt and trainers and a five-day stubble. He looks too young and too good-looking to make suitable deputy mayoral material to me, but he speaks with the passion and authority of someone who has to deal with the daily practicalities of the situation. 'If we find someone in trouble on the sea, we do what we can to help. That's the way it's always been. So when we find a boat full of refugees, our instinct is to see what we can do. It's just a human response.'

Many people now living on Lampedusa, he goes on, originally came from Tunisia and Libya, from where most of the immigrants now travel. 'They still have relatives there. Of course we want to we can.'

'When it was fifty, sixty, seventy people a week, there was no problem. They'd arrive. Some stayed. Others eventually would leave. But now there are thousands a month. It requires significant organisation to deal with the numbers arriving these days.'

He explains that any refugees arriving on the island are taken to an old army camp designed to hold 5,000 people at any one time. It's managed by a combination of NGOs and local officials. In theory, the refugees are held there for two to three days for medical checks and to have their papers checked, if they have any. Then they're sent on to other centres on Sicily via the ferry for Porto Empedocle.

'The system is fine as long as the flow is controlled,' says Sferlazzo. 'But from time it gets overwhelmed by the sheer numbers of people. It's not just Lampedusa. Kos and other Greek islands have the same problem. And see what happened in Hungary.'

'On the whole,' he says, 'the islanders accept the situation. There are always one or two who complain, but most islanders see this as part of their humanitarian responsibility. They're just angry with politicians who don't seem able to deal with the situation. This is a problem that's been building up for years. It's not just suddenly happened.'

But recent media coverage of the situation has a serious effect on the Lampedusan economy. 'This is a very small island with very few resources,' Sferlazzo says. 'Our economy's fragile. We've just got fishing and tourism.'

Any stories about problems with the refugees, mass drownings, even ones in which the islanders play a heroic part in rescuing refugees from sinking boats, tend to have a negative effect on people thinking about Lampedusa as a site for a carefree holiday.

'This may seem selfish,' he says, 'but it's the reality.'

Clearly a good deal of trouble is taken over segregating the refugees from the main part of the island. Non-European faces are a rare sight on the island. The people walking up and down the via Roma in the evening are middle Italy on holiday, ordinary folk taking advantage of post-August, off-peak prices to soak up the sun on the beaches of golden-blond sand, crowd onto pleasure boats and sport in the clear waters, out to forget about La Crisi, political shenanigans, football failures and the gruelling business of life.

When I ask some what they think of the situation, they respond with tolerance.

'If they can work, let them.'

'I've got nothing against them.'

'They need shelter. Why shouldn't they come?'

The generosity and lack of rancour makes me ashamed of my fellow countrymen. In general, the calmness and acceptance of responsibility by the people I talk to contrasts strongly with the hysteria and outright viciousness of public utterance and press comment in the UK that I've been following online. For months there's been an absolute lack of measured assessment, rational argument or the basic human decency shown by the people of Lampedusa. Yeats's line about 'The best lack all conviction while the worst/Are full of passionate intensity' seems peculiarly pertinent.

And yet the refugee phenomenon should come as no surprise. As Damiano Sferlazzo said, it's been building for over twenty years; twenty years in which to recognise what's going on, to come up with some kind of co-ordinated policy, to create pan-European structures and systems. Simply telling people who have spent all they have and risked their lives to come to Europe, to go back home, is not an option. As Sferlazzo points out, 'The Berlusconi government tried to turn off the tap, and just send them back, but that didn't work at all.'

'Lampedusa is simply a portal to the rest of Europe,' he says. 'The situation can only be dealt with on a European basis. Of course we should accept those facing political persecution or exploitation in their own countries. That's our humanitarian duty. Perhaps the answer for economic migration is to invest in the countries they come from, to create jobs for them there so they don't need to come here looking for work.' He acknowledges that this is a long way off.

As he says goodbye, he adds, 'We came across some refugees in a boat when I was out sailing with some friends earlier this year. We couldn't just leave them. You can't.'

I park Nicoletta beside the road and go to look for a place to swim. On the map I'd identified a long narrow inlet, a cala, and I'm fairly certain that there's a path hereabouts that'll lead me to it. As I wander along an escarpment looking for the beginning of the path, a reddish, sweating, sunburnt man in shorts and a sweat-stained shirt suddenly pops up out of the scrub like a rabbit. His appearance is as startling as it's improbable. He stares at me and mutters away in a dialect so particular I can't understand a word he's saying. I explain that I'm looking for the path. He obviously understands me better than I understand him. He gestures for me to follow, dashes off over the edge of the escarpment, and vanishes among the bushes.

I follow him gingerly, and find him in a kind of makeshift camp tucked away under the lea of the slope. He gestures that I should follow him again, and again, I scramble after him, following a barely discernible path winding between low-growing trees and shrubs. He bounds down the almost vertical slope with the agility of a mountain goat, moving with astonishing speed and surety of foot. I descend more decorously on my bottom, and there's the cala, calm and blue and inviting. I find a shelf above the sea and spend a tranquil afternoon with mask and snorkel patrolling the warm, clear waters. There're rich pastures of Posidonia oceanica (Neptune grass) waving languidly, but surprisingly few fish. Maybe, as Giuseppe Mascoli told me, the sea's become so warm close to the land that the fish have decamped to cooler waters.

Some hours later, I see my guide once more as I pass him at the road. He asks for a lift into town. Unfortunately, I'm heading in the opposite direction for the Trattoria Terranova da Bernardo on the outskirts of town. What is he? A hermit? A leprechaun? His appearance was so odd that for a moment I wonder if I imagined him.

Trattoria Terranova da Bernardo is clearly Lampedusa's destination restaurant, to judge by the cars outside. It's a cavernous place, smart rustic, and has an old-fashioned antipasto buffet, which is the kind of thing I like.

I pile my plate with Russian salad and marinated anchovies and roasted peppers and other matters of that kind. I clear it with pleasure. The appearance of Russian salad throughout Italy is something of a mystery. No one I've asked about it has come up with an explanation for its popularity. That doesn't make it any the less welcome. Personally, I love the stuff, all nuggets of gravelly veg slathered in mayonnaise, with tinned tuna mashed into it, if you're lucky. It goes along with hard-boiled eggs, another mild addiction of mine.

While I'm eating I overhear a man at a nearby table begins hectoring the waitress.

'Couscous! I don't want Taliban food!' he declares noisily.

The waitress giggles and explains that couscous has nothing to do with the Taliban. It's Sicilian. He's having none of it.

'I'm just a simple farmer and I don't want Arab food,' he insists. The waitress raises her eyebrows and sighs and directs him towards some definitely un-Islamic pork.

Then I'm sandbagged by a lasagna of mussels and clams. I'm not convinced that something that looks like a vast, pallid mattress, feels like flannel and tastes of mussels and clams, is ever going to be hailed as a classic. Of course I finish it because I'm that sort of guy, but it rather casts a shadow over an equally generous portion of fried squid and prawns, which actually are very good, their natural crunch boosted by being coated with fine polenta before being fried. I finish that, too, but with a sigh of relief rather than a sigh of content.

Back in town I console myself with an ice cream from the Gelateria Gola, a cornet of ginger and fondant chocolate, painstakingly shaped to look like a rose. It seems a pity to demolish this work of gelato craft, but I do so without any hesitation and much pleasure as I wander back to my quarters.

———

There's something deeply agreeable about the simplicity of Lampedusa. It feels more like the Isle of Wight than the Isle of Capri. It has few pretensions. Its airs and graces are modest ones. People are decent and kindly and hard-working, doing as many jobs as are needed to keep bread on the table and wine in the glass. They're friendly, too – the man in the laundry shop, the young woman in the Gelateria Gola, the chap serving me at the trattoria. Lampedusa may be closer to Africa than Europe, but it feels more Italian than Pantelleria or Trapani.

But the weather's turned capricious – sunny, grey, rainy, sunny again by the hour. The light takes on an astonishing clarity and purity, washed clean of evaporating water and dust particles by the rain, giving a certain fractious quality to the land. The wind continues to scupper my plans to visit Linosa, more of an isoletta than an isola, where jellyfish-eating leatherback turtles breed and where the great singer and composer of 'Volare', Domenico Modugno, used to spend his summers. I don't relish the prospect of dodging the showers and sheltering from the wind. If you can't lie in the sun or play in the sea, there's not a lot to do on Lampedusa. Much as I like the island, I decide that I'd be better off pushing on.

I go for a last dinner at the Trattoria Pescheria Azzurra on the via Roma, Lampedusa's Regent Street. A massive antipasto appears. It's a buffet in its own right – mini tuna burger; tuna in agrodolce; salted tuna with a slice of pear; fried, breadcrumbed red mullet fillet; potato, octopus and green olive salad; polpette di ricciola, amberjack rissoles, with peas and carrot strips; rings of very thinly sliced squid with fennel, red pepper and carrot strips. This is very sharp cooking. Each mini-dish sings clearly. I rather take for granted that the quality of the fish is going to be pretty glittery, but the skill and thoughtfulness behind each element comes as a fine surprise.

Lampedusa marks the end of one section of my odyssey. It's the last island of the Tyrrhenian Sea on the western, Mediterranean side, of Italy. After this, I'll be heading for the Tremiti Islands in the Adriatic, a different sea. I'll be moving from what was, historically, the Arab sphere of influence to the Byzantine and Ottoman sphere. This gives Lampedusa some kind of emblematic significance.

I peer at the slab of roasted ricciola, amberjack, a member of the tuna family, tiled with potato scales in front of me. Outside, couples and families saunter past, not dressed in the billowing finery of more fashionable islands, but in smarter versions of their daywear.

The fish is taut, fine textured with a delicate veal flavour, and the potato scales are crunchy with toasted breadcrumbs. I've eaten quite a bit of fish since I set out on this odyssey, and the food on Lampedusa, at the Trattoria Pescheria Azzurra in particular, is some of the most imaginative I've come across. Contemporary Lampedusan cooks show a sense of adventure tempered by common sense and skilful precision that makes some of the more highly touted eateries on other islands look distinctly pedestrian. Finally, lemon sorbet cleans my mouth of any fishy aftertastes. So civilised.

On the ferry back to Porto Empedocle is another consignment of refugees, kept off limits in the air-conditioned saloon area. I see them peering out of the windows as I make my way along the deck. They smile and wave, but I can't help but think of slaves being transported. How will their dreams of Europe and a new life match up with reality?

Sicily (again)
The next clutch of islands, the Tremiti, lies off the coast of Puglia

on the far side of Italy. As I look at the map, I realise just what a long way it is from Villa San Giovanni, on the other side of the Straits of Messina, to Termoli to catch the ferry. Too far to negotiate by Vespa. In order to get to Villa San Giovanni I'll have to get to Messina and in order to get to Messina, I'll have to cross Sicily.

Since I first came to Sicily in 1973, it has always struck me as one of the most singular places on earth, an island of great loveliness and full of extraordinary monuments, Greek theatres and Roman villas, Baroque towns and Norman churches and gracious, generous people. It's also an island of astounding ugliness and depressing urban development, of mounds of rubbish piled beside the road, vicious criminality and bureaucratic corruption. It's the only place I know where you come into contact with 5,000 years of history on a daily basis through its food, places, names, language and the attitudes of its people. That history has made Sicilians the masters of elliptical observation. The whole island seems to exist at a tangent to the rest of the world, a passionate, ironic comment on it.

On return to Porto Empedocle I feel that perhaps I've been a bit intemperate about the place. I don't think it'll ever be a place of beauty, but if I'd spent a little time earlier on the vast expanse of beach running from the town to the extraordinary stratified, multicoloured cliff face of Scala dei Turchi, like one of those glass tubes filled with different coloured sands, but on a colossal scale, or discovered that potent pastry, la rustichella, my earlier reactions might have been more measured.

La rustichella, as made at the Café Elisir, is a sweet dainty of beguiling charm. The pastry is ineffably light and crumbly, with that hidden richness produced by using strutto (pig fat) in the pastry. The base of the filling is chocolate, not too dark, but not milky. Above that is a billowing cushion of curdy ricotta, ewe's ricotta very specifically. The top is set with toasted almonds, with a faint edge of burnt bitterness and plosive crunch. And they're dusted, perfumed rather, with ground pistachios. Crunch, munch, crumble, cream, sweetness, balm, beauty, seduction – they're all there.

So, properly fortified, it's into the saddle once more, and off we set, Nicoletta and I.

———

I arrive in Caltanissetta, a large town almost slap bang in the middle of Sicily, in a state of despair. As I approached the city, I discovered that the notebook covering the last six weeks of travel had fallen from my back pocket somewhere between Canicatti some thirty or so kilometres back, and, well – where? The enormity of the loss is overwhelming, far worse than the earlier one on the ferry to Naples. The chances of recovery are zero. I've no one to blame but myself. Once again I'm torn between exasperation at my own incompetence, fury at the Fates, and the wretchedness of loss. I'm in a sombre mood as I set out to wander around neighbourhoods familiar from when I'd last passed through Caltanissetta almost ten years ago.

Almost immediately I come across a scene that would've been unimaginable then. The main square, the Corso Umberto, is full of kids playing table tennis, table football, chess, fencing, doing archery, weight lifting and chucking around a rugby ball – yes, a rugby ball, in central Sicily. They're kick boxing in the Municipio, the town hall, and there're gymnastics and football shooting practice in a sidestreet.

When I first visited, Caltanissetta was very depressed. Once it'd been the richest and most magnificent city in Central Sicily, built on the wealth of the sulphur mines. They'd long gone, the last mine closing in 1980, and the grand town houses, those monuments to capitalist greed and good taste, were crumbling away. There were no new industries to provide work, and a general air of gloom and despondency hung about the town. The only notable event in Caltanissetta's recent history had been the trial of Toto Riina, the murderous capo di tutti capi who declared war on the Italian state in 1995.

I don't know what's happened recently, but I get the distinct impression that Caltanissetta, if not exactly thriving, is definitely on the up. The market in the Via Consultore Benintende, that I remember with such affection, may be a shadow of its former bustling, thriving self, but perhaps that's because it's a Saturday afternoon. On the other hand, many of the town houses have been restored, the streets colonised by some major brands, and people walk around as if life means something rather than just being a burden. More than just a sprinkling of Muslims have obviously made their home here, which seems not inappropriate as the original Arab name of Caltanissetta was Qal'at al Nisa, meaning Fort of the Women. The cycles of history.

I go into one of my favourite buildings in Sicily, the Cathedral of Santa Maria Nova. It's handsome enough from the outside, if plumed here and there by shrubs growing at random in its upper reaches. But inside it's an intoxicating whirligig of baroque and rococo, cherubs and cherubims, swirls and twirls, flowers and leaves, mouldings and trompe l'oeil in gold leaf and ice-cream colours – strawberry pink, chocolate brown, fior di latte cream, pistachio green. And there, in a side chapel, is the bust of Johannis Jacono, Bishop of Ragusa and Caltanissetta, his arm flung out, his mouth agape, his mitre as firmly on his head as the helmet of a knight about to go into battle, his chins flowing down over the collar of his vestments, the very embodiment of the Church Militant and the Church Gourmand. He makes me laugh as he did before, remarkable as I'm still grieving the loss of the notebook.

The following morning, having been sunk in gloom for twelve hours, I decide I have to make at least some effort to find the vanished notebook, and I set about retracing my route of the day before. It's a very, very, very long shot, but I can't just let it go. So back down the Agrigento–Catania highway I go to Canicattì, about thirty kilometres, and start searching. I scan the sides of roads, gutters, verges as I go by as slowly as I can manage, trying to be philosophical, but in reality my spirits sinking lower and lower. Unlike previous losses, where the search areas had been clearly defined, the notebook with its brown leather cover could be anywhere along kilometres of both highways and by-ways. The probability of being reunited with it is slim to the point of impossible. This doesn't stop every scrap of litter, every gleam in the roadside scrub producing a surge of hope, and then a relapse to gloom. The verges become a blur. All shreds of optimism fade.

And then, blow me down, bowl me over, unbelievably there it is, lying on the verge beside a very minor road between Canicattì and Serradifalco, forlorn and a little scuffed, but otherwise none the worse for its adventure. At first I can't trust my senses. It isn't until I pick it up that I breathe out and say a word of thanks to all the powers that be. What's that bit in the Bible about the father rejoicing about the son who was lost and is found? I know just how the father felt. It's enough to suggest that the Age of Miracles is still with us.

Greatly cheered, I make my way to Agira, along some of the dodgiest roads I've yet come across. Some great beast appears to have bitten chunks of tarmac out of some. Earth has casually slipped away from underneath others, causing alarming dips and sags in the smooth tarmac. I pass through some countryside so remote and primitive it feels raw and brutal, a throwback to a different time. It's almost impossible to think of humans in such a space it's so elemental, and yet everywhere there are the signs of agriculture, sheep and cattle grazing furiously, stubble and tilled earth. As I pass a dark, low barn; a man emerges and watches me with stony-faced suspicion.

———

Agira is clamped to the top of one of the pinnacles that erupt from time to time from the Sicilian central plain. Around it spreads a vast undulating panorama. John Irving had told me that the local sport of Agira consists of throwing stone pins at stone balls on a hillside. He swore that he'd once seen men in flat caps playing it, around 1980. It seems entirely probable.

Agira was the birthplace of the historian Diodorus Siculus sometime in the first century BC. Not many people remember Diodorus Siculus but he wrote a universal history generally referred to as 'monumental', and was the first man to use the Olympic Games to date historical events. This might not seem much in itself, but bearing in mind the stop-start nature of our ability to measure time, it's not unimportant. The town prospered under the Arabs, and in the thirteenth century the Hohenstaufens rebuilt an earlier Arab/Byzantine castle, the fractured remains of which are silhouetted against the sky as I look up. Since then, Agira seems to have dozed in a gentle agricultural torpor.

My resting place, Case Al Borgo, is on the Via di Gesù, somewhere near the castle. That much I know from studying the map. The road leads up and up and up, and round and round, and up and round and then back on itself, but it doesn't lead where I need to go. The narrow, cobbled Arab/medieval streets weave in and out of each other with baffling complexity, like a ball of wool. I stop to ask various folk for the Via di Gesù. Men shake their heads. Women purse their lips. No matter how far up I get or how many times I go round, I can't get any closer. I'm getting desperate. I stop a man who's getting out of his car.

'I'm just back from work and need a shower,' he says. 'Hang on for half an hour and I'll lead you there.' I wait for half an hour, and then, to my surprise and relief, he returns. I follow his car through the streets around and around and up and up again until suddenly we come out at the back of Agira, near the remains of the medieval castle and there's the Case Al Borgo. My guide checks that there's someone in reception to look after me before driving off. I'm so overwhelmed I forget to ask his name. It's a poor reward for such graciousness, kindness, thoughtfulness.

My room is an eyrie perched high above the land across which I've just travelled. What appears to be the whole of the central plain of Sicily spreads out like an immense billowing bedspread below me, with Etna to my left, and reaching to Siracusa and the sea beyond a hundred kilometres away. The tinkling of sheep bells rises through the still air, sounding remarkably like the ring of a mobile phone. There's a curious disjunction between the individual, intimate precision of the bells and the immensity of the landscape.

I eat a fine dinner in a canteen below my room including slices of potent pork in an orange sauce with onions agrodolce and a frittata. It seems an improbable combination, but it's oddly effective. Or maybe it's simply the pleasure of eating meat again after weeks of nothing but fish.

After breakfast the next morning, the cheerful and beautiful Viviana manning reception deserts her post to guide me back down the town to the road to Bronte. Selfless generosity seems a common characteristic of the people of Agira. Without the kindness of Viviana and my nameless guide of the day before, I'd probably be going round and round and up and down still.

Wilson, Flynn, Pointe, Gauthier, Parkhurst, Gates, Bouchard, Sabbut run the names on the headstones, each identical but for the inscription below the name and the occasional Star of David among the crosses. The headstones are drawn up precisely aligned in parade-ground order and set in narrow beds cut in the trimmed green turf. Flowers grow in and around them. There are no weeds.

A Canadian War Cemetery set back from the road between Agira and Bronte, formal, neat, tidy, an orderly memorial in a disorderly landscape, shaded with pines, tranquil and beautiful and utterly quiet but for the sound of the wind in the trees, birdsong and the distant sound of a dog barking. How odd it must have been, for these young men to have come from Alberta, Winnipeg, Saskatoon and fought their way across this extraordinary island. How sad that they died here rather than seeing it as I'm seeing it.

I sign the visitors' book and head for Bronte.

Waves of eggy, smoky, boiled milk incense – I smell them before I realise what they are – pistachios.

The road that runs along the valley of the Simeto between Adrano and Bronte is hemmed by pistachio groves, the trunks of the trees leaping at random out of black volcanic rubble, gangling and untidy, branches twisting and curling, as if petrified in the middle of some mad dance. Clusters of nuts, pink teardrops, hang among the dusty, holly-green leaves.

I can hear, and occasionally see, groups of men and women among the trees bringing in the harvest. Some of the picking team bash the branches with bits of wood, causing the nut clusters to cascade onto the ground. Family members, friends and hired hands do the back-breaking business of picking them up.

'It's hard work,' says a young man, one of the pickers. 'But they are the best pistachios in the world.'

'What makes them so good?' I ask.

'The volcanic soil,' he says. 'It's full of minerals. Just enough water. The sun. And our passion for them.' It's an explanation I've heard before, but it's probably true. You need to have a certain passion to attend to the gruelling labour of picking up the fallen nuts. Given the nature of the terrain, it's impossible to envisage a machine capable of doing the same thing.

The nuts are put into sacks and the sacks transferred to a processing area. I say processing area. There may be splendid, hygienic, computer-controlled modern industrial units around Bronte, but the one I watch is outside a small house beside the road. Two women heft the sacks and pour the freshly picked fruits into an ingenious machine that shakes them all about, separating stalks and leaves from the nuts, and getting rid of the husks. The pistachios begin to look like the familiar nuts to which I'm addicted. They're spread out on the sheets to dry in the sun. For how long will depend on the sun, the heat, the nature of the harvest and the level of moisture in the kernels. They may be shelled and even skinned after that.

'Can I chat to you about pistachios?' I ask a woman raking out nuts on sheets in the sun in front of a house. I want to find out how you rate pistachios, what makes one pistachio superior to another, whether there are differences, how much they fetch, and whether this traditional form of harvest is under threat in any way, like the salt farmers at Trapani.

'No,' she snaps. 'I'm working.' She turns away and begins raking again.

That's that.

You couldn't accuse the Brontesi of not making the most of their famous nuts. They put them into absolutely everything – pastries, ice creams, salamis, cheeses. They're turned into sauces for pasta and used to make a crust on a piece of pork. Nothing, it seems, can't be dolled up by pistachios whole, pistachios chopped, pistachio crumbs, creamed pistachios. That mild, curiously penetrating, slightly sweet, perfumed flavour is absolutely inescapable.

The town of Bronte is strung out along a long slope. It's not beautiful, but it is interesting. In 1860 it was the site of one of the most atrocious episodes of Garibaldi's liberation campaign. Brigandage and civil unrest had afflicted much of the island in the vacuum after the expulsion of the Bourbons and their functionaries. Encouraged by notions of liberty and more equable distribution of land, there had been an uprising among the peasants of Bronte demanding land rights. Garibaldi sent his trusted lieutenant, Nino Bixio, to deal with it, which he did with great severity, summarily shooting several of the leaders. This act of barbarity is still remembered.

Among the estates the peasants demanded should be handed over was that of Maniace, owned by the Bridport family, descendants of the original owner, Admiral Horatio Lord Nelson, scourge of the French, hero of the nation, and Duke of Bronte. Nelson had been awarded the title, house, estate and vassalage of the peasants living on it, by a grateful King Ferdinand of Bourbon, after the admiral had deployed the power of the British fleet to help restore him to the throne of Sicily and Southern Italy.

I'm not sure that this was Nelson's or England's finest hour. Ferdinand was neither a good king nor a nice man. Nelson behaved with unusual brutality to Caracciolo, the leader of the short-lived Parthenopean Republic that had replaced Ferdinand, neither allowing him a fair trial, nor to be shot as requested when he was found guilty. He was hanged by Ferdinand's minions within twenty-four hours of the verdict. Nelson went on to hang a number of other supporters of the republic.

More to Nelson's credit was another, less trumpeted, effect on Sicilian history. After the Battle of the Nile in 1798 the admiral ordered up several hogsheads of Marsala, the fortified wine, from his friend, John Woodhouse. This gave the officers and men of the British fleet such a taste for the stuff that Marsala became the tipple of choice of the British upper classes, and fortunes were made by the Princes under the Volcano, as the Marsala dynasties were known, including that of the Florios, whose tuna canning factory on Favignana I had admired so much.

Although he signed himself Nelson Bronte, the admiral never visited his Sicilian retreat, which is about eight kilometres from the town of Bronte itself. It was inherited by Charlotte, a niece, who married Alexander, Viscount Bridport. The Bridport family continued to live there until 1982, when they sold the house and the estate to the commune of Bronte. Astonishingly, the vassalage of the local peasantry remained, a medieval survival, until the agricultural reforms of the 1950s.

Even here the Nelson estate behaved in a thoroughly reprehensible manner, according to Carlo Levi, whose account of peasant life in a remote corner of Calabria, *Christ Stopped at Eboli*, is a classic of clear-eyed reportage. In an equally remarkable book, *Le parole sono pietre* (Words are Stones) published in 1955, he recounts how the Nelson estate was forced to sell off a percentage of the land to tenant farmers under the reforms designed, in part, to break up the latifundia, the frequently gigantic estates owned by ex-patriot landlords, and managed by unscrupulous managers under the iniquitous gabelotto system. The Nelson trustees negotiated a high price for their land, sold it as directed, waited for the tenant farmers who had borrowed heavily to buy it to go bankrupt, and then bought it back at knockdown prices.

Over the years, the Bridports turned the property into a curious hybrid. The exterior is that of a handsome Sicilian country villa overlooking a central yard, while the interior is that of an English country house, with outside English lawns divided up by box hedges in the French style. All this has been lovingly restored by the Bronte Council.

The phrase 'lovingly restored' is something of a cliché, but it seems apt as I wander through the rooms that look out on the long, rectangular yard in one direction, and over the garden on the other. It might not be Blenheim, which the grateful British nation gave John Churchill, First Duke of Marlborough, but I imagine it was a damn sight easier to live in, and whatever the rights and wrongs of the behaviour of the Nelson estate, the commune of Bronte is clearly determined to make the best of the Nelson connection.

Each room is given a distinctly ornate, Sicilian accent by the floor tiles from Caltagirone, but all the furniture, paintings and pictures, glasses, decanters, knick-knacks, bits and bobs are those I'd expect to find in an English country house of the eighteenth and nineteenth centuries; a bit stuffy, a bit predictable, and very, well, English. There's a decanter and two glasses that belonged to Nelson. I wonder if he ever drank Marsala out of them. Our excellent guide can't say. Even the wallpapers are of the period and have the right feel to them. The only tiny detail I can find with which to take issue are the curtains. The materials are correct, but surely they'd have been interlined, rather than simply left as a single layer. The bathrooms are unusually large for the period, too.

It's like wandering through a vaguely familiar house in which the members of the family have just popped out for a walk or to change for dinner. I wouldn't be the least surprised to see copies of *The Field* or *Country Life* on a table, or a Labrador lying in front of the fire. There's even Virginia creeper covering most of the courtyard-side wall of the house facing onto the courtyard.

At the other end of the courtyard is what's left of the Benedictine Abbazia Maniace, a delightful Gothic-Norman church, austere by Sicilian standards, and made beautiful by its proportions and the light streaming through the plain windows. The nave soars upwards on pillars of dark, volcanic stone to a magnificent hammer-beam roof. The side naves are almost equally high. A fine Byzantine icon, purportedly painted by St

Luke, hangs on one wall. I haven't been aware of his artistic talent hitherto. The simplicity and spirituality of the building and the icon are rather at odds with a life-sized statue of an anguished-looking Jesus in questionable taste inside a kind of presentation case of hideous kitsch.

———

Mariano Brischetto rings me to say that he's going to appear in a performance of *La Bohème* in the Teatro Antico in Taormina that evening. Would I like to go? Why not? The Teatro Antico. Taormina. A performance of *La Bohème*. A warm summer's night. What else have I got on that's half as interesting? I tell Mariano to count me in.

The Teatro Antico at Taormina is spectacular in the evening light; a happy synthesis of Greek aesthetics and mastery of acoustics and Roman engineering, of stone and brick, of time and place. Curved banks of stone seats line the hillside. In a gap in the middle of the wall of Roman brick behind the scena, the lights of Giardini di Naxos and Calatabiano glitter beneath Etna. A plume of gas streams from its summit. A tiny slice of moon is just beginning to show in the darkening, velvet sky. It's a dreamscape of incomparable beauty, as dramatic as any production in the theatre. I wonder if Sophocles or Aeschylus had sat where I'm sitting, supervising production of their plays.

All, however, is not quite so harmonious down at the performance area.

'I've only just been told I'm singing Marcello,' says one tenor.

'But you've sung it before,' says Ross, the Welsh chorus master of the Teatro Massimo Bellini, and the man in charge of the Catania contingent.

'Oh yes. But I haven't been told who's singing Mimì.'

A woman comes up looking cross. 'There aren't any costumes for the band.'

'What do you mean?' says Ross.

'We were promised costumes and there aren't any.'

'Oh God. Perhaps you can play off stage,' suggests Ross.

There's a tremendous crash followed by a tinkling sound. The frame holding the tubular bells has fallen over. For a moment everyone looks rather embarrassed, and then the hubbub of preparation rises up again.

'This is meta-theatre,' Mariano says cheerfully, as he goes off to check his costume and changing room. 'Theatre within theatre.'

'I'm not religious,' says Ross, 'but, do you know, I've only been in this job for seven months, and they've got me believing in fate, destiny, the whole shooting match.'

The production is part of the Taormina Lirica Festival, a co-operation between the Taormina Musical Festival organisation and the Teatro Massimo Bellini of Catania. In theory the Teatro Massimo Bellini is providing the chorus and orchestra, the Taormina Lirica Musical Festival organisation is supplying everything else – the conductor, soloists, costumes and changing rooms. The Festival Puccini di Torre del Lago near Viareggio is responsible for the scenery. I ask Ross if involving three separate companies is normal practice in opera productions. He's about to answer when Mariano returns, no longer quite so cheerful.

'There aren't any changing rooms for the chorus.'

'No changing rooms for the chorus!' says Ross. 'But there must be! That was expressly specified in the letter we sent them. I'm sure it'll be fine. I'll go and talk to the director.'

It's about 7 p.m. and the performance is due to start at 9.15 p.m. As the three opera forces have never met each other before, it strikes me that this seems to be leaving such essentials as rehearsals and staging until rather late in the day. Still, they know what they're doing. Don't they?

Ross comes back. It's clear that, while the two organisations might know what they're doing, they don't necessarily know the same thing. The professional warmth is curdling to professional animosity. Mariano's becoming increasingly pessimistic.

'The trouble is,' he says, 'if we don't feel that they respect us, look after us properly, why should we care about the performance?'

Ross returns. His early affability has turned to outrage.

'I asked the festival director why he had ignored everything we had specified in the letter. Do you know what he said? "And why have you ignored all the things we requested?"' Ross's voice rises in indignation. 'He said that he'd never come across such an unprofessional company as the Teatro Massimo Bellini. Yes, he actually said that. I couldn't believe it.'

'When I asked about changing rooms for the chorus,' says Mariano, 'the conductor said, "The Berlin Philharmonic don't ask for changing rooms."'

'The conductor's an idiot. The Berlin Phil don't wear costumes,' snaps Ross.

They go back to their respective battles. I retreat to the higher reaches of the seats high above the fray.

There's a tremendous banging going on on the stage as the carpenters erect the scenery kindly provided by the Festival Puccini di Torre del Lago. The lights over the music stands begin to shine brightly. The orchestra coming to life issues genial burbling sounds. A man walks past me and waves in a friendly manner as if I'm a colleague. I've never seen him before. I assume that he assumes that I'm part of the great enterprise, too. I'm flattered. Would Aeschylus or Sophocles have recognised the scene below me? I rather think they would. I don't suppose the tropes, dramas and artistic tensions of theatre life have changed much in a couple of thousand years.

Lighting tests begin. Various sections of the stage suddenly leap into brilliant relief and then vanish into darkness. The evening is warm and humid. I wonder if there's going to be enough willing suspension of disbelief to carry us through 'Che manina gelida'.

A short, plump man balanced precariously on a chair keeps trying to adjust a light at the top of a high stand. He stands on his tiptoes. His fingers keep just brushing the lower rim of the shade. He does it over and over and over again. I wonder at his obstinacy and persistence and futility. The French horns begin their warm-up routine. Parp, parp-parp, parp-parp-parp. Then the trumpets and the strings. What a splendid, civilised cacophony.

At 7.45, the conductor turns up. He's slender, fiftyish, long hair curling over the collar of his open-necked shirt. He appears crisp and autocratic. He takes the orchestra through various parts of the overture. The soloists appear looking nonchalant. The conductor moves on to key arias and staging of Act One. Everyone eases into their role as if they're sliding their feet into old slippers. They must have done this hundreds of times. Not with this conductor, perhaps. It takes a little time before the maestro's happy. Act Two: ditto. There's just time to run through Act Three, but not, sadly, for Act Four.

By this time it's 8.40. I see Ross and Mariano for the last time before the performance. They are not in the best of moods. Still no changing rooms for the chorus.

How did the rehearsal go?

'Not so good,' says Mariano.

'He [the conductor] didn't even notice the set for Act Two wasn't the right one,' hisses Ross.

When someone asked George V which was his favourite opera, he replied, '*La Bohème.*'

'Why is that, Your Majesty?'

'Because it's the shortest.'

His majesty would have been disappointed in the Lirica production. It begins at 9.40. I realise we're in for the long haul when the carpenters reappear after Act Two, and spend the best part of forty minutes constructing the set for Act Three, the Barrière d'Enfer, in front of our eyes. The audience clap warmly when they finally finish and march off stage.

The music tugs at the heartstrings. The chorus is magnificent and the children particularly impressive. Mimi finally expires around 12.25 a.m., Rodolfo's grief-stricken and it's all over. The rather diminished audience give enthusiastic, if rather relieved, applause. And, of course, I enjoy it all hugely, the theatre and the meta-theatre. Who wouldn't? It's not often you get to see behind the scenes of any production, and witness the battles for artistic integrity at first hand. It's all pure delight, stretched out over six hours. Forget *Die Meistersinger von Nürnberg*. Give me the dual drama of a production of *La Bohème* involving three opera companies any time.

As Mariano drives me back to Bronte, I tell him that I was surprised that Mimi hadn't died of old age long before consumption took her.

Nicoletta and I glide out of Bronte, heading for Capo d'Orlando, the last staging post before Messina. The road leads across fields of pumice towards Randazzo, 'City of Wine' as it declares itself. It was the headquarters of Peter I of Aragon during the Sicilian Vespers rebellion of 1282, and the town still has a distinctly medieval aspect, which is remarkable given that it was hit by something like 1,200 bombing raids during the war.

The road continues across the Alcantara Valley and up into the hills of the Nebrodi beyond, an area of Sicily more like the bosky uplands of the Aspromonte in Calabria than the rest of Sicily's largely woodless interior. Thick stands of holm oak, cork trees, Sicilian pine, ash, beech, maple and hazel cast cool shadows across the road. Somewhere among them scamper and forage the suino nero dei Nebrodi, the Black Pig of the Nebrodi that, a few years back, had provided the sweetest, most exquisite slice of cured ham I've ever eaten in my life. Every now and then the forest gives way to clearings in which creamy cattle munch on mountain grasses, and to villages clinging to the sides of hills.

Even though it's deliciously sunny, there's the slight murmur of autumn in the air, of mists and mellow fruitfulness. Rose hips and crab apples, as bright as Christmas lights, light up the verge. Wild pears, blackberries, hazels and walnuts crowd the tangle of vegetation. The leaves on the maples are just, just starting to turn, the faintest tinge of yellow infusing the green.

Presently I pass a man bent over in a rough field gathering something. Cicoria, he says. Wild chicories. They look like the flattened clumps of leaves you see around the base of a dandelion flower, but slightly furry rather than shiny.

'Are they good to eat?'

'They're good for cows,' he replies. 'They must be good for us.'

I don't challenge his logic, but ask if I can taste one.

He trims off the earthy root with a sharp, worn knife, bracing the plant against a gnarled thumb.

'These are the first of the season,' he says. 'They're best right now, just after a bit of rain.'

The leaves are subtly fleshy and crunchy and slightly bitter.

'How do you eat them?'

'Raw, like a salad,' he says, 'with oil and lemon. And cooked, boiled.'

He goes back to picking, and I go back to the road, following its switchbacks until it comes out by the sea and the highway that leads to Capo d'Orlando.

———

A melancholy sweetness and quiet has descended on the town. When I passed through in July, it'd been pulsating with the unconstrained energy of holiday-making. The beach had been all but invisible beneath groves of sunbrellas. The sea had been a playground, the air raucous with the seagull cries of children. Bars bustled. Restaurants turned away customers. Traffic streamed along the promenade without cease. The streets hummed with folk bent on having a jolly time.

All that's ebbed away. Only one or two sunbrellas dot the tawny sand, brightly coloured, abstract circles. The sea is flat blue. The sky is flat blue. The occasional car trundles along the seafront. Some of the restaurants are shut up. In others waiters go about their business in a listless fashion, more in hope than expectation. The scene has the stillness of one of those long takes designed to express the ennui of life in such films as *L'Avventura* or *La Notte* directed by Michelangelo Antonioni.

The Ristorante Odeon, where I'd had that splendid dinner with Anna Venturi and her husband, is open, even if hardly a quarter full. I settle to zuppa di ceci e vongole, earthy with chickpeas, sweet with clams, rife with garlic, fruity with tomatoes; and then something called piatto rustico, a splendid hurly-burly of bits of sausage, strips of egg, shreds of green chicory and battlements of fried bread. What a splendid pub dish this would make.

The following day I make for Messina, where I meet up with Mariano Brischetto once more, and we settle down in a café, Irrera 1910, that I first visited in 2005. I renew my passionate affair with the sublime granita di caffè con panna e brioche, fall almost as deeply in love with a sospiro di monaca (nun's sigh) a kind of ethereal macaroon; and satisfy my lust for Irrera's incomparable pistachio and coffee ice creams. Ah me, what bliss. I tell Mariano about the hours I'd spent in Irrera's laboratorio, where these incomparable delicacies are created by gnarled, sceptical, passionate craftsmen.

For logistical reasons I have to leave Nicoletta in Messina. She's going to be transported by truck to Termoli in Puglia on the far side of Italy, where we'll be reunited after I've finished with the Tremiti. I'm travelling by train. It's time to go, to say goodbye to the bosom of the Madre Mediterranea that's sustained me for so long.

In his majestic study, *La Mediterranée*, Fernand Braudel proposes the concept of la longue durée, which I roughly interpret as 'the long haul'. Braudel's theory, as I understand it, is that there are various levels of time: geographical time; social, economic and cultural cycles; and the histoire des évènements, the events that impact on transitory, ephemeral lives of individuals. The last months reflect all three aspects of Braudel's longue durée.

Of course Mediterranean isn't simply one, but a mosaic of multiple seas – Tyrrhenian, Adriatic, Aegean, Ionian, Balearic and even small sub-set seas such as the Ligurian, the Levantine, the Saharan, the Sardinian, the Thracian, the Myrtoan, the Icarian – each of which has its own particularity to the people who live by it. It's a kaleidoscope rather than a jigsaw, as the relationships between them are forever in flux, fracturing, shifting, changing and exchanging.

At the same time, the Mediterranean has a physical unity, a discrete identity, a wholeness which is appealing to the outsider. In the end, the Mediterranean is as much about the lands surrounding it as it is about the water. Land and water together create a vast canvas on which the history of conquest, trade, social change, migration, scientific progress and religious conflict has been acted out. They've shaped the narrative of Western Europe, which, in turn, has shaped, for good or ill, the rest of the world. The Mediterranean Sea, itself, is active and passive. It breeds myth and legend, and enforces harsh realities. Its characteristics open the way to a vast diversity of possibilities and have affected the course of history. It is both frame and picture, fable and reality.

Braudel might have treated the Mediterranean as a subject of study, something about which to be coolly analytical and objective, but I'm not coolly analytical or objective. I'm a sentimental kind of chap. I feel warmly towards the Mediterranean. Of course I know it isn't sentient, any more than Iddu is, and yet, just like those cool, intelligent, rational professional folk on Stromboli, I find that I've developed a kind of relationship with Her. She's been ample and kind and provided a fabulous panorama in which to travel, explore, experience, in which to swim, beside which to lie and dream.

Cardinal Newman wrote the hymn 'Lead Kindly Light' after crossing the same straits in a storm; his ship was guided to safety by the lighthouse at Messina. Thank heavens no storms are forecast, and ferries are busy, unsentimental things. They carry their passengers irrespective of their emotional condition. Thirty minutes from Messina to Villa San Giovanni on mainland Italy. Chop-chop. No time for regret or mourning. None of that sentimental nonsense. I hardly get on before I get off, and suddenly, there I am, sitting on the platform at Villa San Giovanni station, waiting for the train to take me on the first leg of my journey to Termoli, and the Tyrrhenian Sea part of my Mediterranean odyssey is over. I don't even have Nicoletta for company.

San Domino

There's a stiff wind. The sea's fluid chipped slate. A shaft of sun illuminates a patch of water a kilometre or so away, for a moment giving the surface the silvery glimmer of chain mail. The aliscafo heading for San Domino sways back and forth, heavily laden with weekenders, mostly in their forties and fifties. It's some relief when we dock.

I settle into the Hotel Rossana, which looks out over the harbour towards San Nicola, San Domino's sister island. The day is cool and pale, with silver-grey clouds threatening rain. It soon clears however, the sun comes out and I head off to explore.

San Domino is an exquisite, irregular hump, capped with a canopy of brilliant green Aleppo pines. They fill the warm air with the sharp perfume of resin. Their trunks form screens around functional, white-painted, cuboid holiday villas. Pathways wind between them, leading from cala to cala – cove to cove. They're architectural and sculptural, aesthetic and practical.

San Domino is really just one large resort, artfully decked out as an island covered in beautiful pines. You can swim in the pristine waters. You can lie on the rocks in the sun or on the sand of the few beaches. There're some fine, easy-paced walks. The adventurous can go diving. There's a day trip to San Nicola, a five-minute water taxi ride away. There's a bar or two, and that's San Domino done. No night life to speak of, no cinemas or playgrounds or other distractions other than eating. There're plenty of restaurants, and some are pretty good, but compared to the islands on the Tyrrhenian side of Italy, the Tremiti are virgin territories when it comes to shopping opportunities and other diversions. As on Ventotene, people come here to get away from all that stuff, to slip into neutral, soak up primal delights and chill.

Most of the villas and hotels stand a little way back from the shore perimeter. A few just peek through the green canopy; sensible family places, not unhandsome in a way, linked by broad streets paved with wavy bricks, just suitable for wheeling baby buggies and the odd car and van delivering luggage or other essentials. There's a village of San Domino with a square that functions less as a common space and more as a gap around which cluster bars, gelaterias, trattorias and the island's few mini-markets.

Away from the designated roads and paths, in what the locals call 'il paese', the countryside, I stumble across a rather different San Domino – encampments of mouldering mobile homes, caravans and shacks, piles of rusting machines, stashes of pipes and bricks, pick-up trucks, pens with chickens and geese, abandoned boats higgledy-piggledy, guarded by formidable women and men. There're orchards and patches for growing vegetables, parts of the support system for the thousands who rent the houses or stay in the hotels every year, carefully tucked away out of casual view.

Curiously for a short time, San Domino was the only place in Europe at that time where gays could be openly gay. Between 1938 and 1939 Mussolini sent homosexuals there. That, in itself, is curious, because homosexuality wasn't officially recognised by the Fascist state. It was deemed inconsistent with Italian virility. Out of sight, out of mind. By all accounts the living conditions had more in keeping with a boot camp than a holiday camp, but there must have been worse places to be imprisoned (in Germany, open homosexuals were sent to concentration camps).

I settle down to chill, too, writing, lying about, snorkelling, walking, reading, dozing, eating and dozing some more. The weather is becoming more changeable by the day, cool and blowy and damp one moment, hot and sunny the next. Little by little the island is beginning to shut up shop for the season. After the weekend, the crowds thin. One or two of the bars and eateries have already closed. The remaining holidaymakers are scattered across the tables that, only a week or so ago, were crammed with folk. The cale, the inlets, that appear to have been designed by nature for sun and sea bathing, are usually empty by 5 p.m., the paths deserted, the roads quiet. Twice a day, the road to the harbour below my room in the Hotel Rosanna resounds to the clatter of suitcases on wheels and the flap-flap of flip-flops coming down to catch the ferry.

San Nicola

The energy, the determination, the willpower, the sheer blinding confidence, that's what strikes me about San Nicola. There, on the crest of the island, the archipelago's nominal administrative centre, is a fortified, castellated, towered and postern-gated abbey, the Abbazia di Santa Maria a Mare, a powerful statement of the Church Militant. Walls merge into the vertical sides of the island. A steep, narrow, walled path leads to a fortified postern gate. Any invading force would struggle to get two abreast. Just before the gate, the path takes a sharp left turn, so that any attacking momentum would have to check and swivel before carrying on.

The abbey was founded by Benedictine monks in the ninth century. They built the core of the existing structure and walls in 1045 to guard against Muslim incursions. Later Cistercian monks took over guard duties, although not as effectively as they might as the abbey was sacked by the Dalmatian 'pirates' from Omis in 1334. In 1442 the Lateran Canons bought the islands and set about rebuilding and improving the defences to such effect that they managed to hold off an attack by the Ottoman Navy in 1567.

Later the monks were thrown out by King Ferdinand of Naples, who, in 1843, turned the island into a colony for the criminals and prostitutes deported from the slums of Naples to start new lives, with a view to letting them create and run their own society in quiet seclusion. There may have been a thought that, left to their own devices, they would create an Eden-like sanctuary, full of equality, liberty and sisterly and fraternal love. Sadly, that was not how things turned out. Some became fishermen, but in a few years the island became so chaotic and violent that the king had to send in the military to establish order.

It's difficult to associate modern-day San Nicola with such

a seamy past. The older buildings aren't exactly in pristine condition, and the more modern ones are crumbling away, and there's quite a lot of unsightly pipework and scaffolding around the place. But the scraps of the medieval original and subsequent monkish additions – a chapel, a long arcade with fine elegant pillars, and, I'm pleased to see, a substantial and spacious refectory – show how impressive the place had once been.

The chapel, in particular, is a handsome structure built of creamy stone, with an exhilarating sense of space. It has an unusual square nave with a wooden roof above, decorated with biblical scenes and supported on massive quadrifoliate pillars, and below, a Byzantine mosaic floor of geometric patterns and symbols in cream, black and umber. These mismatched elements have been blended into a moving whole by the passage of time and the force of the history.

A group of some thirty Poles file in, arrange themselves in a semi-circle and begin to sing. Their unaccompanied voices fill the space, austere and richly textured at the same time, plaintive and celebratory, communal and singular, past and present woven together in faith by faith. I'm transported to a time when the abbey thronged with martial monks and such plainchant was commonplace. It's odd to think of the prostitutes, jades, robbers, cutpurses, bagmen and murderers of nineteenth-century Naples capering around the place.

An undulating flat area of stone and low-growing sea shrubs extends well beyond the part enclosed by the fortifications. It ends at a rather rickety monument to 1,300 Libyans who were sent to the island between 1911 and 1912 for resisting Italian colonial rule. Most of them died there.

From the crest of San Nicola, I look out over the narrow stretch of sea to Caprera. In theory it isn't inhabited, although I can see one house. Another mystery. As I walk back along the path, I smell goats. But that's absurd. Why on earth should there be goats on San Nicola? And then I see them, far below me, scampering along the rocks by the sea's edge, jet black, and with magnificent, corkscrew horns. How the devil had they got here?

San Domino (again)

I lie on my back in the amethyst water of the Cala Matana, looking up at the rim of crinkled sandstone rock just above sea level, at the billowing clouds of Aleppo pines, their tops turning green-gold in the evening sun, and think 'This is it. This is why people come here. This is what they come for. Loafing. Idleness. Escape.'

How rarely do we treat ourselves to the luxury of such simple indulgence, a luxury that costs nothing. 'Thoughtless' is generally seen as a pejorative adjective, and yet the absence of thought opens the way for instinct, for pure pleasure, for the cool silk of the sea on your skin, the warmth of sun upon your head, the scent of pine resin, the oscillating lattice of light over the rocks, the canopy of intense green needles, the limitless blue sky above; just hanging there in the water, not moving, without motivation, compulsion, responsibility, the modern imperative for action.

I climb out of the sea and lie in the sun and listen to the suck and rustle of the waves. Presently a lean, muscular, tanned and tattooed young man emerges from the water. He could be some mythical, oceanic creature were he not clutching a plastic bag. He takes a limp octopus out of it, and begins bashing it on the rocks. He's joined by his girlfriend, who'd been sunbathing higher up the shore. She comes leaping from rock to rock like a chamois, with that utter surety of the young. She could be as mythical a creature as he until she starts berating him, shrill as a parrot. He pays her no attention and continues bashing the octopus.

Is the Adriatic Sea so very different from the Tyrrhenian Sea in, by or on which I'd spent the earlier agreeable months? Aren't they both simply two of the many seas that make up the Mediterranean? It seems to me that they each have a very distinctive character. The Adriatic doesn't have the presence of the bigger sea. The mainland never seems very far away. It feels more like a lake than a sea, safer, sensible, more delicate. The Mediterranean is Madre Mediterranea, big-bosomy, active, muscular. The Adriatic feels like the Mediterranean's softer, milder sister. All nonsense, of course. A sea is a sea is a sea, impersonal, powerful, occasionally violent. It's odd the directions solitude and sunlight can spin your mind.

The sun's sinking now, a broad golden blade gliding across the smooth surface of the water. Colour's slowly draining from the world. The shades of blue on the sky coalesce, grow more uniform, denser. The rocks turn solid black. The sea shifts from teal and gold to teal and silver. Cooler air is stealing in. In a day or so I'll be heading up the Adriatic coast to Venice.

There's still a way to go, but I have a sense that this wonderful journey, this window in life, is beginning to draw to a close. For five and a half months I've been a single traveller, an individual, simply following the dictates of my own desires. I haven't had to subscribe to any group ethic or dynamic. Of course there have been periods of loneliness and moments, places or episodes when I'd thought 'I wish so and so was here to share this,' but taken all in all, it's been sublime, the sense of freedom exhilarating. Still is exhilarating even though, little by little, the fetters of a more ordered, responsible, humdrum existence are beginning to snap into place.

I go to Da Pino up in the village for a last supper of zuppa di pesce. Like all the trattorias and eateries on San Domino, Da Pino is decorated in the disarming style of the 1980s – naff, chintzy, fussy, cluttered, a touch gloomy. There's a group of three at another table: a balding, bearded young man; a slightly older woman, hair pulled back from a lovely, open face; and a deeply tanned, older man in red trousers and white shirt and with round, blue spectacles, white stubble and a white skull. I can't work out the dynamics of the relationships. Who's with whom? Is the woman the lover of the younger man? Or the wife of the older? Or younger sister, perhaps? Or parents with a son? Unlikely. The ages aren't right. And there are small signs of subtle currents. The older of the two men is the dominant force at the table, but the woman seems to exert a subtle influence over the other two. Their conversation is sporadic as the woman and the older man spend a good deal of time consulting their smart phones, while the young man stares silently into space. How I love the theatre of public eating.

The zuppà di pesce arrives in the same kind of terracotta bowl as Riccardo d'Ambra insisted was suitable for cooking coniglio all'Ischitana. It's a seething magma of intense tomato and marine goo cloaking chunks of bream, red mullet, and eel. A claw of a langoustine extends out of it like the arm of a drowning man, blue shells of mussels gape, and chunks of toasted bread rise in amber pinnacles. A fall of grassy parsley freckles the surface. It has the florid tartness of tomato and the fleshy sweetness of marine life. It's all I need.

As I walk back down to the Hotel Rossana, vertical strikes of lightning fracture the sky over the mainland every few seconds. Definitely time to go.

Mainland Italy

I head north towards Venice along the Strada Adriatica, SS16, on Nicoletta. The weather's turned distinctly autumnal. Soon it begins to rain so hard I have to take refuge in a station until the worst has blown through. Only a few days before I'd been wandering around in a pair of bathing trunks and nothing else. Now I'm wearing two T-shirts, a waterproof jacket and socks. I would be wearing long trousers, too, but I only have one pair and I can't take the risk of them becoming spattered with mud as I need them in pristine condition in a day or two. So shorts it is, and cold my knees and legs are. It doesn't bode well for the next 400 or so kilometres.

The Adriatic coast is forlorn and desolate now the season's done. Cloud and wind drain the colour out of the landscape. The sand is dull fawn, the sea a murky grey-green, the sky ashen and full of ragged, racing clouds. Most of the bars and restaurants along the foreshore are closed and shuttered. In one or two the owners and their friends sit and gossip, not seriously expecting any business, going through the motions. Various gaudy banners look grubby and tattered. Clusters of plastic boats rest on the shore, amidst the poles that would've carried bright sunbrellas a week or so before. The hotels are closed up, too, their windows blank and dead. Solitary walkers form black silhouettes on the beaches, sometimes with dogs, sometimes not. Kilometre after kilometre after kilometre of sand, sand, sand from which the wind has removed the traces of footsteps.

The Strada Adriatica runs parallel to the coast, through one seemingly endless ribbon of dreary development – shops, factories, hotels, holiday apartments. Resorts are marked on the map – Ortona, Francavilla al Mare, Montesilvano Marina, Roseto degli Abruzzi, Giulianova – but it's difficult to tell where one begins and the next ends. They blur into each other, drab and cheerless. Devoid of blithe families and shouting children, they feel like the discarded husks of a lost civilisation.

There are pretty bits and handsome towns, too. I like Fano, and the centre of Pesaro with its core of a Renaissance town centre. There's a lovely stretch of landscape just between Termoli and Vasto, and just before Ancona, where the road turns inland away from Numana and Siriolo. How beautiful this stretch of country, fought over again and again down the centuries, must have been once.

Generally, it's day after day of hard pounding to Rimini, where I'm going to rest before advancing on Venice. I check into the aptly named Grand Hotel, an architectural pavlova designed by Paolo Somazzi and lovingly kept in pristine condition by the Batani family. Although opened in 1908, it's a majestic monument to late nineteenth-century hotel luxury, all parquet flooring, Venetian glass chandeliers and creamy French grandiloquence. It's the first time on this journey I've spent a night in anywhere so luxurious, and it's little short of transcendental to subside into the billows of comfort, another stage in the process of re-entry into the real world.

Rimini was the power base of the brutal, cultured Malatesta family between the thirteenth and fifteenth centuries, and then changed hands with remarkable frequency until it reinvented itself as a resort in the nineteenth century. It suffered badly during the Second World War, but has gradually rebuilt itself as the conference centre of the Adriatic.

Personally, I find the story of how Rimini captured the Adriatic conference market rather less than gripping. However, for whatever reason, Rimini is the birthplace of a remarkable number of creative figures, among them Hugo Pratt, Italian in spite of his name, graphic novel genius and creator of Corto Maltese, a sailor-adventurer, the son of a Cornish sailor and a prostitute/witch known as 'La Nina de Gibraltar'; Massimo Tamburini, the genius behind the fabulous, lithe Ducati 916; and, most famously, Germaine Greer's lover, Federico Fellini, who lovingly evoked the characters and places of his native town in many of his films.

Now I'm ready for Venice, sadly without Nicoletta. I can't take her into Venice. I arrange for her to be shipped back to England. The tachometer says that we've done 5,166 kilometres together. Never a complaint. Never a cross word. Never an upset. She's been steady as a rock on good roads and bad, on piste and off, up hill and down dale. I feel about her as a racehorse owner must feel about a favourite, successful thoroughbred when its racing days are over. I can't bear to sell her. She'll be ferried back home to spend a well-earned retirement, pottering around the lanes of Gloucestershire when I get back. Still, it's a tearful parting.

8
ON ARRIVAL IN ITHACA

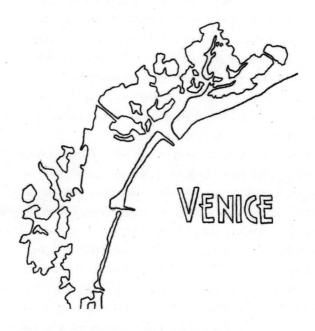

OCTOBER 2015

Venice

Venice

There he is, standing by the pillar with a lion on top in St Mark's Square, as he'd said he would be.

It seems rather improbable now, that my friendship with Rory Gibson was forged on the rugby fields around Berkshire thirty or so years ago; cold, muddy afternoons followed by sessions in a succession of pubs where cold and bumps and bruises were dispelled by drink and laughter.

Age has been more than kind to him. He may have made a pre-emptive strike against baldness by shaving his head, but he's still instantly and completely recognisable as the same person. The muscular body is looking remarkably trim. Above the shoulders, a thick neck, head shaped somewhere between a rugby ball and a football, deep-set eyes full of quizzical expression, irony and good humour beneath a slightly overhanging forehead. He embraces me as if he's a drowning man and I'm a life-jacket. Lois looks on with amusement.

'Matt, you old man.'

'Drink?'

'Oh, yeah!' he says with the faintest curl of his upper lip, and a slight wag of the head.

It's difficult to give the exact quality of that 'Oh, yeah!' There's the slightest of pauses between the 'Oh' and the 'yeah' before the emphasis falls heavily on the second word. The 'yeah' is slightly elongated, 'yeeaah', Rory's inflection rising towards the end, expressing both enthusiastic endorsement of the suggestion and absurdity that it's been made in the first place.

Rory leading, we make our way across St Mark's Square and into a labyrinth of narrow streets beyond, each more clogged than the last with map-and-water-bottle-wielding, backpack-loaded tourists. After a few minutes, he ducks into the Devils Forest Pub, a kind of bar-cum-pub already raucous with rugby fans of all nations, gathered to watch England versus Australia in the Rugby

World Cup. By good fortune we find an unoccupied corner and settle down, torn between a flood of happy reminiscence and the drama of the game unfolding on the TV screen.

Venice marks the end of my odyssey, my last port of call, my Ithaca. In some ways it's the summation of island culture. The city, itself, is built on several islands, and its cultural hegemony embraces over a hundred others. But there's a unique conceptual unity to it that sets it apart. Venice is as much a place of legend and imagination as it is of fact and history. Looking at it from across the lagoon, at its cupolas, domes, towers, palazzi and houses, set flat along the skyline, it seems preposterous that it exists at all. It is fantastical and dreamlike, something lifted from an antique fable. Autumn in Venice, days of mists and mellowness, of golden sunshine and the soft dying of summer, it seems the proper place to end my progress.

When I planned this, I hadn't taken into account either the Rugby World Cup or Rory. Initially, they seem at odds with the narrative that had formed in my head, but happenstance, serendipity, fortune is part of the texture of travel. They simply add another seam of richness to the journey.

Lois has come to join me for an extended weekend, and it seems right that she should be here. She's been the heartbeat of the journey. Whenever I've wavered, she has given me encouragement. If I questioned my motives for undertaking this indulgent fantasy, she said that she was proud to have a dad who would do these things. If I got fed up or felt lonely, as occasionally I did, she told me that self-pity didn't suit me, that I was bloody lucky to be doing what everyone else dreamed of doing and I should generally buck up my ideas. Anyway I thought she would probably enjoy Venice and its oddities. The evening surfs through on a breaker of mirth and nostalgia.

The next morning we all walk from the Rialto Market to Fondamenta Nuove to take the water bus to Torcello. It's a brilliant, warm, sunny day. The city is looking at its most seductive. The faded pinks, browns, umbers, creams, yellows and streaky greys glow. The winding lanes of water, the hump-backed bridges, the endless variety of windows, doorways, door frames, wrought-iron gates and wind guards, tiny gardens and formidable fronts, and the varying heights of the buildings seem juxtaposed with perfect aesthetic judgement. Even decay – crumbling plaster, exposed bricks, braces preventing walls from sliding apart, blistered paint, decaying stonework – has an exquisite lustre. Every twist and turn of our walk throws up another and another perfectly composed cliché of buildings and canals, boats moored or moving at random as if placed just there by some artistic master hand.

Quite by accident, just before we get to Fondamenta Nuove we stumble across the Chiesa dei Gesuiti strongly recommended by my brother Johnny. 'Not to be confused with the Chiesa dei Gesuati. Not nearly so interesting,' he'd said sternly.

It's as astounding as he said it would be, not for intrinsic architectural merit or even beauty, but for the singular craftsman-ship of the marble work. Johnny had been particularly taken with the steps leading up to the altar, where the marble is carved to look like a carpet flowing down over them. That is singular, but even more so are the curtains swagged and bagged either side of a pulpit balcony halfway down the nave. It takes me a minute or two to realise that they're marble, too, and not cloth of some kind. Aside from these wonders, every wall is covered with black-and-white marble patterns of such bold intricacy that they remind me of Maori tattooing. The motifs rise to a nave and apse gilded and painted with hallucinogenic opulence. I might question the aesthetic judgement, but the exhibition of decorative skill is utterly captivating.

Rather excited by this unexpected glory, we catch the

water bus that goes to Torcello by way of Murano, Burano and Mazzorbo. The novelty of travelling by water bus never wears off. The very act of being apart from the land produces different perspectives, and there's something soothing and leisurely about the movement of the boat. At the same time I have a sense of adventure from witnessing the skill and nerve of the bus driver negotiating the busy waterways, and from admiring the easy expertise of the conductor as he or she loops the mooring rope around the stanchions at each stop and uses the momentum of the boat to draw the bus into the correct part of the station so that we can embark or disembark.

Most of the passengers disembark at Murano to look at glass blowing or Burano for cloth making. A few get off at Mazzorbo. By the time we get to Torcello after about forty minutes, the passengers have been reduced to a rump.

Ernest Hemingway spent some months on Torcello in 1948 writing *Across the Water and into the Trees* (an unreadably bad book). It's a good place to write because there aren't many distractions, but on such a day as this, filled with cheer and excitement, with the sun shining and all very right with the world, Torcello is the only place to be. A path leads alongside a narrow canal, past a number of minor trattorias, to the Locanda Cipriani and its gardens, generally acknowledged to be one of the prettiest, if not the prettiest, restaurant to eat at in the whole Venetian lagoon.

And so it is, flower beds lambent with colour, bosky and shaded. The Locanda has the easy, muscular confidence of a place that knows exactly what it's doing and is doing it extremely well. It isn't about the food so much, although the food is pretty good, but about that rare and happy synthesis of the senses, when pleasures at several levels fuse together into seamless experience.

We sit in the shade. The flowers glimmer around. The tablecloth is crisp with starch, and as brilliant as the egrets on

Asmara. The glasses and cutlery glitter. Waiters, dressed in traditional white jackets and black ties, move easily back and forth in that ordered choreography that I find as delightful to watch as it is to be served by. A great restaurateur told me once that perfect service should pick you up in a smile as you come through the door, and hold you in it until you're placed gently back on the mat ready for departure. That's the Locanda Cipriani.

We're cosseted. We're flattered. We're soothed. We're managed with faultless professionalism and charm. A bottle of Prosecco, please. Brut, signore? Not so dry, please. Extra dry is better, signore; and it is. And so's the Pinot Bianco that our waiter chooses when I suggest Pinot Grigio, and cheaper. And so are the gnocchi with scampi and chanterelles; and the John Dory with tomatoes and capers; and the pancake filled with sweetened ricotta flamed in Cointreau – my darling, so old fashioned.

It isn't great food, challenging or innovative, but it's very good food. The flavours are genial and generous. Lois scoffs tagliatelle with Gorgonzola and prosciutto, and follows up with turbot with funghi porcini. Rory sets about fish soup and then monkfish and then apple and custard tart. We have a second bottle of the Pinot Bianco. We have grappas. We have coffee. We have fun. There's an aura of sublimity about the day. It's a time and a place for chat, for happy reminiscence, story telling, laughter and deep pleasure in life.

We pay and wander round the corner to the elegant and handsome Cathedral of Santa Maria Assunta, a Venetian-Byzantine church of red brick, and home of the skull of Saint Cecilia, the patron saint of music. It was founded in AD 639, renovated in AD 864 and then again in AD 1008. It contains some striking mosaics, some of the oldest in the lagoon, one a particularly energetic version of the Last Judgement, a rather disturbing Harrowing of Hell, the magnificent calm of an eleventh-century Virgin Hodegetria framed against a sheet of golden mosaic, and a wonderful hammerbeam roof. There's just enough culture to instil a scintilla of serious purpose to offset the delicious indulgence of lunch.

Possibly indulgence won out in the end, because, when we return to Venice proper, we go for a gondola ride. Brutally expensive, so naff, such fun.

———

It's a story of easy days, easy company. Each morning Lois and I walk from the flat I've rented in Dorsoduro; find breakfast of coffee, orange juice and buns filled with prosciutto and cheese; meet Rory; journey by water ferry, potter on foot; take a glass of Prosecco whenever we pass a bar; eat cicchetti, those little Venetian savoury nibbles of ham, mortadella, or cheese or salami or this and that at Al Merca, washing them down with un' ombra, a glass of white wine; lunch at Al Corvo (indifferent); and dinner at Antico Pizzo Risorto, a curious dive near the Rialto, where we discover that the smart thing to do is to eat not what's on the menu, but what's off it.

Lois and I pay homage to the Rialto Market, she marvelling at the brilliance of the vegetables and wrinkling her nose at the fishy smells. We wander through the Palazzo Ducale, so elegant on the outside, so opulent within. It isn't difficult to imagine the great trading empire being controlled from these rooms, walls hung with monumental paintings by Carpaccio, Bellini, Pisanello and Titian celebrating the glory of Venice and its rulers, ceilings illuminated by Tintoretto, Tiepolo and Veronese, with their plasterwork of luxuriant exuberance, their carved wood and marble floors. The sense of prestige and pragmatism is palpable. Here the courses of argosies were chartered, delegations from Ottoman emir, Persian satrap, Russian czar and French king were received, listened to, politely dealt with, money lent, trade deals struck.

'You couldn't do it now,' says Lois after a long silence.

I don't suppose you could. Those were the days when wealth was put on public display, the outward and visible sign of power and commercial dominance.

What an extraordinary creation Venice had been, a City State with an elected governing body and an elected leader, even if the Doge was president for life, and a bureaucracy that matched that of the EU – Doge, Council of Ten, Signoria, (the Minor Council), Quarantia (the Grand Council), Sapientes, Consiglio de Pregadi (the senate), Savi and Savi Grandi, magistratura and so on and so on, layer upon layer of ledger-keepers, note-takers, archivists, customs officers, fetchers and carriers, made up from the great merchant families, the Rezzonicos, Foscaris, Pandolfos, Barbaros, Ghisis, Morosinis, Loredans and Veniers, whose colossal wealth built the palaces, houses and churches – monuments to Mammon as much as God – that still flank the canals, consummate façade after consummate façade.

In the course of the eighteenth and nineteenth centuries Venice gradually ceased to trade in goods and began to trade on its history. It translated the legacy of its commercial past into the commercial present. The city's mythology was perpetuated as the basis for its economic survival. Once its highways and byways were a Babel of Turkish, Persian, Lebanese, Indian, English, French and Spanish, the languages of the Baltic states, foreigners come to trade, borrow money, sell. Little by little they gave way to a babble of languages from around the world as tourists came to gawp at the legacy of Venice's glory, and take away souvenirs of it.

For Venice has turned itself into the most beautiful shopping centre in the world. Its innumerable thoroughfares scintillate with shops peddling goods for all tastes and occasions. Glassware and tableware, fancy pens and fancy papers, fancy fabrics for fancy houses. There're clothes shops and shoe shops, bag shops and scarf shops, shops festooned with Murano glass, shops piled high with unimaginable dross, workshops and antique shops. And then there're gelaterias and bars, cafés and trattorias in which to refresh between jousts with culture and commerce. The streets are one vast Milky Way of enticements to buy, the calls to spend ubiquitous and constant.

It would be easy to dismiss this insistent commercialism as vulgar and degrading, as the dying mutter of Venice's glorious trading past, but I prefer to see it in a different light: as evidence of the Venetians' determination to survive, of their tenacity to keep their city going and to continue to live in their city by whatever means possible. In other words, the endless shops are evidence of a vital spirit, not the gesture of a dying culture. For beneath all this commercial armoury lies the steel will of the Venetians. They're survivors. Permanent inhabitants may have dropped from around 100,000 to 55,000 since the 1970s, but those who do remain turn their hand to whatever business is necessary to keep the city alive.

We have lunch at Antiche Carampane in Sestiere San Polo, handsome, well set up, and, like the Locanda Cipriani, confident by habit. We're each given a little paper cornet of tiny fried shrimps. They crunch like cornflakes and taste of the lagoon. They pop up again, worked into polenta as thick as double cream, with fleshy slices of funghi porcini on top. Then moeche (or molecche), tiny soft shelled crabs, dipped in egg and fried; not drowned in egg and parmesan and then fried, as was once the way. A practice frowned upon these days, so I'm told, but still carried on at home. These are soft and crunchy, the egg and cheese in which they've been dipped just nudging the delicacy of that seaweed-and-shrimp sweetness of the crustacean. It's proper, old-school Venetian cooking, artfully building on the inherent qualities of the ingredients, perfected through repetition, season by season.

Venice may be filled with pizzerias, spaghetterias, bars and eateries of every hue peddling gastronomic junk that keeps the vast majority of its visitors happy, but when it comes to the culinary pleasures of its permanent residents, there're still plenty of places that keep to the old ways

We take the water bus back to the flat, struck, as every visitor to Venice is struck, by the changes darkness brings to the city. By day a gallery of aesthetic delights, by night it metamorphosises into an eighteenth-century theatre of mysteries. The precise forms of the buildings vanish into darkness. Only a doorway here, a window there, a hump-backed bridge over a silver-threaded canal are framed by some adjacent light. The black, slick water flickers and undulates, stirred by the sulphurous orange-lit boats moving along them, pulling into bright stops, caves of light, for passengers to disembark and others to embark.

There're other rambles, further bottles of wine and extended lunches and dinners with Rory, and then, suddenly, it's time for Lois to go. We hug and hug on the landing stage as the water bus for the airport draws in. I long for her to stay, but these three days have been a gift and perhaps given her a taste of the city. She can always return when she's older, perhaps share it with her own children one day. At least she knows of it and about it.

She rings from the airport in distress. Susan, who's been minding my elderly dog, Joe, while I've been away, has rung her as she couldn't get through to me. Joe has a burst eardrum caused by a growth behind his eye, and is in great pain. He has to be put down. Do I want to come back to be with him? I'm devastated. I do, but I know I can't get there for at least two days. Joe will continue to suffer all that time. I tell Lois that it would be better for Joe to go as soon as possible. She agrees. We're in tears. Joe has been a constant in our lives, a dog of inherent sweetness and occasional snappiness. I feel bereft.

I make my way back to the flat in deep sadness. Joe is the latest of several friends who've died in the course of these travels. The losses are distressing, not simply because the particular ease and warmth of affection, conversations and exchanges covering decades bound up in them have come to an end, but also because I sense the sum of humanity shrinking and time sneaking up on me.

For a moment my natural solitude turns to loneliness. For the best part of six months I've been travelling alone, by choice. Friends have joined me briefly. I've forged friendships along the way, but most of the time I've been on my own, and been happy with it. It seems to me that solitude is different from being alone in the same way that being alone is different from loneliness.

> 'What I am none cares or knows,
> My friends desert me like a memory lost:
> I am the self-consumer of all my woes –
> They rise and vanish in oblivious host...'

So begins John Clare's poem 'I am', surely the most melancholy lines in all British poetry and ones that define the essence and egocentricity of loneliness.

Solitude, on the other hand, is the chosen state of the solitary. It is both active and passive. Solitude doesn't preclude relating to what is going on around, but it's unlikely that the solitary will feel entirely a part of it. While I enjoyed the concert by the ex-Broadway star on Favignana, I never felt the full weight of the communal experience. I remained outside it, and was happy to return to being alone afterwards.

Perhaps solitude is one of the defining conditions of being a writer. By nature, I'm pretty gregarious, but writing is something I have to do on my own. No one else can do it for me. Travelling, too. The moment someone else joins me, the whole dynamic of travel is altered. Their company, their personality, their responses provide a different prism through which a particular experience is reflected. If I'm strictly honest, they're a distraction, too. How much easier it is to chat away to them than it is to note what's going on around me. I'm aware that the observations in my notebooks drop by about 75 per cent when there's someone else about.

At the same time, my various companions have added immeasurably to the texture and pleasures of my travels. There have been times when having someone with whom to share events and experiences has provided me with pleasures that I would never have had on my own. Nevertheless, I've been happy when they're gone and I can resume my solitary rambles.

It's easy to slip from solitude into being lonely. Being lonely means you've lost the habit of communicating with others. You've retreated into yourself. You have to guard against slipping from being alone into loneliness. 'If you're lonely when you're alone,' said Jean Paul Sartre, 'you're in bad company.'

Venice is a good city in which to feel bereft. There's a melancholy about it, particularly at this time of year. Summer's at an end. In the early morning the canals and the buildings are cloaked in mist. There's a slight chill in the air at night. I continue my rambles around the city, solitary now – Rory left shortly after Lois – to Cannaregio, and Castello, to the Giudecca, to the Rialto to take pleasure in the smells and colours of the market once more. It seems to me that Venice is uniquely constructed to absorb what, at times, appears to be a limitless number of tourists. We can be dispersed throughout that vast labyrinth of calli, sotoporteghi, rami, salizzarde, fondamente, rughe and rughette, campi, campielli and corti, or along the watery canale and rii, or sent off to innumerable churches, palaces and museums spread across the seven districts or dispatched further to the islands scattered like odd-shaped plates across the lagoon.

I do what tourists are supposed to do and gorge on the city's beauty as I might on a vast box of chocolate truffles of unforgettable richness. I fall under the spell of the Basilica dei Frari, its vaulting red-brick spaces, its combination of power and grace, and with the *Pesaro Madonna* by Titian in particular. In the bottom right-hand corner of the painting, among a group of kneeling figures, is a boy, a teenager perhaps, looking directly out of the picture, solemn, owlish, challenging. His fierce gaze draws me into the scene.

I listen to a man playing Vivaldi's *Four Seasons* on a glass harmonica made from wine glasses, the eerie, resonant notes hanging in the air. I eat grilled eel and polenta at the Osteria di Quatro Ferri, the flesh of the eel melting beneath a crisp lacquer of skin, the polenta oozy and neutral. I go to the Guggenheim Museum, and am refreshed by the iconoclastic vitality of twentieth-century art after the smothering opulence of the seventeenth and eighteenth centuries.

One afternoon I sit next to a most graceful old lady on a water bus. She has silvery white hair, a trim blue suit and a walking stick. She tells me how the city's changed since she grew up in it.

'Foreigners have always come here,' she says. 'It's good that they love Venice.'

'But do they love it too much?' I ask. 'Are there too many of us? Is Venice ever quiet?'

'No,' she says, 'not any more. It used to be, in winter, but not now. People come here all year.'

'What's that meant for you?'

'The old communities have gone. You find a bit of the old ways in Cannaregio and on the Giudecca. You know, calli where you know your neighbour and meet for a chat in the street. But it's difficult. Most of the local food shops have gone. You make more money selling jewellery or souvenirs than food.'

'You can always shop at the Rialto Market,' I say.

'That's not so easy for me,' she says. 'Venice is a wonderful city when you're young. Not so good when you're old.' She gestures to her walking stick.

I thank her for her company, and get off at San Marco Zaccaria. As I stand there getting my bearings, she suddenly appears at my elbow. Am I sure where I'm going? She wants to make certain. Just up that calle, left at the end and there's the church I'm looking for, she says. I thank her and watch her make her way gently through the crowds. Old Venice, I think. Graceful even in decline.

I cross the water to Palladio's Chiesa di San Giorgio Maggiore, monumental in every sense of the word, and yet elegant and full of natural light. I go to a concert of the music of Vivaldi, Pachelbel and Albinoni, all composers born in or associated with Venice, and hackneyed though the programme is with the players dressed in eighteenth-century finery, there's a kind of magic in hearing the well-known pieces in the city where they were composed. Monteverdi, Vivaldi, Gabrieli – the history of the music of Venice is as richly textured as every other aspect of this city's life in the fourteenth, fifteenth, sixteenth and seventeenth centuries.

A day later I take the ferry to Sant'Erasmo. I've wanted to visit the island since I discovered that it's the market garden for the Rialto and many of the city's restaurants. It's famous for its purple artichokes and asparagus, both of which are out of season, of course, but I'm sure that there're other vegetables to take their place.

It's a bright, sunny day, with a faint breeze just stirring the waters of the lagoon. From a distance Sant'Erasmo doesn't exactly look a garden of plenty, but it's bustling with activity. Quite by accident, my visit coincides with the Sagra Del Mosto, a festival to celebrate must (grape juice). There's something of a regatta going on as I disembark, mini-gondolas fizzing through the water, propelled by young men and women dressed in blue and white standing fore and aft paddling away with a will, encouraged by a loudspeaker commentary.

'Forza! Forza! Aaah. Vignotta vinci! Sempre Vignotta!' The crews in a couple of the boats have given up and trail in well after the winners, still encouraged by their enthusiastic families.

There are several long tables set out in the square by the landing stage, and stalls where food is being prepared. I join a queue buying tickets for the dishes and then another queue to collect them – deep-fried salt cod, a bun with musetto, a boiling sausage for eight euros – and then join a third queue to collect a ticket for barbecued pork ribs, sausage, grilled polenta and fennel salad, another eight euros, that I collect from a fourth stall. It's all cheery and chatty.

I sit down at one of the long tables. Presently several families join me – 'È occupato?' 'No.' 'Bene. Ragazzi, sedetivi. Grazie signor,' children milling about, boys playing with model dinosaurs, girls drawing. Someone plonks a bottle of wine on the table. A small boy watches fascinated and unmoving as a small bottle of liquid soap for blowing bubbles falls over and decants its contents over the table and then onto the bench beside him. His mother mops it all up with a napkin without breaking off her conversation with her friend. Another boy knocks over a plastic box spilling crayons and other toys onto the ground. He looks at the empty box for a moment, and then picks it up and, furious, hurls it on top of the spilled toys and stomps off. His little sister stares after him, and then patiently begins picking everything up.

The queues at the stalls selling the food tickets grow ever longer, the crowds round the food stalls, themselves, grow ever thicker, the benches along the tables become ever more closely packed. No one seems to mind. The banter between the food servers and their customers is good natured and familiar. The lagoon is a piece of silk the colour of lichen. Beyond it, in the far distance, I can see the Alps, some of the peaks white with snow.

I wander off, and find another set of stalls behind the church selling jams, honeys, vegetables grown on the island, things made by the schoolkids. There's an angular metal structure like a gantry with rubber harnesses and trampolines. Children in the harnesses are bouncing up and down, five, eight metres into the air shrieking with fright and delight.

It all has very much the same jaunty, communal feeling as a village fête in England. Perhaps the view is more spectacular, and the food is unquestionably better and people lack that peculiar English social diffidence, but the day out, people congregating, sharing, blessed by yearly habit – 'something people do', as Philip Larkin put it in 'Show Saturday' – that's just the same.

The houses soon come to an end and the road runs straight to the further edge of the island, there turning into a series of paths snaking between pools, flighting ponds, streamlets. Between the watercourses and their surrounding ruffs of reeds, alder, birch and scrub, are patches of vegetables, tiny aubergines, fennel, cabbages, leeks and chillies in neat rows. It's odd to grow chillies here. They're part of the cooking in Calabria and the south, not of the north. Then I remember seeing bouquets of chillies, as brilliant as sparklers, in the Rialto Market, and tourists buying them as edible or decorative mementoes, just another Venetian trading product.

I pass several fields of the celebrated Violetto di Sant'Erasmo, the purple artichokes of Sant' Erasmo, one of the island's most cherished products and treasured nationally even in a country where artichoke-worship is pretty much universal. Sadly, the season for these fresh vegetable delights is long past. They're at their best from April to June, but the distinctive coronets of feathery grey-green fronds stretch in lines the length of the fields, giving promise of next year's harvest. Once they would've been fertilised with crushed crab and other shells to counterbalance the natural acidity of the island's soil. Only a few, mostly elderly, growers still keep to the old ways.

The Violetti are quite small and spiny when they're picked, and have a tender crunchiness and a distinctive, meaty flavour.

308

The most treasured are castraure, which are the very first buds of the artichoke that are cut off in a certain way to 'castrate' the plant, hence the name. They are so tender they can be eaten raw with just a sprinkle of olive oil and lemon. In their heyday, the Violetti were greatly favoured by Venice's Jews, a reminder of the culinary debt Italy owes to its once vibrant Jewish communities.

When I get back to the church, the ranks of festival-goers have thinned. There're still plenty of people eating and talking, but the initial energy has dissipated. Sant' Erasmo has that post-celebration torpor; and so do I.

My adventure is almost at an end. Tomorrow I leave for England, hearth and home. I feel restless and sad, anxious and expectant. Time has caught up with me. I have meetings fixed back in London, arrangements made, friends and family to see. The old, familiar pattern is reasserting itself, and I'm not entirely unhappy about it.

I come out of the Chiesa di Santa Maria della Salute. It was built to celebrate escape from the clutches of the Black Death, and is all very splendid but a bit overwrought for my taste. The evening sun lights up the Grand Canal churned by a constant traffic of water buses, water taxis, water vans, water trucks. Water restless, rippling; waves gurgling, splashing against the quays and walkways, gives the city an edgy energy. I can just make out the voice of a singing gondolier over the noise of water traffic. Someone's having the full Venice experience.

The light is just beginning to go as I make my way along the Fondamenta delle Zattere. Palladio's masterly Chiesa della Redentore in the Giudecca, also built to celebrate yet another deliverance from yet another outbreak of the plague, glimmers across the choppy, silver-white-silver-blue expanse. It has a certain familiarity, maybe because its white façade was inspired by one of my favourite buildings in Italy, the Pantheon in Rome; or maybe because I've seen a thousand photographs of it.

I pass a fisherman on the quay, holding his rod, as unmoving as a heron; waiters laying tables; a man with three long-haired dachshunds on leads chatting to a terrier walker; several couples pushing buggies; the odd jogger (obviously not Venetian); other evening strollers. The buildings across the water in the Giudecca are growing dim. A subtle quietness is settling over the scene. Shadows begin to gather in the narrower calli and canals, darkness filling the spaces.

People are filing into Santa Maria del Rosario, elegant with Tintorettos, Tiepolos, Riccis and Torrettis. Pink slowly suffuses the evening light. Along the Zattere al Ponte Longo, past the Sotoportego Fioravante. Now gold ribs the pink, settling on the chimneys of the chemical plants at Mestre beyond the fringes of Venice, another world. No matter how cynical I try to be about the city, about the way it commercialises its past, trades on its history, I can't resist its beauty and its charm and the richness of its existence.

It's almost dark by the time I turn away from the Canale della Giudecca, cross the Campo San Basegio and make my way along the Calle Nuova. The lights of bars, shops and trattorias are sharp and bright. Velvety darkness cloaks the buildings. How seductive and mysterious the city has become, a world of shadows and blackness broken here and there by the anonymous brilliance of a hotel foyer, the amber halo of a street light, a lambent ribbon across the rippling surface of water. A passing water taxi leaves a molten scar that heals and vanishes in an instant; more blackness, shadowy shapes, blank façades, doors and windows until the light of a lamp or chandelier through an uncurtained window illuminates a ceiling of sumptuous flamboyance, creamy plasterwork, gleaming gilt, plump, rosy-faced cherubs balanced easily on airy clouds; glimpsed, passed, and then darkness again.

I sit on the Ponte de l'Avogaria at the head of the calle leading to the flat. My journey is done. It's been an extraordinary odyssey, rich in people, places, experience and food, beyond anything I had imagined. How lucky I've been, I think. True, my summer in the islands has been split over two summers, but that, in itself, has only added to the texture of the whole. Perhaps Tom was right after all. I've lived a time of rare privilege, a time without a care in the world, except, perhaps, where my next meal was to come from, where I was to lay my head. It makes me realise just how my life before this journey had been hemmed in by humdrum realities, regimented by dates and diaries, dominated by responsibilities. How refreshing it's been to escape from all of that.

'Many flowering islands lie/In the waters of Agony', wrote Percy Shelley about Italy's islands. Well, I had visited many flowering islands, but experienced precious little Agony. All the flowering islands have given me pleasure, food to eat and food for thought. I warmed to some more than others, but everywhere I've found beauty, curiosity, idiosyncrasy, oddity. Everywhere I've found delight and content. Looking back, I can conjure image after image, landscape after landscape, person after person, the photographs of memory – pigs lying in the sun and the beekeeper on Gorgona; Stefano Farkas looking out over his vines, telling me 'one thing'; Giglio and Francesco and Gabriella Carfagna bickering over fish stew and Lois with her head thrown back in laughter and the wayward vines of Altura; the quizzical cave rabbits on Ischia and the human zoo on Capri; easy-paced meals and rambling conversations with John Irving on Ponza; Iddu and the superstitious rationalists of Stromboli; Kiki on Salina and Lisa on Alicudi; golden days and golden wine on Ustica; the diverting absurdities of the Villaggio L'Oasi on Favignana; the humanity of Lampedusans; even the shimmering waters and the resinous perfume of the pines on San Domino.

I remember the sea of ever-mutating blue (I've been obsessed with trying to render its colours and nature in exact words; and failed), the fossicking fish, languid anemones, hazy sunlight filtering down to pastures of posidonia, the shy octopus, the tremulous pink jellyfish. And climbing out of the sea, to rest on black volcanic rock or crunchy tufa or lumpy pebbles, to feel the sun warm my skin and soak into my bones, to doze, dream and slip back into the water again.

My mind drifts back once more to that first summer, in Cervia, almost sixty years ago, where this romance has its origins, to those sunlit, carefree days, to the riotous familial laughter of many summers in Licenza, to my early explorations of Sicily and Salina, and trips to Tuscany and Lombardy and Piedmont, to Calabria, Campania, Basilicata and Le Marche. I look back over all the people with whom I've shared those times: my parents, my brothers and sister, my wife, my uncle and aunt, my nephews and nieces, and friends beyond counting, and, above all, my daughter. They weave a brocade of extraordinary variety, splendour and happiness. I'm no Apollonian bard, but I have travelled in realms of gold, to homes and prisons, to refuges and forts, places to escape from, and places to escape to, realities and dreams.

When I set out, the islands had a romantic allure. They were largely unknown to me, each separate and unique. I saw them as individual bodies. They seemed accessible and approachable, and, indeed, so they proved to be. But as I got to know them better, delved more deeply into their history and character, I realised that they weren't really discrete entities. The life on them spilled over, to other islands, countries and continents, and vice versa. I might have gone looking for some simple, mythical, paradisiacal past, but what I've found is far more complex, dynamic and fascinating.

Every island has been touched by appropriation, piracy, political control, poverty, migration and now tourism, but each has developed a different narrative out of these experiences. So many of the comings and goings of Greeks, Romans, Turks, Saracens, French and Spanish are still remembered keenly, and celebrated on the islands; great events in circumscribed lives. Yet each island has been different, a separate room, a chamber, perhaps furnished with many of the same elements, but still utterly distinct one from the other. Perhaps each island represents a different aspect of 'Il Continente', of Italy as a whole – pragmatic, romantic, practical, delusional, playful, serious, tough and generous.

There's no doubt that Italy and its islands are changing, and will change much, much more. A great deal has been eroded or lost – communities, the historical connections they embodied, communal memories, social lore, knowledge of land and what it produces – but much also remains if you look for it. I feel that this is a part of the world I could go on exploring until I die, and never come to the end. The fascination will always be there.

And yet, much as I feel pleasure and astonishment at what I've been doing for so many months, I know it's time to go home. I miss the familiarity of home, the comfort of family and friends. The leaves of the woods on the hills either side of the valley in which I live will be turning yellow, brown, gold, withering around their edges, falling. The fields will be shrouded in mist in the early mornings. It's the time of apples and pears, medlars and quinces, for mushroom hunting and blackberry picking. I wonder if there's anything left in my vegetable beds, whether the tomatoes are still ripening, how my quince tree is faring. Suddenly I long for a pub, a pint, a packet of pork scratchings, a fire, companionable conversation in my own language.

I feel drawn back to Britain, the island from which I started out. Perhaps that's what binds island dwellers together, something that people who live on vast masses of land can't share or understand. Like sheep, we're hefted to a specific landscape. This particular piece of earth, rock, magma reaches out into us. That's why so many people born on the islands return to them after periods, even generations, in some other country.

Like all personal enterprises, realising them, and coming to the end of them, is the hardest part. I have a sense of sadness and loss. I've accomplished what I dreamed of for so many years. And...?

According to Robert Fox, the Mediterranean was known as the Inner Sea by early Arab and Jewish cartographers, and I feel it is just that, in a personal as well as in geographical and historical senses. I have discovered 'not only the exterior world, but also that which lies within us,' as Stefan Zweig admonished.

I call to mind an entry I made in my notebooks when I was on Ischia: 'Some times I have wished that I was making the journey younger, that I had made it when I was twenty-seven or thirty-seven rather than sixty-seven. Now I'm profoundly glad, not that I didn't do it then, but that I'm doing it now. Each ripple on the sea, each flicker of sunlight sparks another memory, another sense of sweetness, of pleasure, of gladness for the past, and an exquisite sense of the present.'

ACKNOWLEDGEMENTS

None of this would have been possible without the generosity, first of all, of those who subscribed to the book through the good offices, literal and figurative, of Unbound. They – you – have shown remarkable faith and patience, for which I will always be grateful. Secondly I had five sponsors – Pizza Express, Fortnum & Mason, Lavazza, HS1 and Sacla UK – whose backing was a kindly act of faith and meant I was spared financial anxieties, particularly during the several months when I was completely incapacitated.

I must also thank Justin Pollard of Unbound for the unstinting enthusiasm he showed for the project from the outset, and for his constancy through every hesitation, setback and flip-flop; to Isobel Kieran (or Frankish as she was when she began nudging me towards completion); to John Mitchinson, who finally took the book over the line; to Lauren Fulbright, who handled production with precision, tolerance and kindliness; to Anna Simpson who tactfully but firmly shepherded me through the latter stages; to Louise Haines, whose wise counsel, advice and generous encouragement have been invaluable aids.

Somewhere in the narrative I quote John Keat's poem 'On First Looking Into Chapman's Home': 'Much have I travell'd in the realms of gold/ And many goodly states and kingdoms seen.' That's all true, but it was the people I met along the way, who talked to me about their lives, fed me, poured wine and wisdom into me, put me in touch with their friends, showed me unstinting generosity, who brightened my days: Commissario Mario Salzano; Stefano and Gabriella Farkas; Francesco and Gabriella Carfagna; Lina Casu; Ian and Henny; Peppino and Raimonda Sanna; Giovanni Ruffa, Bruno Bego and Marco Bianchi and Nadia Durando for sharing their passion for the corner of Sardinia around Santadi; Riccardo and Silvia d'Ambra; the kindly staff at the Hotel Villa d'Orta; Umberto who helped me see the Capri underneath the tourist hordes; Matteo Rugghia who shared the delights of the Pontine Islands; Carlo Vespa and his generous friends on Stromboli; Maurizio Di Dio and Nino Calamuneri for their help in finding accommodation on Salina and Filicudi; Kiki McDonogh and Giuseppe Mascoli, whose presence illuminated Salina; Lisa Hilton, who brought such fun and glamour to Alicudi and Filicudi; Anna Ventura and her husband, Bill; Mariano Brischetto of the burnished tenor voice, unquenchable generosity and irrepressible sense of adventure; Damiano Sferlazzo, the vice sindaco (deputy mayor) of Lampedusa; and Rory Gibson who travelled halfway around the world to join me in Venice at the end of the summer. Many thanks also to Marcello Marengo of the University of Gastronomic Sciences in Pollenzo for his help with all the bookings.

But there are two people to whom I owe even greater gratiude – John Irving and my daughter, Lois.

John kept me company from start to finish, quite literally, even if he was actually physically present for a few days only. He was the one who sorted out all the paperwork involving buying, licensing and insuring a Vespa in Italy; who kept an eye on ferry timetables, booked me into hotels and B&Bs, put me in touch with friends and friends of friends, sorted out confusions and provided a running commentary on my progress. Equally valuable has been his contribution to this book. With characteristic diligence and taste he has corrected my Italian, my innumerable misspellings, contradictions and repetitions, checked facts and rectified them when I'd got them wrong. Any correct Italian is down to John. Anything wrong is down to my own incompetence. I owe him a debt I can never repay.

But most of all I'm indebted to Lois, my daughter, who is simply the most extraordinary human being I know. She encouraged me when necessary, chivvied me when necessary, joined me for periods, provided me with perspective, love and support, and it is to her I dedicate this book.

INDEX

SUPPORTERS

Unbound is a new kind of publishing house. Our books are funded directly by readers. This was a very popular idea during the late eighteenth and nineteenth centuries. Now we have revived it for the internet age. It allows authors to write the books they really want to write and readers to support the writing they would most like to see published.

The names listed below are of readers who have pledged their support and made this book happen. If you'd like to join them, visit: www.unbound.com.

T. J. Galvin
Beth Gardiner
Anna Gazeley
Catherine Gazzoli
Amro Gebreel
Harriet Geddes
Hugh Geddes
Irene & Silvano
  Giraldin
Kevin Goodall
Bob Granleese
Lynne Gray
Henry Chevallier
  Guild
Simon & Judith
  Gunn
Fiona Hadfield-Hart
Louise Haines
Caitlin Harvey
John Hatt
Nigel Haworth
Glen Hewitt
Sandra Hinderaker
Kit Hodgson
Pam Holley
Lucy Hopkins
Tom Hostler
Natasha Hughes
Jimmy Hunter
Ray Hunter
John Irving
Sacla Italian
S L Jackson
Lucy Jameson
Melanie Jappy
Ian Jesnick
Signe Johansen
Gilly Jolliffe
David J. Jones
Mark Jones

Nikki Jones
Halina Kessler
Dan Kieran
Mary Killen
Alastair Kimbell
Vanessa Kimbell
Valya 'Tomato'
  Kozyreva
Landlord Manor
  House Inn
Jimmy Leach
Jeremy Lee
Prue Leith
John A Letham
Beth Lewis
Paul Lewis
Fiorenza Lipparini
Tamasin Little
Oliver Lloyd
George Lutz
Elizabeth Lynch
Paul Lynch
Claire Macdonald
Mark Marshall
Rebecca Mascarenhas
James Maskell
Timmy Milk-Toes
Maureen Mills
John Mitchinson
Nicola Moody
Rob Moore
Siobhan Moore
Sue Moore
Diana Morgan
  Social Media
  Marketing for
  food businesses
Phil & Pat Morton
Carlo Navato
Donald Neil

Peter and Shelley
  Nelson
Mike O'Brien
Zoë O'Brien
Alan Ogden
Alicia Okines
Keith Okines
Pete & Jen Oldfield
Jake Overton
Jane Overton
Jonathan Overton
Talia Overton
Mary Padfield
Sarah Chalmers Page
Geoff Patterson
Jeremy Paxman
James Pembroke
Robert Phillips
Abigail Pitcher
Emma Playfair
Sarah Playfair
Justin Pollard
David Pritchard
Fiona Pritchard
Paolo Proto
Emma Ramsbotham
Louise Rice
Karen Riley
Neil Roberts
Jill Champion
  Rosenlund
Sue Samuel
Christine Asbury
  Şendenel
Uğur Şendenel
Bevelie Shember
Steven Short
Anne Skulicz
Stephen Sloat
Larry Smith

Jeremy Sowden
Aleksander Stanley
John Steed
James Steen
Peter Stevenson
Martyn Streeting
Tessa Stuart
Alasdair Scott
    Sutherland
Geraldine A.
    Sylver-O Malley
Vinay Talwar

Elspeth Tavaci
Mark Taylor
Sheila Thewlis
Ian Thomas
Amelia Thompson
Andrew Thompson
Ian Thompson-Corr
Mitchell Tonks
Peter Tooley
Richmond Towers
Julia Tratt
David G Tubby

Justine Tweddle
Richard Tyson
Oona van den Berg
David Verey
Richard Watson
Nick Watts
Julie Whalley
Alun Williams
Dennis Willison
Ed Wilson
Amanda Wright
Rachel Wright